ANOTHER PERSPECTIVE

A View from the Mercy Seat

ANOTHER PERSPECTIVE

A View from the Mercy Seat

Wilbur Schwartzendruber

All Scripture references are taken from the King James Version of the Bible unless otherwise noted.

ISBN 10: 1-59571-107-4
ISBN 13: 978-1-59571-107-6
Library of Congress Control Number: 2005938229

Word Association Publishers
205 5th Avenue
Tarentum, PA 15084
www.wordassociation.com

To The Glory Of God
"of which we cannot now particularly speak".
Hebrews 9:5

CONTENTS

INTRODUCTION

As necessity is the mother of invention, as a drowning man searches for a refreshing gasp of pure air, as enveloping darkness requires us to seek for light, so does abject Spiritual poverty motivate the soul to look for Spiritual freedom.

The darkness of my soul is what motivated this author to search the Scriptures for the purpose of life. Although I had searched in many places for meaningful identity, I found no peace until the Scriptures revealed to me what God had made me, through His will, to be in Him.

A personal tragedy at a very early age unfortunately, graphically taught me that the so called "fathers" of the denominational church, in their legalistic enthusiasm, had no Spiritual sensitivity to hear the cry of a broken heart. Through no fault of my own I was ostracized from the church of my youth and, in my own mind, separated from the hope of being included in the body of Christ. For many years I was totally convinced that I was hopeless, that Jesus Christ came to save all sinners except myself. I thought that I alone was the exception, that I was not eligible for redemption. I fully identified with Jonah;

> And said, I cried by reason of mine affliction
> unto the LORD, and he heard me; out of the belly
> of hell cried I, and thou heardest my voice.
> For thou hadst cast me into the deep, in the midst

*of the seas; and the floods compassed me about:
all thy billows and thy waves passed over me.
Then I said, I am cast out of thy sight; yet I will
look again toward thy holy temple.
The waters compassed me about, even to the
soul: the depth closed me round about, the weeds
were wrapped about my head.
I went down to the bottoms of the mountains; the
earth with her bars was about me for ever: yet
hast thou brought up my life from corruption, O
LORD my God.
When my soul fainted within me I remembered
the LORD: and my prayer came in unto thee,
into thine holy temple.
They that observe lying vanities forsake their
own mercy.
But I will sacrifice unto thee with the voice of
thanksgiving; I will pay that that I have vowed.
Salvation is of the LORD.* (Jonah 2:2-9)

It was only when I realized there was no true meaning or
eternal purpose in the present, physical, visible existence, was I
open to receive the thought that, perhaps the true meaning and
purpose of life would be found in the Word of God, in the Bible.
I determined to search the Scriptures for myself to see if they
would offer an answer as to the meaning of the purpose of life.
There are no words to describe the glorious answer to the
meaning of life which the study of the Scriptures revealed to my
heart. It is only through the study of God's revealed Word that I
have found my true identity. It is only through response to His
revealed Divine Purpose for mankind, contained in His Word,
that my eternal Spirit has found rest in Him. This transformation
of life only came about as I discovered, through the study of His
Word, as revealed to my heart by the Holy spirit, that to be made
alive in Christ is to be continually reminded of the vanity of the

old life of self-purpose, and of the deadness and hopelessness of the present world system.

> *But what things were gain to me, those I counted loss for Christ.*
>
> *Yea doubtless, and I count all things but loss for the excellency of the knowledge of Christ Jesus my Lord: for whom I have suffered the loss of all things, and do count them but dung, that I may win Christ,*
>
> *And be found in him, not having mine own righteousness, which is of the law, but that which is through the faith of Christ, the righteousness which is of God by faith:*
>
> *That I may know him, and the power of his resurrection, and the fellowship of his sufferings, being made conformable unto his death;*
>
> (Philippians 3:7-10)

However, fortunately, God's Holy Spirit directed me to find a new heart in the strength and grace of His Word. It was only after several years of searching the Scriptures that I was convicted of the Holy Spirit to kneel beside my bed and ask God to "take my heart", it was there at my bedside that He, through the witness of the Holy Spirit, made me dramatically aware that His gift of salvation was intended for me also.

However, although now having been fully accepted into His Kingdom, much of the hurt and guilt of my earlier negative church experiences still remained on my conscience. I could not fully forgive these church "fathers" who had inflicted these deep hurts. Only after, again being led of the Holy Spirit, to memorize the entire book of Hebrews, that the Lord, through the revelation of His present High Priestly ministry, gave me the necessary Spiritual strength and insight to forgive the organized church for "shooting their wounded." It was only after having the doctrine of the High Priestly ministry of Christ, along with the realization that God had made all believers the seed of Abraham, as revealed in His precious Book, that God instilled in me the Spiritual strength to face these people, and attempt to share with these "church fathers" the victory over the spirit of unforgiveness, which had set me free. It was also the Spirit revealed truths contained in the Book of Hebrews that opened my eyes, that lifted the inner veil, to see all Scriptures, both in the Old and New Testaments as being in total unity. Redemption of all believers, from Adam and Eve onward, was given them by grace through faith in the sprinkling of the blood of Jesus Christ on the Mercy Seat in Heaven.

So then it is the hope and prayer of this author to bring to the forefront of any and all believers consciousness, the importance of accepting several foundational doctrines as revealed through the study of the eight Covenants God made to mankind, the first principles of the oracles of God.

This book is meant to lead the reader, through the witness of the Holy Spirit, through a comprehensive study of Scripture, which will reveal to the believer a new and further, inner veil, experience and awakening of God's Holiness and will for mankind. If and when this awakening occurs to the individual reader, the believer will see Scriptures in a whole new light, every passage of Scripture when taken in context, will confirm the same message to the heart, the message which was from the beginning, from the time of Adam and Eve onward, which is that all believers have been saved by grace through faith in the blood of Christ, and have been separated from the law of sin and death. This awakening reveals to us that the Gospel message is, first and foremost, to simply accept and appreciate what God has done, and is continually doing for us through the High Priestly ministry of Christ, that of giving believers His very own unconditional righteousness. What we, as believers, can do for Him is a secondary response, a response which only becomes a Spiritual reality when we first understand and appreciate what was on

God's heart when He made promise to our father Abraham. All believers, past, present and future, are the Spiritual seed of Abraham.

However an antinomian label will not apply, this author fully recognizes that "not one jot nor one tittle will in no wise pass from the law," the ten commandments, until all be fulfilled. The author recognizes that it is the law, written on tablets of stone, which is the schoolmaster of future heirs of the Kingdom of God. However, the author also recognizes that the Scriptures reveal to us, that the law is not made for a righteous man, but for the unredeemed.

> *Now the end of the commandment is charity out of a pure heart, and of a good conscience, and of faith unfeigned:*
> *From which some having swerved have turned aside unto vain jangling;*
> *Desiring to be teachers of the law; understanding neither what they say, nor whereof they affirm.*
> *But we know that the law is good, if a man use it lawfully;*
> *Knowing this, that the law is not made for a righteous man, but for the lawless and disobedient, for the ungodly and for sinners, for unholy and profane, for murderers of fathers and murderers of mothers, for manslayers,*
> (1 Timothy 1:5-9)

The receiving of His righteousness fully meets and exceeds all the demands of the law.

It is the cry of this authors heart that all believers, and future believers, be shaken and awakened to the unconditional sinless and righteous nature of God which indwells all those who have their faith rooted in the perfect blood propitiatory sacrifice of Jesus Christ. It is the cry of this authors heart that all believers come to realize, through the witness of the Holy Spirit, that the Spirit of Christ which indwells them has separated them from the law of the flesh, and the Holy Spirit which lives within them cannot sin. I identify with the heart of Ezekiel as stated in the Scriptures below; if I warn the righteous that they are righteous and because they are righteous they sin not, I have delivered my soul.

> *When I say unto the wicked, Thou shalt surely die; and thou givest him not warning, nor speakest to warn the wicked from his wicked way, to save his life; the same wicked man shall die in his iniquity; but his blood will I require at thine hand.*
>
> *Yet if thou warn the wicked, and he turn not from his wickedness, nor from his wicked way, he shall die in his iniquity; but thou hast delivered thy soul.*
>
> *Again, When a righteous man doth turn from his righteousness, and commit iniquity, and I lay a stumblingblock before him, he shall die: because thou hast not given him warning, he shall die in his sin, and his righteousness which he hath done shall not be remembered; but his blood will I require at thine hand.*
>
> *Nevertheless if thou warn the righteous man, that the righteous sin not, and he doth not sin, he shall surely live, because he is warned; also thou hast delivered thy soul.* (Ezekiel 3:18-21)

Also:

> *He that committeth sin is of the devil; for the devil sinneth from the beginning. For this purpose the Son of God was manifested, that he might destroy the works of the devil.*
> *Whosoever is born of God doth not commit sin;*

for his seed remaineth in him: and he cannot sin, because he is born of God.
In this the children of God are manifest, and the children of the devil: whosoever doeth not righteousness is not of God, neither he that loveth not his brother. (1 John 3:8-10)

FOREWORD

The eight Covenants as outlined in Scriptures were meant by God to be the superstructure of His church, the pillars of His dispensations to mankind. If we, as believers, see church history as recorded throughout the ages, as a record of man's response to His will, rather than seeing His church structure and history simply upheld by His Word and the leading of the Holy Spirit, regardless of mans responses, we ignore what His unadulterated will and love is for individual believers. If we see men such as Augustine, St. Francis, Luther, Calvin, your local pastor, or any other mere man, or human organization as pillars which uphold church history, then we miss the simple fact that the pure spotless bride of Christ, His mystical church, is built upon the love of God and each believers individual response, in faith, in the churches cornerstone, Jesus Christ.

The pillars of the mystical church are the first principles of the oracles of God, that is, His Covenants.

We will explore these Covenants in an attempt to simply accept, through His Spirit and His Word, what was on God's heart when He spoke them to mankind throughout the ages. It is important to understand that these Covenants still apply to every believer, TODAY. We will attempt to look at these Covenants from God's infinite eternal perspective, as recorded in the Bible, separated from the view of man's finite mind.

The fiercest enemy of God's mystical body is the pre-conceived mind set, those presumptuous sins of individual believers whose faith is grounded in the traditional denominational dogmas which are the cause of the many schisms in the organized church. Who can conceive in his mind a mystery such as His glorious church, Christ's pure spotless bride? Is it not Spiritually discerned? God does not change, neither is Jesus Christ divided, Jesus Christ is the same yesterday, today and forever. If there be any divisions or misunderstanding as to what God's will and love for mankind ordains believers to be in Him, it is because of the great transgression of being blind and deaf to what God has said to us in His Word, through His eight Covenants. Speaking of Old Covenant, as well as New Covenant High Priests, the Scriptures say:

> *And being made perfect, he became the author of eternal salvation unto all them that obey him;*
> *Called of God an high priest after the order of Melchisedec.*
> *Of whom we have many things to say, and hard to be uttered, <u>seeing ye are dull of hearing.</u>*
> *For when for the time ye ought to be teachers, <u>ye have need that one teach you again which be the first principles of the oracles of God;</u> and are become such as have need of milk, and not of strong meat.*
> *For every one that useth milk is unskilful in the word of righteousness: for he is a babe.*
> *But strong meat belongeth to them that are of full age, even those who by reason of use have their senses exercised to discern both good and evil.*
> (Hebrews 5:9-14)

The present High Priestly ministry of Jesus Christ began when, He as an High Priest in the order of Melchisedec, offered bread and wine to Abraham. Until the importance of this foundational doctrine is revealed to the heart of the believer, he remains on a restrictive Spiritual diet of milk, not on the more satisfying solid food of Spiritual meat. Hopefully, through the study of God's Word, and the gifts of His Covenants, and Christ's ever present High Priestly ministry at the right hand of the Father, the anointing of the believer into the fulness of God's perfect unconditional righteousness, will be revealed to every heart. Only through the knowledge of the power of the sprinkling of the blood of our High Priest, Jesus Christ, on the Mercy Seat in Heaven, are believers made aware of their Spiritual position in Heavenly places. Only here at the Mercy Seat in Heaven, within the second veil, not on the cross, are believers purged from a guilty conscience, and thus strengthened in the Spirit, to totally accept forgiveness for themselves and consequently toward all others. It is through the knowledge of, and coincidence of the Abrahamic and New Covenants, and what was on God's heart when He spoke them, that the believer is made aware of his positional boldness to enter and dwell in God's very presence, within the Holy of Holies. In order to experience this Spiritual blessing the believer must understand there is only one mediator between God and man, our High Priest at the right hand of the Father, no longer on the cross, the resurrected Christ Jesus. Only when dwelling within the secret place of the Most High, consciously aware of being separated from his flesh and freed from guilt, does the believer become aware that both his Christian position and experience are perfectly united in one Spiritual entity in God's Grace, mercy, and glory.

Another major stumbling block to Spiritual freedom is the pre-conceived mind set, the false doctrine which teaches that Spiritual positional perfection cannot be achieved except through experiential perfection of the flesh. This humanitarian view of the believers position in the gift of God's perfect righteousness is due to looking at church history through man's eyes and not through the heart of a Sovereign God as revealed in His Word, whether it be in the Old Testament or in the New Testament, both are Covenants of God's Grace, providing for the believers experiencing the gift of God's perfection and righteousness. Were believers given a new spirit of life in Christ after we experientially, through the will of the flesh, made ourselves worthy of this gift of salvation, or were we saved through faith in our God given position in what God had on His heart for us? "For God so loved the world that He gave...." We will search the Scriptures, hopefully with an open mind, as to whether the Spirit of Christ, which dwells within the heart of every believer, dwells within us positionally or experientially, or both.

The word "Covenant" is one of the many words, often used by Christians, the meaning of which has not been clarified by present day teachings. The true meaning of this word is pivotal, in order to Spiritually discern what God had on His heart, when He made these Covenants to mankind. The mystery of the pure spotless bride of Christ is revealed to us only when we see His Covenants viewed from God's perspective, His Word, not on looking upon it through the eyes of mere men. The word "Covenant" means; a compact made by walking between two pieces of divided flesh. The author will hopefully clarify this as we go.

The overall theme of the Bible is simply to believe in faith through grace. All that a loving God requires of believers is to simply accept the gift of His perfect unconditional righteousness, only then will the indwelling Holy Spirit motivate the heart of the believer to do God's works. If we read His Word with an open mind which simply asks: "What did God the Father have on his mind and heart when He established His Covenants for mankind?" Then He will lead us through the second veil, to dwell with Him in the very Holy of Holies, the secret place of the Most High, the city of rest.

Jesus Christ was made to be sin for us on the cross, this knowledge too is foundational to bring sinners to repentance and the gift of God's unconditional righteousness, however Christ is no longer on the cross, He is seated at the right hand of the Majesty in the Heavens. God the Father turned His face from His very own Son on the cross, because He could not look upon the face of sin. Just as the serpent which Moses lifted up in the wilderness represented the sin of the Israelites, so the cross of Christ represented the sin of all believers. The cross, the present day symbol of Christianity, is a reminder to all of the believers past sin nature which Jesus so dearly paid to have done away with.

And as Moses lifted up the serpent in the wilderness, even so must the Son of man be lifted up: (John 3:14)

Why then do believers, and Bible teachers as well, chose to remember Jesus on the cross, in His desperate struggle with sin on our behalf, rather than to be ever grateful for the victory and glory He shares with us, in the Throne Room of Grace and Mercy, as our High Priest in the order of Melchizedek? Jesus Christ, and the Father willingly, even gladly, paid a very high price to separate believers from our sin nature through the blood of the New Covenant. During communion in the partaking of His blood and body, I am reminded that Christ continually presents me in His righteousness and sinless nature to the Father.

1
CHURCH HISTORY
The Covenants

Church history may only be understood through accepting the Spirit and intent of God's Word through the Covenants He made with man. Unlike other history, Church history cannot be revealed by the record of man's reaction and response to world events, for the true Church is the Spirit of God which mysteriously indwells the heart of all believers, not a bibliography of man's opinion of who God is. Jesus Christ is the foundation stone of the true church and through whom also God the Father has confirmed and fulfilled all of His Covenanted Promises. The foundational Covenants and the Holy Spirit led history and future of the true church are all framed by the Word of God, the Bible. When God spoke, His Word immediately became history, history past, present and future. Although His mercies continue to be new every morning, they were fore ordained from the foundation of the world, and confirmed to man and made manifest by the faithfulness of the blood of Christ upon the cross. Therefore, in order to know God's purpose for mankind we must be aware of what He has revealed to us, of His nature, through His Covenants contained in His Word, <u>the first principles of the oracles of God.</u>

God revealed His faithfulness to His people through the fathers and prophets of old, in order that believers of all ages might be led to understand the nature of God. The fathers and prophets of old exemplified the relationship and fellowship between God and man.

> *Moreover, brethren, I would not that ye should be ignorant, how that all our fathers were under the cloud, and all passed through the sea;*
> *And were all baptized unto Moses in the cloud and in the sea;*
> *And did all eat the same spiritual meat;*
> *And did all drink the same spiritual drink: for they drank of that spiritual Rock that followed them: and that Rock was Christ.*
> *But with many of them God was not well pleased: for they were overthrown in the wilderness.*
> *Now these things were our examples, to the intent we should not lust after evil things, as they also lusted. (1 Corinthians 10:1-6)*

If believers would grow in grace, we need again to become aware of the knowledge of the first principles of the oracles of God, especially the principles He established through our father Abraham. Church history can only be understood if we know of what God first spoke as being His principles, and the oracles or messengers with which He reveals His very being. As is stated below:

> *For when for the time ye ought to be teachers, ye have need that one teach you again which [be] the first principles of the oracles of God; and are become such as have need of milk, and not of strong meat.*
> *For every one that useth milk [is] unskilful in the word of righteousness: for he is a babe.*

But strong meat belongeth to them that are of full age, [even] those who by reason of use have their senses exercised to discern both good and evil. (Hebrews 5:12-14)

The unconditional Covenants speak of the Sovereign Grace and the all encompassing love of God toward His creation, mankind. The unconditional Covenants include the Covenants He made to Adam and Eve, to Noah, the Old and New Covenant He made to all believers through Abraham, and the Covenant He made to the nation Israel through David. Unconditional Covenants are upheld by God alone, whether or not we appreciate His provisions of love and grace does not deter Him from being faithful to uphold the provisions of these Covenants, nor diminish or nullify His Holy omnipotent love and concern for all humanity.

What advantage then hath the Jew? Or what profit is there of circumcision?

Much every way: chiefly, because that unto them were committed the oracles of God.

For what if some did not believe? shall their unbelief make the faith of God without effect?

God forbid: yea, let God be true, but every man a liar; as it is written, That thou mightest be justified in thy sayings, and mightest overcome when thou art judged. (Romans 3:1-4)

Unconditional Covenants are upheld by God's will, for in these Covenants He promises and emphasises "I will". His will supercedes all other wills and excludes the will of man, otherwise Jesus would not have shown us how to pray "thy will be done on earth as it is in heaven". The will of man is of no consequence in determining truth, faith or the way to justification, for the will of natural man is directly opposed to God's Will. In the final analysis, man is justified and finds truth and life only through belief in the grace and faithfulness of God. To the extent we look at God and the history of the organized church through "our faith" we distort and limit our perception of God's faithfulness. God alone is faithful and true, not man's opinion or creeds, for the faithfulness of God is not an opinion, but righteousness revealed by the Spirit of His Word.

Probably the most difficult aspect of Christianity is to simply accept the unconditional gift of righteousness which He imputes to believers through His Grace and mercy. Grace being the gift of God's righteousness which believers did nothing to deserve, mercy expiating or setting aside His wrath which all unbelievers do deserve. Our belief, and faith in God, is limited by the lack of the knowledge of His unconditional righteousness and love toward us as revealed in the Covenants, especially the everlasting Covenants.

Unconditional Covenants are upheld by God through the faithfulness of the blood of Christ, the degree to which we receive righteousness through these Covenants, is dependant upon our faith in the power or efficacy of His blood. The unconditional Covenants are the core of the Gospel of the Good News of God's Grace toward all who believe. The degree to which the believer experiences the indwelling gift of the righteousness of God is dependent upon how much the believer appreciates his positional perfection given him through the knowledge of the shedding and sprinkling of Jesus' blood, and the oaths of the unconditional Covenants sworn by God.

> *For when God made promise to Abraham,*
> *because he could swear by no greater, he sware*
> *by himself, Saying, Surely blessing I will bless*
> *thee, and multiplying I will multiply thee.*
> *And so, after he had patiently endured, he*
> *obtained the promise.*
> *For men verily swear by the greater: and an oath*
> *for confirmation is to them an end of all strife.*
> *Wherein God, willing more abundantly to shew*

unto the heirs of promise the immutability of his
counsel, confirmed it by an oath:
That by two immutable things, in which it was
impossible for God to lie, we might have a strong
consolation, who have fled for refuge to lay hold
upon the hope set before us:
Which hope we have as an anchor of the soul,
both sure and stedfast, and which entereth into
that within the veil; (Hebrews 6:13-19)

The two immutable unconditional everlasting Covenants are the Covenants God made to us through Abraham and the New Covenant, which will be expounded upon as we go.

There are also conditional Covenants made by God, the ten commandments and the Palestinian Covenant, these were made only after man refused to believe and receive the love and grace of His unconditional Covenants. The conditional Covenants were made to convict man that he had fallen from the grace of the unconditional Covenants. Conditional Covenants were made to show man his fallibility and to demonstrate to man that his will power was not adequate to meet the requirements of a righteous God. Conditional Covenants were typified by "thou shalt" perform God's will, which is impossible for the carnal man to accomplish. For if righteousness came by trying to adhere to "thou shalt" then Christ's death, resurrection and present High Priestly ministry is of no consequence.

Conditional Covenants however were only conditional until the believer awakens to the unconditional Covenant of Promise. Conditional Covenants are of the letter of the law as distinct from the unconditional Covenants of Grace.

For example: the purpose of the ten commandments is to lead us to the knowledge of the redeeming blood of Christ, through which we as believers experienced initial justification. Justification is a declaration by God of the unconditional gift of His indwelling righteousness.

> *For the law was given by Moses, [but] grace and*
> *truth came by Jesus Christ.* (John 1:17)

Also;

> *But we know that the law [is] good, if a man use*
> *it lawfully; Knowing this, that the law is not*
> *made for a righteous man, but for the lawless*
> *and disobedient, for the ungodly and for sinners,*
> *for unholy and profane, for murderers of fathers*
> *and murderers of mothers, for manslayers,*
> (1 Timothy 1:8,9)

God originally made only unconditional Covenants with man, such as the Covenant God made to us through Abraham. It was only after man had demonstrated his unwillingness to receive of God's gift of righteousness through the unconditional Covenants that the conditional Covenants were imposed upon them, such as the ten commandments.

> *Now to Abraham and his seed were the promises*
> *made. He saith not, And to seeds, as of many; but*
> *as of one, And to thy seed, which is Christ.*
> *And this I say, [that] the Covenant, that was*
> *confirmed before of God in Christ, the law,*
> *which was four hundred and thirty years after,*
> *cannot disannul, that it should make the promise*
> *of none effect.*
> *For if the inheritance [be] of the law, [it is] no*
> *more of promise: but God gave [it] to Abraham*
> *by promise.*
> *Wherefore then [serveth] the law? It was added*
> *because of transgressions, till the seed should*
> *come to whom the promise was made; [and it*
> *was] ordained by angels in the hand of a*
> *mediator.* (Galatians 3:16-19)

The message which the law and the prophets were continually trying to impress upon the Israelites was: "Remember your deliverer and return to God's Covenant of Grace". The message still remains the same today.

> *But now hath he obtained a more excellent ministry, by how much also he is the mediator of a better Covenant, which was established upon better promises.*
>
> *For if that first [Covenant] had been faultless, then should no place have been sought for the second.*
>
> *For finding fault with them, he saith, Behold, the days come, saith the Lord, when I will make a new Covenant with the house of Israel and with the house of Judah:*
>
> *Not according to the Covenant that I made with their fathers in the day when I took them by the hand to lead them out of the land of Egypt; because they continued not in my Covenant, and I regarded them not, saith the Lord.*

(Hebrews 8:6-9)

Believers are encouraged to remember this Covenant and to drink to it through the sacrament of His Table. Believers are encouraged to remember Jesus Christ's body and blood, they are not encouraged to reflect back on their sins. (Covenant and Testament being the same Greek word.)

> *After the same manner also [he took] the cup, when he had supped, saying, This cup is the new testament in my blood: this do ye, as oft as ye drink [it], in remembrance of me.*

(1 Corinthians 11:25)

In order that the believer be weaned off of the milk of the Word and be exercised in the meat of righteousness that comes from the knowledge of the first principles of the oracles of God, the following pages expound, however inadequately, in order, the eight Covenants and dispensations as revealed in God's Word, the Bible. Only the Holy Spirit, through God's Word, can reveal to the heart of the believer the purposes and intent of these Covenants. The Holy Spirit alone is able to motivate the heart through grace. For this reason the Scriptural references are included in the text of this book because what a mere man writes is not necessarily anointed of God, only His Word is anointed to teach.

> *But the anointing which ye have received of him abideth in you, and ye need not that any man teach you: but as the same anointing teacheth you of all things, and is truth, and is no lie, and even as it hath taught you, ye shall abide in him.*
> (1 John 2:27)

2

Edenic Covenant
Innocence

The Edenic Covenant is the historical record of Adam and Eve's fall from innocence and the first promise of redemption through faith in the sacrifice of Christ's blood. Redemption means not only to be bought back from the results of the fall but to be bought back from the fall itself, to be restored to the perfect state of Parrhesia, the innocence Adam and Eve had before they partook of the tree of the knowledge of good and evil.

> And the LORD God took the man, and put him into the garden of Eden to dress it and to keep it.
> And the LORD God commanded the man, saying, Of every tree of the garden thou mayest freely eat:
> But of the tree of the knowledge of good and evil, thou shalt not eat of it: for in the day that thou eatest thereof thou shalt surely die.
> (Genesis 2:15-17)

When God instituted the Edenic Covenant and the dispensation of innocence, when God created Adam and Eve and placed them in the Garden of Eden, their only consciousness was that of God's continual presence through the indwelling Holy

Spirit. God's gift of His indwelling perfection and everlasting righteousness was the strength of their very being in Him. This continual state of Parrhesia, the privilege of being anointed to commune and fellowship freely with their creator eternally was God's gift to the first of His chosen creation. There was no unrighteous outside influence, distractions nor guilt consciousness to disturb the tranquillity of perfect, continual, and the possibility of eternal communion with their God. However, as we see in the Scripture above Adam and Eve were commanded not to partake of the tree of the knowledge of good and evil being warned of God that to do so would destroy their state of Parrhesia and be replaced with the curse of the knowledge of physical death. Adam and Eve's partaking of the fruit of the tree of the knowledge of good and evil set in motion the ageing process, resulting in eventual physical death, in all future generations of mankind. This was not a harmless apple tree, as is often depicted, but the tree of the knowledge of life and death, and was not to even be touched.

> *But of the fruit of the tree which [is] in the midst*
> *of the garden, God hath said, Ye shall not eat of*
> *it, neither shall ye touch it, lest ye die.*
> *And the serpent said unto the woman, Ye shall*
> *not surely die:* (Genesis 3:3,4)

The partaking of the tree of the knowledge of good and evil separated Adam and Eve from the gift of God's gracious Sovereign Covenant for them, innocence. Here is the first example of the division between the believers two natures, through belief, living in the Spirit of God's will, or through unbelief, catering to the will of the flesh. Had Adam and Eve simply accepted God's Covenant of Grace, which was freely given to them, they would not have been tempted to look upon and yield to the desires of the flesh. This same principle is also true of today's believer. If believers choose to look back upon the law of sin and death, the letter of the law, the ten commandments, we ignore God's Covenant of Grace through faith in Christ's blood. The law is a schoolmaster to the unbeliever and was never intended for the redeemed.

It was through the unbelief of God's Word that their downfall came about, and consequently the downfall of the entire human race that was to be born of their union, for Eve was the mother of all living.

And Adam called his wife's name Eve; because
she was the mother of all living. (Genesis 3:20)

Confusion and a sense of unreality and separation from perfect communion with God was, and still is, the consequence of unbelief of God's revealed Word. Unbelief and unbelief alone separates mankind from the perfection of the knowledge of God's gift of unconditional righteousness. God and man were in perfect Spiritual harmony until that harmony was broken by the sin of disobedience and unbelief. As a result mankind took upon himself the fallen sinful nature of vanity and the need to attempt to validate himself, in his own eyes, through the search for self righteousness. Adam and Eve rightfully saw themselves as complete in God's presence and Glory, and they had no knowledge of separation from God nor the meaning of a lie nor any inclination to hide because of guilt, until sin was conceived. Through their cardinal sin of unbelief the consciousness of God's unhindered presence and the awareness of living in the illumination of His Glory, was removed from them.

Before their fall from grace Adam and Eve were joined as one flesh in the Spiritual institution of marriage, they had no sense of sin or guilt, and they walked in the garden of Eden naked and unashamed before God.

And Adam said, This [is] now bone of my bones,
and flesh of my flesh: she shall be called Woman,
because she was taken out of Man.
Therefore shall a man leave his father and his
mother, and shall cleave unto his wife: and they

shall be one flesh.
And they were both naked, the man and his wife,
and were not ashamed. (Genesis 2:23-25)

After the fall of Adam and Eve, who are the representative heads of all mankind, because they had doubted the love of the truth and the supreme reality of God's Word, found it necessary to try and hide their nakedness and newly acquired sinful flesh nature from God. Unbelief had fostered a sense of alienation in exchange for the parrhesia of their first estate. Guilt and resultant sin consciousness had now prompted them to try and devise a means whereby they might try and hide their fall from God's gift of righteousness. They foolishly fashioned garments of fig leaves, with their own hands, in an attempt to hide their newly acquired sense of nakedness before God.

> *And the eyes of them both were opened, and they knew that they [were] naked; and they sewed fig leaves together, and made themselves aprons.*
>
> *And they heard the voice of the LORD God walking in the garden in the cool of the day: and Adam and his wife hid themselves from the presence of the LORD God amongst the trees of the garden.*
>
> *And the LORD God called unto Adam, and said unto him, Where [art] thou?*
>
> *And he said, I heard thy voice in the garden, and I was afraid, because I [was] naked; and I hid myself.*
>
> *And he said, Who told thee that thou [wast] naked? Hast thou eaten of the tree, whereof I commanded thee that thou shouldest not eat?*
>
> *And the man said, The woman whom thou gavest [to be] with me, she gave me of the tree, and I did eat.* (Genesis 2:7-12)

Adam and Eve disobeyed because they had not fully appreciated God's dispensation of innocence, as a consequence they were expelled from the Garden of Eden. However, before they were expelled from the garden, God in His abundant mercy, with His own hands, clothed them with the righteousness garment of a slain animal. The skin of the slain animal testified of God's righteousness imputed to all men who have faith in the propitiatory blood of Jesus Christ. God clothed Adam and Eve with the garments of righteousness before they were expelled from the Garden of Eden, typical of how God gives his righteousness to all believers at the time He delivers them from the guilt of sin and death. It was the garment of righteousness placed on Adam and Eve through the grace and mercy of God, not made by human hands, that set aside and made useless the aprons of fig leaves with which they had clothed themselves in an attempt to hide their guilt.

Unto Adam also and to his wife did the LORD God make coats of skins, and clothed them.

(Genesis 3:21)

God's intent in replacing their clothing is quite clear, although their human bodies would now be relegated to return to the dust of the earth through physical death, they were given hope of eternal Spiritual life through faith in the blood of the righteousness garment which God had placed upon them by His Sovereign Grace. The garment of the slain animal testified of the Gospel of God's gift of perfect redemption for the fallen, it spoke of the future coming of the second Adam, Jesus Christ. Adam and Eve were given the Covenant of restored righteousness through faith in the blood of the promised redeemer, having now been cast out of the Garden of Eden.

In the verse below we see that God also gave believers a promise that the power of the tempter would be destroyed by the seed of the woman, Jesus Christ, who would purge the Heavenly Tabernacle with the blood of His perfect sacrifice. The promise also implied that Satan, along with his angels, would eventually be cast into the pit of Hell that has been prepared and reserved for them.

God, in addressing Satan for having deceived the woman, promised that the seed of the woman, Jesus Christ, would crush his head on the cross. Satan had only inflicted the bruise of physical, but not Spiritual, death upon the flesh of mankind.

> *And the LORD God said unto the serpent, Because thou hast done this, thou [art] cursed above all cattle, and above every beast of the field; upon thy belly shalt thou go, and dust shalt thou eat all the days of thy life:*
>
> *And I will put enmity between thee and the woman, and between thy seed and her seed; it shall bruise thy head, and thou shalt bruise his heel.* (Genesis 3:14,15)

Through Adam's seed his sinful nature was now to be passed onto all future generations of man because he was the father of all mankind. All men since Adam have a need to be redeemed, to be fully reinstated, from the fallen nature we inherited through Adam. No one can enter the kingdom of God unless he is reborn of the incorruptible seed of the second Adam, Jesus Christ.

> *For if by one man's offence death reigned by one; much more they which receive abundance of grace and of the gift of righteousness shall reign in life by one, Jesus Christ.)*
>
> *Therefore as by the offence of one [judgment came] upon all men to condemnation; even so by the righteousness of one [the free gift came] upon all men unto justification of life.*
>
> *For as by one man's disobedience many were made sinners, so by the obedience of one shall many be made righteous.* (Romans 5:17-19)

We inherited Adam's sin nature by God's design, but it was God's Sovereign Grace, through Christ, who came to set aside that sin nature. If God was so abundantly willing to set aside the original sin of Adam and Eve, which put into jeopardy the salvation of all mankind, why would we who were born of a sin nature, through no fault of our own, not also consider ourselves eligible for the utmost salvation? We need not feel guilty for having inherited a sin nature which was beyond our control.

However we all have a choice of believing and receiving the new nature of the righteousness garments of Christ which comes only from recognition of Jesus' completed work through the cross, and His ascension to the right hand of the Father. Our original sin nature with which we were born was not our fault, even though we must suffer the consequences of our human nature while in this body. The new righteous nature of Christ however, is given believers through individual choice, that is through simple belief and acceptance of God having separated us from our sin nature, through faith in the blood of Christ.

Adam and Eve came to the knowledge of sin by disobediently partaking of the fruit of the tree of the knowledge of good and evil, that is they became aware of the deadly sin of disobedience by ignoring God's Covenant with them. God's Covenant with them did not condemn their humanity until they became aware of their humanity, and they were not aware of that humanity until they became aware of the knowledge of good and evil by partaking of the fruit of the forbidden tree of good and evil.

I would like to suggest that the same is still true today. If we, through the knowledge of the law, attempt to govern our lives through the knowledge of good and evil or condemn ourselves for our negative reactions to God's law, then we ignore His everlasting Covenant of Grace which sees only the righteous Spirit of Christ within the redeemed. As God has stated in the promise of the New Covenant which Jesus Christ made manifest.

For I will be merciful to their unrighteousness,
and their sins and their iniquities will I
remember no more. (Hebrews 8:12)

Also:

And they shall teach no more every man his

neighbour, and every man his brother, saying,
Know the LORD: for they shall all know me,
from the least of them unto the greatest of them,
saith the LORD: for I will forgive their iniquity,
and I will remember their sin no more.
(Jeremiah 31:34)

For if we as believers are led of the Spirit then we are no longer under the law.

[This] I say then, Walk in the Spirit, and ye shall
not fulfil the lust of the flesh.

For the flesh lusteth against the Spirit, and the
Spirit against the flesh: and these are contrary
the one to the other: so that ye cannot do the
things that ye would.

But if ye be led of the Spirit, ye are not under the
law. (Galatians 5:16-18)

Is it possible that until man first tastes of the inheritance of vanity through the knowledge of sin that he cannot appreciate God's gift of righteousness? Could it be that Adam and Eve sinned because they had no idea of the consequences of sin? Could it be that God intended us to first taste of sin, so that we might then long for His gifts of righteousness?

For the creature was made subject to vanity, not
willingly, but by reason of him who hath
subjected [the same] in hope, (Romans 8:20)

Are not the above Scriptures final evidence that the good news of the Gospel of Grace was made evident and available to all mankind beginning with God's first chosen creatures, Adam and Eve? Is it not evident from the above Scriptures that the unconditional gift of the righteousness of God has been offered freely to all believers through faith in the blood of Christ, from the beginning, and to all subsequent generations? Was the Gospel, in all its fullness and glory not preached to Adam and Eve as depicted in the above Scriptures?

Moses was the author of the Pentateuch, the first five books of the Bible or the Scriptures that are known as the Torah. Is it not then evident that Moses' writings in Genesis as pertaining to Adam and Eve, began with Grace and The Good News of the Gospel of Jesus Christ? It is true that God spoke the cruel law of the ten commandments, through Moses, but this was because the children of Israel no longer believed in and had forgotten the Covenant of Grace God had unconditionally given them through the Covenant He made to all believers through Abraham, by which they were delivered from Egypt.

And God spake all these words, saying, I am the LORD thy God, which have brought thee out of the land of Egypt, out of the house of bondage.

(Exodus 20:1,2)

It was because of their transgressions that God found it necessary to remind the children of Israel, 430 years after the Covenant of promise was given to them through Abraham, that the tree of the knowledge of good and evil is very distasteful and so He imposed upon them the ten commandments, at their own request.

And this I say, that the Covenant, that was confirmed before of God in Christ, the law, which was four hundred and thirty years after, cannot disannul, that it should make the promise of none effect.

For if the inheritance be of the law, it is no more of promise: but God gave it to Abraham by promise.

Wherefore then serveth the law? It was added because of transgressions, till the seed should come to whom the promise was made; and it was ordained by angels in the hand of a mediator.

(Galatians 3:17-19)

Surely it is evident; that although the Edenic Covenant speaks of mankind falling from grace, the theme of the Edenic

Covenant is that man will always be restored to the very righteousness of God through faith in the redeeming power of the blood of Christ, the Lamb that was slain from the foundation of the world. In the future all those who will worship the anti-Christ will be those who have not given recognition to the Lamb of God who was slain from the foundation of the world.

> *And all that dwell upon the earth shall worship him, whose names are not written in the book of life of the Lamb slain from the foundation of the world.*
>
> *If any man have an ear, let him hear.*

(Revelation 13:8,9)

3

God's Covenant
Through Adam
Conscience

While still in the Garden of Eden, although they tried of their own will, Adam and Eve were not able to clothe themselves with a garment of righteousness suitable to meet God's righteous requirements, but merely clothed themselves in fig leaves in order to hide their new found knowledge of nakedness. Because of their willful disobedience, Adam and Eve could no longer be accepted by a righteous God. However, God in grace and mercy, did make provision to reestablish Adam and Eve back into His righteous Kingdom by providing and clothing them with the skin of a slain animal. The shedding of blood which was necessary to provide these righteousness garments, was a type of the blood of the perfect sacrifice of Christ to come, for Christ is the Lamb who was slain from the foundation of the world.

Adam and Eve now having been expelled from the Garden of Eden and no longer under the dispensation of innocence, were given a totally new set of life circumstances with which to deal. Through the disbelief of Adam and Eve the curse of now having to till the soil in order to sustain life was imposed upon all following generations of mankind.

> *Wherefore, as by one man sin entered into the world, and death by sin; and so death passed upon all men, for that all have sinned:*
> (Romans 5:12)

Now being made aware of the certainty of physical death, through the knowledge of right and wrong, which because of unbelief, was now incorporated into their newly acquired human sin nature of the flesh. They now became dependent upon their faith in the shed blood of a promised redeemer for the remission of the sin of unbelief. When God, in His Sovereign Grace, clothed them in the symbolic righteousness garments of a slain animal (Lamb), they were given to understand that the only way to be reunited with God, into the purity of their former estate, was through the provision of the perfect blood sacrifice of the promised Messiah/Christ.

The soul that is under the dominion of it's original sinful human nature has been contaminated by the inherited guilt and knowledge of death, and it can never receive the righteousness of God's Kingdom through self effort. God's righteous Kingdom can only indwell man if he first and foremost accepts the blood of Christ as being the redeeming, reuniting and sustaining power of the Holy Spirit of Christ within him.

> *Forasmuch as ye know that ye were <u>not redeemed</u> with corruptible things, [as] silver and gold, from your vain conversation [received] by tradition from your fathers; But <u>with the precious blood of Christ, as of a lamb without blemish and without spot: Who verily was foreordained before the foundation of the world,</u> but was manifest in these last times for you, Who by him do believe in God, that raised him up from the dead, and gave him glory; that your*

faith and hope might be in God.

Seeing ye have purified your souls in obeying the truth through the Spirit unto unfeigned love of the brethren, [see that ye] love one another with a pure heart fervently: <u>Being born again, not of corruptible seed, but of incorruptible, by the word of God, which liveth and abideth for ever.</u>

(1 Peter 1:18-23)

Ever since God expelled Adam and Eve from the Garden of Eden, men born of the flesh, the seed of the first Adam, have been relegated to work and till the soil, in order to earn a living by the sweat of his brow. Also the birth pangs of women are a reminder, that all living are now born with the fallen nature of Adam and Eve.

Unto the woman he said, I will greatly multiply thy sorrow and thy conception; in sorrow thou shalt bring forth children; and thy desire [shall be] to thy husband, and he shall rule over thee.

And unto Adam he said, Because thou hast hearkened unto the voice of thy wife, and hast eaten of the tree, of which I commanded thee, saying, Thou shalt not eat of it: cursed [is] the ground for thy sake; in sorrow shalt thou eat [of] it all the days of thy life;

Thorns also and thistles shall it bring forth to thee; and thou shalt eat the herb of the field;

In the sweat of thy face shalt thou eat bread, till thou return unto the ground; for out of it wast thou taken: for dust thou [art], and unto dust shalt thou return. (Genesis 3:16-19)

Having nullified the Edenic Covenant through unbelief and resultant sin, Adam and Eve were expelled from the Garden of Eden. God however, in His Grace and mercy, now made a means of escape from the death sentence of contaminated blood through a New Covenant, the Adamic Covenant.

Implicit in giving the Adamic Covenant, God's loving intent was that future generations would simply accept the gift of His imputed righteousness to all who had faith in the promise of the perfect blood sacrifice of Jesus Christ to come. The Adamic Covenant was to be a dispensation of conscience without the guilt of law. However, the idealistic state of "Parrhesia" and innocence before a Holy God was now only available to fallen man through a new birth, a gift of a new nature of the indwelling Holy Spirit, through faith in the shedding and sprinkling of the blood of Jesus Christ, who would not be made manifest for another four thousand years. Under the new dispensation of conscience, given Adam and Eve, there were no written behavioural boundaries set by God to condemn the guilt of their old sinful flesh nature.

In the sense that there were no God given established laws of the flesh to govern willful behaviour, the Adamic Covenant was unconditional. At the same time however, they were given the provision to experience salvation to the uttermost through faith in the blood of Christ, exemplified by the blood of the slain animal with which they were clothed. Through faith, they were instilled with a God given Spirit of Holiness to guide them and their descendants, as we see in the Scripture example below.

And Abel, he also brought of the firstlings of his flock and of the fat thereof. And the LORD had respect unto Abel and to his offering: But unto Cain and to his offering he had not respect. And Cain was very wroth, and his countenance fell.
(Genesis 4:4,5)

The bible records as typical, the division between Able, who was led of the Spirit through faith in Christ's blood, while his older brother Cain was depended upon natural instincts of the flesh and faith in the work of his hands. When Cain brought the Lord a sacrifice of the fruit of the ground instead of an acceptable blood sacrifice of a slain animal through which he would have been given the gift of God's righteousness, the Lord offered Cain a second chance to repent. Even though he had ignored God's initial offer of justification, the Lord gave Cain another chance to be freed from the unrighteousness of sin, as we read in verses six and seven of the same chapter.

> And the LORD said unto Cain, Why art thou wroth? and why is thy countenance fallen?
> If thou doest well, shalt thou not be accepted? and if thou doest not well, sin lieth at the door. And unto thee [shall be] his desire, and thou shalt rule over him. (Genesis 4:6,7)

As we see in the verses above God gave Cain a second opportunity to offer an acceptable blood sacrifice as redemption from his sin nature. However he rejected this opportunity which would have undone his initial mistake of unbelief and lack of faith in offering an acceptable blood sacrifice, which spoke of a coming redeemer. God only reveals and ratifies His unconditional Covenants to believers through faith in the blood of Christ. God has made the provision for mankind's righteousness through faith in renewing blood, it is up to man simply to accept that offering. Any attempt to receive the benefits of any of God's unconditional Covenants, by human effort, does despite to the Spirit of God's Grace. God however, does not revoke the offer or the benefits of any Covenant to the individual, but until either sinner or saint recognizes that his life is dependant upon the blood of Christ which ratifies the Covenant, the Covenant is of no benefit, and as Cain, he thereby forsakes God's mercy. The believers two natures, that of the Spirit and that of the flesh, are as separated from each other as were the lives of Cain and Abel.

God's unconditional Covenants always promise that "He will" Sovereignly sanctify and cleanse, through His righteous judgements and love for mankind. It is God who has initiated, and continually upholds the offer of unceasing love towards mankind, all that man is required to do is accept that love through belief in His Covenants. The awareness of oneness with God is dependant upon the believers faith in the mediating blood of Jesus Christ, which alone imputes to believers the assurance of His righteousness and Spirit within. The strength and awareness of God's saving love only comes to those who recognize that it is God who first loved them. As believers, our love for God is only in response to God's initial love for us, for He alone is the source of redeeming love.

We love him, because he first loved us.

(1 John 4:10)

And:

And from Jesus Christ, [who is] the faithful witness, [and] the first begotten of the dead, and the prince of the kings of the earth. Unto him that loved us, and washed us from our sins in his own blood, And hath made us kings and priests unto God and his Father; to him [be] glory and dominion for ever and ever. Amen.

(Revelation 1:5,6)

It was not until Cain repeatedly ignored the conviction of conscience, and refused to recognize that shed blood was the only acceptable offering of praise, that God intervened and imposed discipline upon him and all the future generations of his descendants. It was not until Cain yielded to the lust of his own flesh and slew his brother Abel, thereby violating God's Grace and shedding innocent blood, that he was alienated from God. Through Cains refusal to accept forgiveness, Cain and his descendants were cursed, and were relegated to become fugitives and vagabonds upon the earth. So Cain went from the presence of the Lord.

And Cain talked with Abel his brother: and it came to pass, when they were in the field, that Cain rose up against Abel his brother, and slew him.

And the LORD said unto Cain, Where [is] Abel thy brother? And he said, I know not: [Am] I my brother's keeper?

And he said, What hast thou done? the voice of thy brother's blood crieth unto me from the ground.

And now [art] thou cursed from the earth, which hath opened her mouth to receive thy brother's blood from thy hand;

When thou tillest the ground, it shall not henceforth yield unto thee her strength; a fugitive and a vagabond shalt thou be in the earth.

And Cain said unto the LORD, My punishment [is] greater than I can bear.

Behold, thou hast driven me out this day from the face of the earth; and from thy face shall I be hid; and I shall be a fugitive and a vagabond in the earth; and it shall come to pass, [that] every one that findeth me shall slay me.

And the LORD said unto him, Therefore whosoever slayeth Cain, vengeance shall be taken on him sevenfold. And the LORD set a mark upon Cain, lest any finding him should kill him. (Genesis 4:8-15)

The blood of Abel spoke of the only way in which man might become the righteousness of God, that is through faith in the perfect blood sacrifice, which was yet to be made manifest, that of the blood of Jesus Christ.

We see as an example in the Scriptures below, that when the majority of God's people fail to recognize the goodness of God as revealed by his Covenants, God typically raises up and separates unto Himself a remnant who still believe, and continue to have faith in His Word. Abel now having been slain, the

Adamic Covenant was continued through Adam and Eve's third son Seth, one of a faithful remnant who God raised up in place of Abel. Seth then was a type of the resurrected Christ just as Abel was a type of the lamb slain from the foundation of the world.

> *And Adam knew his wife again; and she bare a son, and called his name Seth: For God, [said she], hath appointed me another seed instead of Abel, whom Cain slew.* (Genesis 4:25)

Here we see the meaning of the word "Covenant", the dividing of the two natures of man, the sons of God and the sons of man. Seth was appointed of God to be a progenitor of the sons of God, those who would inherit the way of eternal life. Cain was separated and fled from the face of God and the Spirit of the Lord, and became the progenitor of the son's of natural man and the way of death.

> *And to Seth, to him also there was born a son; and he called his name Enos: then began men to call upon the name of the LORD.*
> (Genesis 4:26).

Note that it was through the seed of the second son of Adam, Seth, whom God had given Adam and Eve in place of Abel, that God chose to continue the blood line of perfection, not through the seed of Cain, the firstborn of Adam and Eve. Typically Christ is the second Adam. We will see this pattern confirmed in many instances as we study His Word, first the natural and then the Spiritual.

In Genesis chapter five, from verse six to verse twenty nine, we can follow the seed of Seth, through to faithful Enoch (Enos) until we come to the birth of Noah. In the verse above we see that it was the descendants of Enoch who began to call upon the name of the Lord, Jehovah, the redeemer to come.

> *By faith Enoch was translated that he should not see death; and was not found, because God had translated him: for before his translation he had*

this testimony, that he pleased God.
*But without faith [it is] impossible to please
[him]: for he that cometh to God must believe
that he is, and [that] he is a rewarder of them
that diligently seek him.* (Hebrews 11:5,6)

And:

*And all the days of Enoch were three hundred
sixty and five years: And Enoch walked with
God: and he was not; for God took him.*
(Genesis 5:23,24)

Enoch also was typical of the faithful remnant whom God
always reserves as a Spiritual seed to propagate a new generation
of believers, prior to separating and invoking His wrath upon an
unbelieving world system. Enoch was sanctified and translated,
or delivered, from the wrathful judgement of the flood which was
about to come upon unbelieving mankind. Enoch, being led of
the Holy Spirit, warned the unbelieving world system of his day
that perfect redemption was available to all who would simply
believe in the provision of the faithfulness of the blood of Christ.

*And Enoch also, the seventh from Adam,
prophesied of these, saying, Behold, the Lord
cometh with ten thousands of his saints, To
execute judgment upon all, and to convince all
that are ungodly among them of all their ungodly
deeds which they have ungodly committed, and
of all their hard [speeches] which ungodly
sinners have spoken against him.* (Jude 14,15)

Also note that the judgement of God's wrath upon a sinful
world, through the flood, did not come until after Enoch had been
translated, and after Methuselah had died. This is also a pattern
of God's nature and typical, as we shall see, as we study His
Word further. God always separates to Himself and delivers those
whom He has judged righteous, because of their faith in the blood
of the Lamb, prior to His judgement of condemnation upon all
unbelievers.

Except for Noah and his family, the unbelieving inhabitants of the earth had become insensitive to God's leading while still under the unconditional Covenant of conscience God had made to Adam. The unbelievers of the world system were about to see the wrath of God revealed, through a world wide flood.

Noah and his family were also of the faithful remnant who God always delivers prior to His judgement of wrath upon the unfaithful. Noah, throughout his days, had counted God faithful and had obeyed the leading of the Spirit of the Lord. He demonstrated this by being obedient in the building an Ark which would be the means whereby he and his family would escape the wrath of the flood and, by being faithful, become heirs of the very righteousness of God.

> *By faith Noah, being warned of God of things not seen as yet, moved with fear, prepared an ark to the saving of his house; by the which he condemned the world, and became heir of the righteousness which is by faith.* (Hebrews 11:7)

Fallen man had demonstrated, once again as did Adam and Eve, their unbelief and lack of appreciation for God's unconditional love. However, God in His mercy, through Noah and his family, gave another Covenant whereby mankind might still be redeemed, a Covenant of human government.

4

God's Covenant Through Noah

Human Government

Before the flood, typically, man being flesh, became dependant upon self and ignored God's second Covenant of conscience which he had given to Adam, by grace through faith in the promised shedding of the blood of the perfect sacrifice to come, Jesus Christ. The inevitable result of ignoring God's principles and oracles is to be overtaken by an imaginative and evil heart. Reality, and a mind free from the fear of death, is given only to those who have confidence and faith in the blood of the unconditional Covenants.

> There were giants in the earth in those days; and also after that, when the sons of God came in unto the daughters of men, and they bare [children] to them, the same [became] mighty men which [were] of old, men of renown.
>
> And God saw that the wickedness of man [was] great in the earth, and [that] every imagination

of the thoughts of his heart [was] only evil
continually.
And it repented the LORD that he had made man
on the earth, and it grieved him at his heart.
And the LORD said, I will destroy man whom I
have created from the face of the earth; both
man, and beast, and the creeping thing,
and the fowls of the air; for it repenteth me that
I have made them.

(Genesis 6:4-7)

God having created man, was not taken by surprise to see that man soon forgot the importance of the blood Covenant He had made with Adam and Eve. As a consequence mankind, except for the faithful remnant, fell from grace. Having ignored the redemption which was his through faith in the blood of the promised perfect sacrifice, his only option was to attempt to, once again, become self sufficient through reliance upon self will. Man once again had forgotten that everything he had enjoyed was given him by God's Grace, and so by default, mankind reverted to the evil of self gratification. God who made man, surely did not want to destroy that which He created for His own pleasure. God, then, as at the present time, only wanted man to awaken to the fact that God was his creator, and that through His Grace, God had given him the gift of eternal life. Mankind, then as now, has no hope of redemption and eternal life in heaven without accepting God's Covenant of Grace, through faith in the shed and sprinkled blood of Jesus' perfect sacrifice.

Noah, being of the remnant and seed of Adam's son Seth, continued the blood line of those who accepted that every Covenant of God's Grace is ratified, through faith, in a perfect blood sacrifice. Again, as is true of His nature, we see that God kept a remnant who continued in grace through faith in the blood Covenant. This remnant, who have faith in the blood of Jesus

Christ to continually cleanse them from all unrighteousness, will be seen throughout the Bible, as the people whom the Lord uses to receive the full blessing and benefits of His Covenants. This faithful remnant will always be used by God to bring the church back to the remembrance of it's first love, back to the awakening of the righteousness which is their inheritance, through the everlasting Covenant of Promise given to the seed of Abraham.

So it was through the faithful remnant, Noah and his house, that the church of his day was purified and brought back to the consciousness of Her righteousness, through the Sovereign will of a Covenant making God.

But Noah found grace in the eyes of the LORD.

These [are] the generations of Noah: Noah was a just man [and] perfect in his generations, [and] Noah walked with God.

(Genesis 6:8,9)

Noah was judged as perfect and righteous by God, the same as all believers, who are justified by grace through faith in the blood of Christ. The meaning of the Hebrew word used here, "tamyim" which is translated "perfect" means complete, full, perfect, undefiled, without spot, whole. The word translated here as "perfect" does not suggest a relative experience but clearly states a perfect positional righteousness in the sight of God. The word perfect is meant to convey the truth that, God has ordained and established His perfect nature into the Spirit nature of those whom He has declared righteous, in those whom He has separated from their original Adamic flesh nature. Redeemed man has two separate and distinct natures, Spirit and flesh. The Spirit nature being of God's perfect gift of righteousness to the redeemed, the flesh nature being that which must eventually die and return to dust.

[This] I say then, Walk in the Spirit, and ye shall not fulfil the lust of the flesh.

For the flesh lusteth against the Spirit, and the

*Spirit against the flesh: and these are contrary
the one to the other: so that ye cannot do the
things that ye would.* (Galatians 5:16,17)

After God had instilled in Noah His very righteous and
perfect nature, He then made it clear that He would destroy those
unbelievers who remained reliant on their original flesh nature.

*And God said unto Noah, The end of all flesh is
come before me; for the earth is filled with
violence through them; and, behold, I will
destroy them with the earth.* (Genesis 6:13)

Also:

*By faith Noah, being warned of God of things not
seen as yet, moved with fear, prepared an ark to
the saving of his house; by the which he
condemned the world, and became heir of the
righteousness which is by faith.* (Hebrews 11:7)

The unregenerated were not condemned without warning.
Noah had preached the full Gospel of Grace to them, they had
been given a choice, but had knowingly rejected the offer of
God's righteousness.

*And spared not the old world, but saved Noah
the eighth person, <u>a preacher of righteousness,</u>
bringing in the flood upon the world of the
ungodly;* (2 Peter 2:5)

However, Noah heeded God's Sovereign warning, because
he wisely counted God faithful to fulfil His Promises. Being
Spiritually motivated, he built an Ark according to God's specific
instructions. The Ark which Noah made was representative of a
type of Christ, the deliverer from God's wrath to those whom He
has declared righteous, while at the same time separates and
condemns unbelievers.

*Make thee an ark of gopher wood; rooms shalt
thou make in the ark, and shalt pitch it within
and without with pitch.*
(Genesis 6:14)

The wood used to construct the frame of the Ark, as in many other instances in the Bible, represented man. The pitch used to join these pieces of wood together and make it water proof, so that Noah and his family would escape the condemnation of the unregenerated, represented the blood of Christ. The Hebrew word ("kopher or kaphar") translated here as "pitch" is translated as the word "atonement" in many other Scriptures in the Bible. For example when the High Priest Aaron entered into the Holy of Holies every year with the blood of animal sacrifices to make atonement for himself and the sins of the children of Israel, this atonement was described by the same word that is translated "pitch" in the above verse. Pitch, as applied to Noah's Ark, was typical of the atoning blood of Jesus Christ, through which God Sovereignly confirmed His oaths and all unconditional Covenants to believing man. It spoke of God's blood Covenants of Grace toward man. It spoke of the blood of the New Covenant which Christ, as the believers High Priest, sprinkled upon the Mercy Seat of the Ark of the Covenant in heaven, after His resurrection. It is only through faith in Christ's atoning blood, sprinkled on the Ark of the Covenant in heaven, that believing man might be forgiven, pardoned, purged and reconciled to God. It also spoke of the expiation or the merciful setting aside of God's wrath upon redeemed man, in this case the eight souls of Noah and his family.

A window shalt thou make to the ark, and in a cubit shalt thou finish it above; and the door of the ark shalt thou set in the side thereof; [with] lower, second, and third [stories] shalt thou make it. (Genesis 6:16)

The word window as in the verse above is described as being a dual or double light and being a cubit above the Ark, could this be representative of the cherubims of glory above the Mercy Seat that is within the Holy of Holies?

And over it the cherubims of glory shadowing

the mercyseat; of which we cannot now speak particularly. (Hebrews 9:5)

The single door of the Ark allowed for only one way to enter into God's provision of grace, for escaping the wrath which He was about to pour out on an unrepentant wicked world. Likewise Jesus Christ is the only door whereby men might be saved.

> *Then said Jesus unto them again, Verily, verily, I say unto you, I am the door of the sheep.*
>
> *All that ever came before me are thieves and robbers: but the sheep did not hear them.*
>
> *I am the door: by me if any man enter in, he shall be saved, and shall go in and out, and find pasture.* (John 10:7-9)

Likewise, there is only one way for the repentant to come into the very presence of God, into the secret place of the Most High, that is through the second veil of the tabernacle. The second veil of the tabernacle was rent from top to bottom at the time of Jesus Christ's perfect blood sacrifice upon the cross, both the veil of the earthly tabernacle, which was a figure of the true, as well as the veil of the Heavenly Tabernacle. It was the rent second veil of the Tabernacle in Heaven, through which our High Priest, Jesus Christ, after his resurrection, entered in order to sprinkle His blood seven times on the Mercy Seat. This sprinkling of His blood, promised from the foundation of the world, made perfect atonement for the sin of all believers. It is through faith in this blood of the New Covenant by which believers are enabled, even encouraged through God's perfect will, to enter boldly through this second veil into the very presence of God.

> *For by one offering he hath perfected for ever them that are sanctified.*
>
> *Whereof the Holy Ghost also is a witness to us: for after that he had said before, This is the Covenant that I will make with them after those*

days, saith the Lord, I will put my laws into their
hearts, and in their minds will I write them; And
their sins and iniquities will I remember no
more.
Now where remission of these is, there is no
more offering for sin.
Having therefore, brethren, boldness to enter
into the holiest by the blood of Jesus,
By a new and living way, which he hath
consecrated for us, through the veil, that is to
say, his flesh; And [having] an high priest over
the house of God; Let us draw near with a true
heart in full assurance of faith, having our hearts
sprinkled from an evil conscience, and our
bodies washed with pure water.
(Hebrews 12:14-22)

After Noah and his family, along with male and female representatives of every living creature of the earth had entered the Ark, the Lord God shut the door behind them.

And they that went in, went in male and female
of all flesh, as God had commanded him: and the
LORD shut him in. (Genesis 7:16)

God "nailed them in" thus demonstrated His immutable oath of salvation to all who continue to have their faith in the blood of the Covenant of Grace, both the Covenant God gave to all believers through the promise of the blessing of Abraham, and the New Covenant which fulfilled that promise.

But with thee will I establish my Covenant; and
thou shalt come into the ark, thou, and thy sons,
and thy wife, and thy sons' wives with thee.
(Genesis 6:18)

As we see in the verse above the Lord God, through His Sovereign will, established a new unconditional Covenant with Noah and his righteous seed, even before they were to witness the destruction of all sinful men who still remained outside the safety of the Ark because of their unbelieving fleshly nature. Here we see confirmed the sharp distinction and utter hopelessness of the sinful nature of natural man, sharply divided and entirely separate from the new Spiritual nature that indwells men who have received the righteousness of God. The full awareness of God's righteousness only indwells those who have faith in the atoning blood of the resurrected Christ who sprinkled His blood on the Ark of the Covenant in Heaven.

Again the provision of ongoing salvation through faith in Christ's atoning blood is typical of our loving God who, even today, continues to provide the faithful remnant a way to escape the destruction which comes to the unredeemed, through the provision of the new Covenant and Christ's ever present High Priestly ministry.

Through Noah's faithful obedience in preparing an Ark, the faithful remnant were saved, and the unbelievers condemned. God gave Noah the invitation to come into the Ark, and in so doing Noah and his family gratefully accepted and entered God's righteous kingdom, thereby mercifully escaping the wrath of God, which came upon the unbelievers through the flood.

And the LORD said unto Noah, Come thou and
all thy house into the ark; for thee have I seen
righteous before me in this generation.
Of every clean beast thou shalt take to thee by
sevens, the male and his female: and of beasts
that [are] not clean by two, the male and his
female. (Genesis 7:1)

After having been separated and delivered from unbelievers through the flood, Noah, in an act of grateful praise, worshiped and praised God. He offered many blood sacrifices of praise to the God, who saved he and his family from destruction. Before the flood Noah was instructed of God to place seven of every clean beast into the ark, in doing so, God had made provision for the wherewithal to sacrifice of the blood of every clean beast and still leave several pairs of every clean beast with which to replenish the earth. Noah's worship, through the blood sacrifice of these animals, was an acknowledgment and grateful testimony of his faith in the power of the blood of Christ to continually separate mankind from the wrath of God. Noah, being led of the Holy Spirit was fully aware of the coming day of atonement, and redemption of believers through faith in the blood of Jesus Christ.

Note that God, in His Grace, had supplied the necessary blood sacrifice with which to offer up the sacrifice of praise, the same as God has given us His son, the Lord Jesus Christ, through which we offer up the sacrifice of praise, through faith in His blood.

And Noah builded an altar unto the LORD; and took of every clean beast, and of every clean fowl, and offered burnt offerings on the altar.

And the LORD smelled a sweet savour; and the LORD said in his heart, I will not again curse the ground any more for man's sake; for the imagination of man's heart [is] evil from his youth; neither will I again smite any more every thing living, as I have done.

While the earth remaineth, seedtime and harvest, and cold and heat, and summer and winter, and day and night shall not cease. (Genesis 8:20-22)

Because of Noah's heart felt sacrifices, God in His abundant mercy Sovereignly promised, "I will not again curse the ground any more for man's sake."

Here again we see the promise of an unconditional Covenant fulfilled without mankind having to offer a plea to God. As with all unconditional Covenants, God out of Sovereign love, graciously gives man yet another opportunity to awaken to His gift of righteousness and perfection to believers. However, Noah received the Covenanted promise of God's protective mercy and grace, only after having been tried through his faithfulness in the building of an Ark, after he had demonstrated that he counted

God faithful to fulfill His promises. Note that it was through faith that he became the heir of God's righteousness.

> *But without faith it is impossible to please him: for he that cometh to God must believe that he is, and that he is a rewarder of them that diligently seek him.*
>
> *By faith Noah, being warned of God of things not seen as yet, moved with fear, prepared an ark to the saving of his house; by the which he condemned the world, and became heir of the righteousness which is by faith.*

(Hebrews 11:6,7)

The Covenant God made with Noah and his descendants is articulated in the Scriptures below. In these Scriptures, as with other unconditional Covenants, please note how often God Sovereignly promises that "He will" supply the power of the Holy Spirit to enable believers to conform to His will. The Noahic Covenant and dispensation of human government which God made with Noah, included His Promise to never again destroy the earth by flood. Also in this Covenant, God gave man the responsibility to govern himself and his environment according to the will of God, through the leading of His Holy Spirit.

> *And surely your blood of your lives <u>will I</u> require; at the hand of every beast <u>will I</u> require it, and at the hand of man; at the hand of every man's brother <u>will I</u> require the life of man.*
>
> *Whoso sheddeth man's blood, by man shall his blood be shed: for in the image of God made he man.*
>
> *And you, be ye fruitful, and multiply; bring forth abundantly in the earth, and multiply therein.*
>
> *And God spake unto Noah, and to his sons with him, saying, And I, behold, <u>I establish my</u>*

*Covenant with you, and with your seed
after you; And with every living creature that [is]
with you, of the fowl, of the cattle, and of every
beast of the earth with you; from all that go out
of the ark, to every beast of the earth.
And I will establish my Covenant with you;
neither shall all flesh be cut off any more by the
waters of a flood; neither shall there any
more be a flood to destroy the earth.*
(Genesis 9:5-11)

Until this day God reminds all mankind of this Covenant He made with Noah, in every rainbow we see after a refreshing rain.

Man was now given the authority to govern his own kind, to subdue violence using the ultimate threat of death, in order to institute community government.

Now once again, in following Noah's genealogy, we see in the dispensation of God's Covenant to believers, how God blesses and upholds a faithful remnant, through the seed of those who count Him faithful. Both Abraham, the progenitor of all believers, (Genesis 11:26), and Jesus the ratifier of the Covenant God made to us through Abraham, (Matthew 1:1), were born through the blood line of Noah's son, Shem.

It is important to see through the sequence of events, and God's provisions for Noah and his family, how God blesses those who accept His Covenants of Grace. God's Covenanted blessings, through Noah, is typical of how, over and over again throughout church history, God Sovereignly predestines a faithful remnant to revive His church.

First: God chose Noah, who understood the significance of the blood Covenant and so found grace in the eyes of the Lord. For it is only by grace through faith in the blood of Jesus Christ that anyone is saved.

But Noah found grace in the eyes of the LORD.
(Genesis 6:8)

Second: By faith he walked with God who judged him just(ified) and Spiritually perfect.

> *These are the generations of Noah: Noah was a just man and perfect in his generations, and Noah walked with God.* (Genesis 6:9)

Third: Noah and his family were delivered from the flood in the Ark which he had obediently built, but a judgement of God's wrath came upon unbelieving man kind.

> *By faith Noah, being warned of God of things not seen as yet, moved with fear, prepared an ark to the saving of his house; by the which he condemned the world, and became heir of the righteousness which is by faith .* (Hebrews 11:7)

Fourth: As we saw in previous scriptures Noah, after having been brought through the flood, offered up sacrifices of the blood of clean, perfect animals, typical of the promised perfect sacrifice of Jesus Christ to come.

Fifth: As we see in the verses below Noah's seed, through Shem, Ham, and Japheth were to became a conduit through which God's purposes for mankind would be continued.

> *And God blessed Noah and his sons, and said unto them, Be fruitful, and multiply, and replenish the earth.* (Genesis 9:1)

Although God had irrevocably judged Noah justified and perfect in the Spirit of righteousness yet, like most of the patriarchs and present day believers, he at times was weak in his natural flesh. Noah, as are we all, was not without sin in the flesh.

> *And the sons of Noah, that went forth of the ark, were Shem, and Ham, and Japheth: and Ham is the father of Canaan.*
>
> *These are the three sons of Noah: and of them was the whole earth overspread.*
>
> *And Noah began to be an husbandman, and he planted a vineyard: And he drank of the wine,*

and was drunken; and he was uncovered within his tent.

And Ham, the father of Canaan, saw the nakedness of his father, and told his two brethren without. (Genesis 9:18-22)

Noah's drunkenness, as a consequence of his lapse into his flesh nature, did not go without repercussions as we see in verse 22 above. Ham in "seeing" his fathers nakedness has deeper implications than merely looking.

And Noah awoke from his wine, and knew what his younger son had done unto him.

And he said, Cursed be Canaan; a servant of servants shall he be unto his brethren.

And he said, Blessed be the LORD God of Shem; and Canaan shall be his servant.

God shall enlarge Japheth, and he shall dwell in the tents of Shem; and Canaan shall be his servant. (Genesis 9:24-27)

Whatever happened between Ham, the father of Canaan, and Noah was significant enough that it caused Noah to put a curse upon his grandson Canaan. The most significant aspect of this incident, was that Ham was removed from the blessing which God had placed upon the family of His blessed remnant, who were gracefully brought through the flood. Ham was excluded from the blessing of grace.

Noah's other two sons, Japheth and Shem, were blessed because they did not consider their fathers nakedness nor regard his flesh nature, but like God, they only knew Noah as righteous and perfect.

And Shem and Japheth took a garment, and laid it upon both their shoulders, and went backward, and covered the nakedness of their father; and their faces were backward, and they saw not their father's nakedness. (Genesis 9:23)

All believers who, from time to time, through lack of faith, lapse into their flesh nature may suffer a momentary loss of Spiritual blessings, however our God does not condemn us. Through faith in the blood of Christ and His High Priestly ministry, within the second veil, God only sees His Spirit of righteousness and perfection within the redeemed.

> *Whosoever committeth sin transgresseth also the law: for sin is the transgression of the law.*
> *And ye know that he was manifested to take away our sins; and in him is no sin.*
> *Whosoever abideth in him sinneth not: whosoever sinneth hath not seen him, neither known him.*
> *Little children, let no man deceive you: he that doeth righteousness is righteous, even as he is righteous.*
> *He that committeth sin is of the devil; for the devil sinneth from the beginning. For this purpose the Son of God was manifested, that he might destroy the works of the devil.*
> *Whosoever is born of God doth not commit sin; for his seed remaineth in him: and he cannot sin, because he is born of God.* (1 John 3:4-9)

There is no middle ground, either God has separated believers from their sin nature or we are still children of the devil. That which is Spirit is Spirit but that which is flesh is flesh.

> *Jesus answered, Verily, verily, I say unto thee, Except a man be born of water and of the Spirit, he cannot enter into the kingdom of God.*
> *That which is born of the flesh is flesh; and that which is born of the Spirit is spirit.*
> *Marvel not that I said unto thee, Ye must be born again.*
> *The wind bloweth where it listeth, and thou*

hearest the sound thereof, but canst not tell
whence it cometh, and whither it goeth: so is
every one that is born of the Spirit. (John 3:5-8)

In Genesis 11:1-9, we read of the results of ignoring the provisions of the blood of the Covenant, and the resultant discord and dispersion of the children of Israel, as depicted in the story of the tower of Babel. The descendants of Noah, in an attempt to make a name for themselves, attempted to make a tower that would reach heaven. It seems they planned to conquer heaven of their own volition. "Let us" had become the prideful motivation of their hearts. Pride of flesh is the only alternative response to life, of those who do not accept the indwelling righteousness of God's Kingdom as their identity.

And they said, Go to, let us build us a city and a
tower, whose top [may reach] unto heaven; and
let us make us a name, lest we be scattered
abroad upon the face of the whole earth.
(Genesis 11:4)

Although God had blessed the righteous descendants of Noah, Japheth and Shem, through the Covenant of self government, their descendants soon forgot who had given them their freedom. They had come to imagine that their lives and salvation was now dependent upon their denominational unity, through self will, and had forgotten the unity of the Holy Spirit which had been given them through their past responsiveness to a gracious God.

Because the generations of Noah had become prideful and self dependant, the Lord confounded their language so that they could not communicate with each other, as a consequence they were not able to finish building their monument to self pride. Each language group then went their own way and were dispersed upon the face of the earth, exactly what they were attempting to prevent by their own will power. They had attempted to build a tower in order to make a name for themselves, but because they ignored God's Covenant, their vision of self fulfilment was shattered.

And the LORD said, Behold, the people [is] one, and they have all one language; and this they begin to do: and now nothing will be restrained from them, which they have imagined to do.

Go to, let us go down, and there confound their language, that they may not understand one another's speech.

So the LORD scattered them abroad from thence upon the face of all the earth: and they left off to build the city.

Therefore is the name of it called Babel; because the LORD did there confound the language of all the earth: and from thence did the LORD scatter them abroad upon the face of all the earth.

(Genesis 11:6-9)

Conclusion:

The present state of mankind is almost identical as was experienced by the decedents of Noah, prideful and self dependent, seeking fulfilment through the lusts of the flesh, through their own understanding. Mankind has once again become forgetful of the Covenants of Grace which God would so willingly reveal to them if they would only listen to His heart through His Word. Mankind is attempting once again to find salvation in a one world government, a new world order. It would be wise for present world leaders to take warning of this Biblical lesson. Mankind in attempting to govern himself through laws of self discipline and social controls ignores and separates himself from God's Covenants of Grace. Historically God shakes man when that happens, and God has not changed. If looking back on world history proves anything, if there is one dominant message of history, surely the lesson to be learned, is that man cannot govern himself.

God loves humanity, especially his church, the mystical body of Christ, whom He has redeemed through faith in the blood of Christ. It is through His Covenants of Grace through which He has established and upholds His pure spotless bride. God desires that all men everywhere, would look unto Him to solve their problems, and find true fulfilment. He would do this if they desired and sought first the Kingdom of God and His righteousness. In the following Scripture we are reminded that the problems of mankind cannot be corrected by faith in the world system, self government. It is up to the people of God to seek His face, and then He will, in return, heal our land. Have we, the institutional church, as the people of God, forgotten who is the land healer? Do we not hear what the Spirit of the Lord is saying? Because of unbelief do we perceive ourselves as being under cruel bondage, as did the children of Israel? Do we as Christians, through faith in political reform, attempt to have our land healed through governmental laws rather than allow His will to be done in us? God means what He says, as recorded in the Scripture below, when He says He will heal our land, if we the people who are called by His name, Christians, will turn from our wickedness of unbelief.

> *If my people, which are called by my name, shall*
> *humble themselves, and pray, and seek my face,*
> *and turn from their wicked ways; then will I hear*
> *from heaven, and will forgive their sin, and will*
> *heal their land.* (2 Chronicles 7:14)

Let present day world leaders be advised, the establishment of a one world state through human government is contrary to God's will, as it encourages man to look to himself for purpose and fulfilment. It is still God's will, as it was in the Garden of Eden, that man remember who made him and who sustains him. God will finally destroy any attempts to build a one world government, because it does not acknowledge and praise Him as giving man an end purpose. God, alone, will institute His own one world government when Christ returns, at his Second Advent, to finally and for all time establish a universal government of righteousness and peace. Present human world governments are built upon laws and situational human moral guidelines and as such ignore God's righteous judgements. At Christ's return he will once again reestablish the Spirit of the "Torah", the first five books of the Bible. The meaning of the Hebrew word "Torah" is God's righteous judgements.

For what nation [is there so] great, who [hath] God [so] nigh unto them, as the LORD our God [is] in all [things that] we call upon him [for]?

And what nation [is there so] great, that hath statutes and judgments [so] righteous as all this law, which I set before you this day?

Only take heed to thyself, and keep thy soul diligently, lest thou forget the things which thine eyes have seen, and lest they depart from thy heart all the days of thy life: but teach them thy sons, and thy sons' sons; (Deuteronomy 4:7-9)

5

God's Covenant Given to all Believers Through Abraham

Promise

It is strongly recommended that the historical account of Abraham's life, first be read from the Scriptures, prior to reading this contemporary viewpoint of the impact of his life, and the Covenant God made to all present day believers through Abraham. It is recommended that the Scriptures from Genesis chapter eleven through chapter twenty-two be read, in order to acquaint the reader with the early history of Abraham.

Beginning in Genesis chapter eleven we see that through the seed of the righteous remnant of Noah, the scarlet thread, the blood of the Lamb slain from the foundation of the world, the seed of the redeemed of the Lord, passed on to Abraham and his seed. For our purposes this account continues until the end of chapter 22 of the book of Genesis. If we are familiar with this historical account of Abraham's life, as recorded in these chapters, the sequence of events in his life with which we will expound, will become more readily understood.

In this chapter we hope to deal with and hopefully shed some light on these questions: In what way does this Covenant have a bearing on my life as a Christian today? What parallel message has the Old Testament, revealed through the Covenant God made with believers through Abraham, have to do with New Testament believers? Does the Covenant God made with believers through Abraham to some degree satisfy the word of Hebrews 5:8-14 where we are exhorted to seek out the first principles of the oracles of God before we are enabled to walk in the meat of the Spirit? What does the understanding that Jesus Christ who was ordained a High Priest in the order of Melchizedek, of whom the Bible through the Holy Spirit has many things to say, have to do with our understanding of the nature and Spirit of Jesus Christ?

> *Though he were a Son, yet learned he obedience by the things which he suffered;*
> *And being made perfect, he became the author of eternal salvation unto all them that obey him;*
> *Called of God an high priest after the order of Melchisedec.*
> *Of whom we have many things to say, and hard to be uttered, seeing ye are dull of hearing.*
> *For when for the time ye ought to be teachers, ye have need that one teach you again which be the first principles of the oracles of God; and are become such as have need of milk, and not of strong meat.*
> *For every one that useth milk is unskilful in the word of righteousness: for he is a babe.*
> *But strong meat belongeth to them that are of full age, even those who by reason of use have their senses exercised to discern both good and evil.*
> (Hebrews 5:8-14)

To begin: Abram and his wife Sarai, who was also his half sister, were called of God to separate themselves from their idle worshipping home in the land of Ur of the Chaldees, and in faith in God, go to the foreign country of Canaan, a land of promise and spiritual fulfilment, a land of peace and rest. The Spirit of God prompted Abram to look for a Spiritual city whose builder and maker was God, not a visible city made with hands, but a city with heavenly foundations, built on the Mountain of God, the heavenly Mount Zion.

> *By faith Abraham, when he was called to go out into a place which he should after receive for an inheritance, obeyed; and he went out, not knowing whither he went.*
>
> *By faith he sojourned in the land of promise, as in a strange country, dwelling in tabernacles with Isaac and Jacob, the heirs with him of the same promise:*
>
> *For he looked for a city which hath foundations, whose builder and maker is God.*

(Hebrews 11:8-10)

All humans since the fall of Adam and Eve in the Garden of Eden, were naturally born into the present evil world system, as was Abram. Through no fault of our own we were born of a corrupt flesh nature that had been separated, through the unbelief and fall of Adam and Eve, from the nature of God's righteous nature.

> *Unto the woman he said, I will greatly multiply thy sorrow and thy conception; in sorrow thou shalt bring forth children; and thy desire shall be to thy husband, and he shall rule over thee.*
>
> *And unto Adam he said, Because thou hast hearkened unto the voice of thy wife, and hast eaten of the tree, of which I commanded thee, saying, Thou shalt not eat of it: cursed is the*

*ground for thy sake; in sorrow shalt thou eat of
it all the days of thy life;*
*Thorns also and thistles shall it bring forth to
thee; and thou shalt eat the herb of the field;*
*In the sweat of thy face shalt thou eat bread, till
thou return unto the ground; for out of it wast
thou taken: for dust thou art, and unto dust shalt
thou return.*
*And Adam called his wife's name Eve; because
she was the mother of all living.*
(Genesis 3:16-20)

We were born and live in a corrupt world city, a world
community where there is no hope of everlasting life except
through Spiritual rebirth. The idolatry with which we naturally
view world leaders, from the viewpoint of our unregenerated
nature prior to Spiritual rebirth, be they political, business
leaders, sports heroes, movie stars and even religious leaders, is
a replica of the idol worshipping environment into which Abram
was born.

*These are wells without water, clouds that are
carried with a tempest; to whom the mist of
darkness is reserved for ever.*
*For when they speak great swelling words of
vanity, they allure through the lusts of the flesh,
through much wantonness, those that were clean
escaped from them who live in error.*
*While they promise them liberty, they themselves
are the servants of corruption: for of whom a
man is overcome, of the same is he brought in
bondage.* (2 Peter 2:17-19)

But like Abram all believers are called through the love of
God, and the working of the Holy Spirit, to look for a city of
peace and righteousness, a city not of this world system. It was
for this eternal city for which Abram sought and eventually

found, through the blessing of the Spirit of righteousness which he received through faith in the blood of Christ. That city is the heavenly Jerusalem and Mount Zion, the heritage of all believers being of the seed of Abraham, as soon as they accept Jesus Christ as Saviour and Lord. All believers have this heavenly home on Mount (Sion) Zion on the provision that they remove themselves from the law of Mount Sinai. Even Moses was distressed by the imposition of the law on Mount Sinai for he feared and trembled.

> *For ye are not come unto the mount that might be touched, and that burned with fire, nor unto blackness, and darkness, and tempest,*
> *And the sound of a trumpet, and the voice of words; which voice they that heard intreated that the word should not be spoken to them any more:*
> *(For they could not endure that which was commanded, And if so much as a beast touch the mountain, it shall be stoned, or thrust through with a dart:*
> *And so terrible was the sight, that Moses said, I exceedingly fear and quake:)*
> *But ye are come unto mount Sion, and unto the city of the living God, the heavenly Jerusalem, and to an innumerable company of angels,*
> *To the general assembly and church of the firstborn, which are written in heaven, and to God the Judge of all, and to the spirits of just men made perfect,*
> *And to Jesus the mediator of the new Covenant, and to the blood of sprinkling, that speaketh better things than that of Abel.*

(Hebrews 12:18-24)

However, Abram, like many believers, after they have received the promise of a new dwelling place in God's Spiritual Kingdom, are lured back into the world system and the natural comforts of the flesh.

After coming into the land of promise Abram experienced a famine and as a result looked for the necessary provisions of life in Egypt, the epitome of the world system. Abram apparently did not believe that God would supply the basic needs of life while he remained in the land of promise.

Believers, those who are born of the Spirit from above, through faith in the blood of Christ, will become Spiritually undernourished if we do not diligently work to feed the Spirit of Christ within us through the study of His Word. If God's Spirit who indwells believers is not continually nourished by the knowledge of His Word, we naturally revert to foolish attempts to experience self righteousness through self improvement programmes and self imposed moral accountability.

> *My people are destroyed for lack of knowledge:*
> *because thou hast rejected knowledge, I will also*
> *reject thee, that thou shalt be no priest to me:*
> *seeing thou hast forgotten the law of thy God, I*
> *will also forget thy children.* (Hosea 4:6)

Also:

> *Study to shew thyself approved unto God, a*
> *workman that needeth not to be ashamed, rightly*
> *dividing the word of truth.* (2 Timothy 2:15)

It was unbelief in God's Word that caused Abram and Sarai to look for life's resources in Egypt, and in doing so they forsook God's promise and as a consequence reverted, to some degree, to their old nature. In the scriptures below we will see that to reenter the world system they had to forsake truth for a half truth.

> *And there was a famine in the land: and Abram*
> *went down into Egypt to sojourn there; for the*
> *famine was grievous in the land.*
> *And it came to pass, when he was come near to*
> *enter into Egypt, that he said unto Sarai his wife,*
> *Behold now, I know that thou art a fair woman to*
> *look upon:*
> *Therefore it shall come to pass, when the*

Egyptians shall see thee, that they shall say, This is his wife: and they will kill me, but they will save thee alive.

Say, I pray thee, thou art my sister: that it may be well with me for thy sake; and my soul shall live because of thee.

And it came to pass, that, when Abram was come into Egypt, the Egyptians beheld the woman that she was very fair.

The princes also of Pharaoh saw her, and commended her before Pharaoh: and the woman was taken into Pharaoh's house.

And he entreated Abram well for her sake: and he had sheep, and oxen, and he asses, and menservants, and maidservants, and she asses, and camels.

And the LORD plagued Pharaoh and his house with great plagues because of Sarai Abram's wife.

And Pharaoh called Abram, and said, What is this that thou hast done unto me? why didst thou not tell me that she was thy wife?

Why saidst thou, She is my sister? so I might have taken her to me to wife: now therefore behold thy wife, take her, and go thy way.

And Pharaoh commanded his men concerning him: and they sent him away, and his wife, and all that he had. (Genesis 12:10-20)

Abram accepted the wealth that he was given of Pharaoh, the leader of Egypt and the central city of the world system. However Abram and Sarai were banished from Egypt when Pharaoh discovered the truth, that Sarai was not just Abram's half sister but really his wife.

There is so much to be learned here from this example that it could be the subject of another complete study. This story is a perfect example of what happens to the present day believer who isn't being fed on the bountiful soul satisfying meat of the Word but only on the meagre starvation diet of milk. So lets try to summerize some of the similarities of this Scripture with the trials of today's immature believer.

First: After the Spirit of Christ comes to tabernacle within the earthen vessel of the believer, we must become convinced through our own experiences, that it is only through the meat of God's Word that the Spirit of our heavenly nature is sustained and satisfied. The nourishing strong meat of the Word only comes to us through the study and awareness of the first principles of the oracles of God, that is, by the knowledge of His eight Covenants given to man through the prophets and patriarchs.

In the Scriptures below the writer of the book of Hebrews, speaking of Jesus Christ and His High Priestly ministry being of the same ordination as that of Melchezedek, writes;

> *Called of God an high priest after the order of Melchisedec.*
>
> *Of whom we have many things to say, and hard to be uttered, seeing ye are dull of hearing.*
>
> *For when for the time ye ought to be teachers, ye have need that one teach you again which be the first principles of the oracles of God; and are become such as have need of milk, and not of strong meat.*
>
> *For every one that useth milk is unskilful in the word of righteousness: for he is a babe.*
>
> *But strong meat belongeth to them that are of full age, even those who by reason of use have their senses exercised to discern both good and evil.*
> (Hebrews 5:10-14)

Secondly: If, through our lack of digesting the meat of the Word we become hungry enough to look for Spiritual guidance through the oracles of man, we exchange the promise and blessing of God for the curse that comes to us through the idol worship of human religious leaders. As we see below, no man is of himself able to teach the heart, only the Holy Spirit is able to anoint truth to the heart through the Word of God.

But the anointing which ye have received of him abideth in you, and ye need not that any man teach you: but as the same anointing teacheth you of all things, and is truth, and is no lie, and even as it hath taught you, ye shall abide in him.
(1 John 2:27)

Third: Abram, in a lapse of faith that God would provide all that He had promised, took matters into his own hands and went to Egypt and thus became dependent on Pharaoh's resources for sustenance. Pharaoh in seeing the physical beauty of Sarai desired her and sought to take her into his harem. Abram, in a selfish attempt to save his own skin, told Pharaoh that Sarai was his sister but neglected to tell him that Sarai and he were husband and wife. Abram who began his journey through the leading of the Holy Spirit temporarily reverted to the will of the flesh. In attempting to deceive Pharaoh he deceives himself.

The believer who does not fully appreciate and respond to the gift of God's righteousness dwelling within him, also forgets and deceives himself as to the full truth of his identity in Christ. To the degree the believer does not awaken to the gift of God's indwelling righteousness he, by default, becomes assimilated with the world system through his flesh nature. Without the strong meat of the Word the believer soon forgets that he has been united in marriage to God, and has become espoused to Him through the indwelling Spirit of Christ. Only through total faith in the blood of Christ and His High Priestly ministry to present believers in His righteousness to the Father do we become members of the perfect church, the spotless mystical bride of Christ.

But ye are come unto mount Sion, and unto the city of the living God, the heavenly Jerusalem,

and to an innumerable company of angels,
To the general assembly and church of the
firstborn, which are written in heaven, and to
God the Judge of all, and to the spirits of just
men made perfect,
And to Jesus the mediator of the new Covenant,
and to the blood of sprinkling, that speaketh
better things than that of Abel.
(Hebrews 12:22-24)

Also:

Be not deceived: evil communications corrupt
good manners.
Awake to righteousness, and sin not; for some
have not the knowledge of God: I speak this to
your shame. (1 Corinthians 15:33,34)

Here again we see this separation, the pure spotless blood washed bride of Christ refers to those who are Spiritual virgins, the flesh nature adheres to the adulterated world system.

Would to God ye could bear with me a little in
my folly: and indeed bear with me.
For I am jealous over you with godly jealousy:
for I have espoused you to one husband, that I
may present you as a chaste virgin to Christ.
(2 Corinthians 11:1,2)

And

For as a young man marrieth a virgin, so shall
thy sons marry thee: and as the bridegroom
rejoiceth over the bride, so shall thy God rejoice
over thee. (Isaiah 62:5)

Fourth: As God used Pharaoh to convince Abram to return to the promised land so God often uses the Satanic world system to bring believers back into His will and instill in them a deeper awareness and appreciation of the promises of His Covenant to them.

We read in Genesis 12:20 above where Pharaoh was angry with Abram for having deceived him and had his men send Abram and Sarai away along with their newly acquired wealth.

And Abram went up out of Egypt, he, and his wife, and all that he had, and Lot with him, into the south.

And Abram was very rich in cattle, in silver, and in gold.

And he went on his journeys from the south even to Bethel, unto the place where his tent had been at the beginning, between Bethel and Hai;

Unto the place of the altar, which he had made there at the first: and there Abram called on the name of the LORD. (Genesis 13:1-4)

In the verses above we come to understand that, through the conviction of the Holy Spirit, Abram is led to return to the land of promise. Here, once again in Bethel, he gratefully returns to the knowledge of the Covenant God has made with him and builds an Altar upon which he offers up a blood sacrifice. Here Abram calls to remembrance what faith in the blood of Christ has done for him.

God, from the beginning had given Abram everything he needed concerning life and Godliness, but it wasn't until his sojourn back into the legalistic world system that he fully realized that life in the Spirit of God and His provisions were much better than reverting to his old way of life, and dependancy upon the law of the flesh. If we as believers were saved by grace and became heirs of the everlasting Covenant of promise God made to us through Abraham, would we not also be foolish to attempt to find purpose in life by reverting to our old sin nature and the life we previously lived through the law of self determination?

O foolish Galatians, who hath bewitched you, that ye should not obey the truth, before whose eyes Jesus Christ hath been evidently set forth, crucified among you?

This only would I learn of you, Received ye the Spirit by the works of the law, or by the hearing of faith?

Are ye so foolish? having begun in the Spirit, are ye now made perfect by the flesh?

Have ye suffered so many things in vain? if it be yet in vain.

He therefore that ministereth to you the Spirit, and worketh miracles among you, doeth he it by the works of the law, or by the hearing of faith?

Even as Abraham believed God, and it was accounted to him for righteousness.

Know ye therefore that they which are of faith, the same are the children of Abraham.

(Galatians 3:1-7)

We will see this same moving of the Spirit of God, using the works of the Devil, to return His chosen to dependency upon God, when we see, in the Covenant God made to His people through Moses, of the deliverance of the children of Israel from Pharaoh's grasp. It was through the many plagues and fear of the death angel, one of the Devil's angels, that the children of Israel were prompted to have faith in the symbolic sprinkling of blood of Christ on their doorposts.

Upon Abram's return to Bethel, where Abram lived prior to his lapse of faith and venture into Egypt, he once again called upon the Lord. Abram was now back where he belonged, that is, in the presence of the Lord, in his own country. The environments of Egypt were now only a bad memory. The guilt of his journey in the flesh was erased when he offered up the sacrifice of praise to the Lord for His mercy and grace. The same is true today, when believers return to the Lord after a lapse of faith, our faith in the sprinkled blood of Christ removes all the guilt of these lapses from our conscience. If the guilt of these lapses of our faith remain upon our conscience, it is because we do not have faith in the blood of Christ to completely cleanse us from all unrighteousness. If we do not have faith in the efficacy of the sprinkled blood of Christ to continually present us to the Father in His righteousness, then we have not received a full understanding of the power of the blood of Christ and His High Priestly ministry. Christ is our High Priest in the Heavenly Tabernacle, not made with human hands, as was the tabernacle of witness which God instructed Moses to build.

> But Christ being come an high priest of good things to come, by a greater and more perfect tabernacle, not made with hands, that is to say, not of this building;
> Neither by the blood of goats and calves, but by his own blood he entered in once into the holy place, having obtained eternal redemption for us.
> For if the blood of bulls and of goats, and the ashes of an heifer sprinkling the unclean, sanctifieth to the purifying of the flesh:
> How much more shall the blood of Christ, who through the eternal Spirit offered himself without spot to God, purge your conscience from dead works to serve the living God?
> (Hebrews 9:11-14)

Because of the size of their herds, and strife between the herdsmen of Lot and the herdsmen of Abram, Abram and Lot now decided to part company, in order that the land might sustain them. Lot took first choice.

> And Lot lifted up his eyes, and beheld all the plain of Jordan, that it was well watered every where, before the LORD destroyed Sodom and Gomorrah, even as the garden of the LORD, like the land of Egypt, as thou comest unto Zoar.

*Then Lot chose him all the plain of Jordan; and
Lot journeyed east: and they separated
themselves the one from the other.*

*Abram dwelled in the land of Canaan, and Lot
dwelled in the cities of the plain, and pitched his
tent toward Sodom.*

*But the men of Sodom were wicked and sinners
before the LORD exceedingly.*

(Genesis 13:10-13)

Although Lot was a man of God and consequently righteous,
he made a very unwise decision in choosing to live in the
unbelievably wicked cities of Sodom and Gomorrah. We will see
the disastrous consequences of a righteous man of God, choosing
to live in an unrighteous social environment, when we look in
more detail at the destruction of these cities by fire and brimstone
sent from Heaven by the Lord.

After Lot, and the distracting influence of his herdsmen were
separated from Abram, the Lord talked to Abram and further
expanded upon the Covenant of Promise which He would
Sovereignly confirm to Abram, when he would meet with
Mechizedek and receive the fullness of the Lord's blessing
through Him.

The Lord promised to give Abram all the land that he could
see in all directions, and asked him to walk through it that he
might see the vastness of the land of promise, which would
become the inheritance of he and his seed, forever.

*And the LORD said unto Abram, after that Lot
was separated from him, Lift up now thine eyes,
and look from the place where thou art
northward, and southward, and eastward, and
westward:*

*For all the land which thou seest, to thee will I
give it, and to thy seed for ever.*

*And I will make thy seed as the dust of the earth:
so that if a man can number the dust of the earth,*

then shall thy seed also be numbered.
Arise, walk through the land in the length of it
and in the breadth of it; for I will give it unto thee.
Then Abram removed his tent, and came and
dwelt in the plain of Mamre, which is in Hebron,
and built there an altar unto the LORD.
(Genesis 13:14-18)

During the time the Lord talked to Abram He also reaffirmed that his seed would become a great nation, that they would become innumerable as the sand of the sea or the stars of the heavens.

The vastness and the richness of the land which the Lord promised to the seed of Abraham has still not become a physical reality to the nation Israel, as of this day. Only at the time of the Lord's return, as promised through the Davidic Covenant which God made exclusively with the nation Israel, will they finally receive full and exclusive possession of the land of promise. More about the Davidic Covenant in a later chapter.

The children of Israel, during the time of Moses and Joshua, had forgotten the unconditional Covenant of promise which God had given them through Abraham, because they had put their faith in the man Moses, rather than in the Covenant of promise itself. Because of their unbelief in God's ability to drive out the Canaanites and the other inhabitants of the promised land, as attested to by the testimony of Joshua and Caleb, the children of Israel were not allowed to enter the promised land through the unconditional Covenant God had made with them through Abraham. Instead, because of their unbelief in the Covenant God made sworn to them through Abraham, the Israelites were only allowed to enter the promise land through the conditional Palestinian Covenant. (We will look at the restrictions of that Covenant later in this writing.) Until this day, the Jewish nation are still living in their land under the dispensation of the conditional Palestinian Covenant because they have chosen to ignore the blessing of the unconditional Covenant of rest and peace promised them through the Covenant God made to them through their Father Abraham.

> *Wherefore (as the Holy Ghost saith, To day if ye will hear his voice, Harden not your hearts, as in the provocation, in the day of temptation in the wilderness: When your fathers tempted me, proved me, and saw my works forty years.*
>
> *Wherefore I was grieved with that generation, and said, They do alway err in their heart; and they have not known my ways.*
>
> *So I sware in my wrath, They shall not enter into my rest.)*
>
> *Take heed, brethren, lest there be in any of you an evil heart of unbelief, in departing from the living God.*
>
> *But exhort one another daily, while it is called To day; lest any of you be hardened through the deceitfulness of sin.*
>
> *For we are made partakers of Christ, if we hold the beginning of our confidence stedfast unto the end;*
>
> *While it is said, To day if ye will hear his voice, harden not your hearts, as in the provocation.*
>
> *For some, when they had heard, did provoke: howbeit not all that came out of Egypt by Moses.*
>
> *But with whom was he grieved forty years? was it not with them that had sinned, whose carcases fell in the wilderness?*
>
> *And to whom sware he that they should not enter into his rest, but to them that believed not?*
>
> *So we see that they could not enter in because of unbelief.* (Hebrews 3:7-19)

A confirmation of Psalms 95:7-11.

The present turmoil in the middle east is a direct result of the unbelief of the children of Israel in the Covenant of promise God had graciously given them through Abraham. They forgot, through willful disobedience, that they had been delivered from the land of Egypt through the Abrahamic Covenant. However, Israel as a nation, will be fully regenerated and grafted into the Covenant God made to them through Abraham, at the return of Christ the Messiah. Paul testified of this in the Book of Romans, when speaking of the temporary disposition of the Jewish nation and the present blessing of Abraham that has come to the Gentiles nations, Paul wrote:

Thou wilt say then, The branches were broken off, that I might be graffed in.

Well; because of unbelief they were broken off, and thou standest by faith. Be not highminded, but fear:

For if God spared not the natural branches, take heed lest he also spare not thee.

Behold therefore the goodness and severity of God: on them which fell, severity; but toward thee, goodness, if thou continue in his goodness: otherwise thou also shalt be cut off.

And they also, if they abide not still in unbelief, shall be graffed in: for God is able to graff them in again.

For if thou wert cut out of the olive tree which is wild by nature, and wert graffed contrary to nature into a good olive tree: how much more shall these, which be the natural branches, be graffed into their own olive tree?

For I would not, brethren, that ye should be ignorant of this mystery, lest ye should be wise in your own conceits; that blindness in part is happened to Israel, until the fulness of the Gentiles be come in. (Romans 11:19-25)

Presently the nation Israel has been temporarily cut off from the blessings of Abraham, until the fulness of the Gentile nations are realized. The Gentile nations, for the present time, have become recipients of the righteousness and the fulness of the blessing that is theirs through faith in the blessings of Abraham.

> *Even as Abraham believed God, and it was accounted to him for righteousness.*
> *Know ye therefore that they which are of faith, the same are the children of Abraham.*
> *And the scripture, foreseeing that God would justify the heathen through faith, preached before the gospel unto Abraham, saying, In thee shall all nations be blessed.*
> *So then they which be of faith are blessed with faithful Abraham.*
> *For as many as are of the works of the law are under the curse: for it is written, Cursed is every one that continueth not in all things which are written in the book of the law to do them.*
> *But that no man is justified by the law in the sight of God, it is evident: for, The just shall live by faith.*
> *And the law is not of faith: but, The man that doeth them shall live in them.*
> *Christ hath redeemed us from the curse of the law, being made a curse for us: for it is written, Cursed is every one that hangeth on a tree:*
> *That the blessing of Abraham might come on the Gentiles through Jesus Christ; that we might receive the promise of the Spirit through faith.*

(Galatians 3:6-14)

God had spoken to Abram and told him to walk through the promised land, in order that he might become familiar with and demonstrate his acceptance of the promise of the blessing of God.

As being the seed of Abraham and heirs of the promise, so we as modern day Christians, will only become consciously aware of the manifold blessings that have Sovereignly been given us, to the extent we walk through and explore the vastness of His Word, and awaken to the righteousness that is our inheritance. It is in becoming aware, and learning to appreciate the precious gift of God's righteousness, through faith in the sprinkled blood of Christ on the Mercy Seat on our behalf, that believers consciences are continually purged, and the thoughts of the quilt of the flesh nature are negated.

Abram's nephew Lot, having earlier made the unwise decision to live in the contaminated world environment of Sodom and Gomorrah, has now been captured and held by the invading kings who overthrew the kings of Sodom and Gomorrah. The invading kings had plundered all the goods, and had taken as hostages all the people of Sodom and Gomorrah, including Lot and his family. One of the hostages escaped and told Abram of this defeat. Abram then mustered troops from his own household, and defeated in battle, all the kings that had invaded Sodom and Gomorrah. Abram, also freed and returned the hostages, along with all the confiscated goods, to the kings of Sodom and Gomorrah, including Lot and his family. Understandably the Sodomite king and his fellows were grateful to Abram and his army for having freed them. However, Abram refused to take any and all the gifts that were about to be offered him by the King of Sodom, because Abram saw them as being contaminated by the world system.

> And when Abram heard that his brother was taken captive, he armed his trained servants, born in his own house, three hundred and eighteen, and pursued them unto Dan.
> And he divided himself against them, he and his servants, by night, and smote them, and pursued them unto Hobah, which is on the left hand of Damascus.

> *And he brought back all the goods, and also*
> *brought again his brother Lot, and his goods,*
> *and the women also, and the people.*

(Genesis 14:14-16)

In the meantime, Melchizedek, the King of Salem and priest of the Most High God, El Elyon, came to meet with Abram and bless him with bread and wine, to further confirm the Covenant that God had made to Abram and his promised righteous seed. Abram recognized that it was not through his own strength that he was able to defeat the enemies of the world system, but it was only through the strength of the Holy Spirit, which the Lord had graciously instilled in him. In grateful recognition of the source of his strength, Abram gave one tenth of his goods to Melchizedek. In spite of this demonstration of the power God imputes to the righteous, Lot still wasn't convinced that he should separate himself from the world system, as we shall see later. Melchizedek had no connection with the Kings of the earth for he himself was a king, King of Salem, to whom Abram chose to be obedient and subservient.

> *And the king of Sodom went out to meet him after*
> *his return from the slaughter of Chedorlaomer,*
> *and of the kings that were with him, at the valley*
> *of Shaveh, which is the king's dale.*
> *And Melchizedek king of Salem brought forth*
> *bread and wine: and he was the priest of the*
> *most high God.*
> *And he blessed him, and said, Blessed be Abram*
> *of the most high God, possessor of heaven and*
> *earth:*
> *And blessed be the most high God, which hath*
> *delivered thine enemies into thy hand. And he*
> *gave him tithes of all.*
> *And the king of Sodom said unto Abram, Give me*
> *the persons, and take the goods to thyself.*

And Abram said to the king of Sodom, I have lift
up mine hand unto the LORD, the most high
God, the possessor of heaven and earth,
That I will not take from a thread even to a
shoelatchet, and that I will not take any thing
that is thine, lest thou shouldest say, I have made
Abram rich: (Genesis 14:17-23)

Although Abraham is the father of all believers, yet we must consider the importance of Melchizedek, as outlined in the next chapter, to whom Abram gave tithes. We will also, in the chapter on Melchizedek, try to expand on the prime significance of Melchizedek's ministry in blessing Abram with bread and wine.

The significance of the blessing of bread and wine surely speaks of the continual atoning ministry of the sprinkling of the blood of Christ on the Mercy Seat, at the right hand of the Father in Heaven. The efficacy of Christ's atoning blood on the heavenly Mercy Seat, is the believers ever present assurance of God's imputed righteousness through which we are encouraged to come boldly to the Throne of Grace.

It has been this writer's experience that the Covenant God made to his people through Abraham, cannot become a Spiritual reality to the individual believer, until he first understands the significance of the High Priestly Ministry of Christ, who was anointed as a High Priest forever, in the order of Melchizedek.

For this Melchisedec, king of Salem, priest of the
most high God, who met Abraham returning
from the slaughter of the kings, and blessed him;
To whom also Abraham gave a tenth part of all;
first being by interpretation King of
righteousness, and after that also King of Salem,
which is, King of peace;
Without father, without mother, without descent,
having neither beginning of days, nor end of life;
but made like unto the Son of God; abideth a
priest continually.

Now consider how great this man was, unto whom even the patriarch Abraham gave the tenth of the spoils. (Hebrews 7:1-4)

We will also explore, in the chapter on Melchizedek, what the Holy Spirit, through the Word of God, had in mind for believers when we consider what determines whether a believer is being bottle fed on milk, or whether he has matured to the point where he thrives on a diet of strong meat. Apparently the answer to this question is dependant upon the degree to which we appreciate the true identity of Melchizedek. As the word says, our belief of who Melchizedek is, will be restricted to the degree we are dull of hearing. Speaking of Jesus Christ the author of the book of Hebrews states:

And being made perfect, he became the author of eternal salvation unto all them that obey him;
Called of God an high priest after the order of Melchisedec.
Of whom we have many things to say, and hard to be uttered, seeing ye are dull of hearing.
For when for the time ye ought to be teachers, ye have need that one teach you again which be the first principles of the oracles of God; and are become such as have need of milk, and not of strong meat.
For every one that useth milk is unskilful in the word of righteousness: for he is a babe.
But strong meat belongeth to them that are of full age, even those who by reason of use have their senses exercised to discern both good and evil.
(Hebrews 5:9-14)

In the previous Scriptures we see portrayed, a very important principal of God, that is, that Abram gave total allegiance and worship to Melchizedek through bread and wine, and also tithes of all his possessions. However, at the same time Abram did not even consider taking as much as a shoe latchet from the King of Sodom, as a reward.

It is very significant to recognize, that Abram made a very distinct and uncompromising choice here. Abram understood clearly that the strength of life itself came through the blessing of eternal Spiritual gifts, as provided to him through Melchizedek, as being totally divided and separate from the prosperity that might come to him through the temporal gifts of the flesh, which had been offered him through the princely powers of the world system. Abram understood that the Spirit of Christ, who indwells believers, and whom we acknowledge through partaking of the blood and body of Christ, has nothing to do with the spirit of the world system, they cannot be mixed. Either the leading of the soul of the Christian is led of the Spirit of Christ or, if by his own foolish works of the flesh, he by default puts himself back under the fleshly law of the world system, there is no compromise. If we attempt to subscribe to both we lose both.

O foolish Galatians, who hath bewitched you, that ye should not obey the truth, before whose eyes Jesus Christ hath been evidently set forth, crucified among you?

This only would I learn of you, Received ye the Spirit by the works of the law, or by the hearing of faith?

Are ye so foolish? having begun in the Spirit, are ye now made perfect by the flesh?

(Galatians 3:1-3)

And again:

For they that are after the flesh do mind the things of the flesh; but they that are after the Spirit the things of the Spirit.

For to be carnally minded is death; but to be spiritually minded is life and peace.

Because the carnal mind is enmity against God: for it is not subject to the law of God, neither

indeed can be.
So then they that are in the flesh cannot please God.
But ye are not in the flesh, but in the Spirit, if so
be that the Spirit of God dwell in you. Now if any
man have not the Spirit of Christ, he is none of
his. (Romans 8:5-9)

Abram had come this far through the leading of the Holy Spirit, and by the testing of his faith, faith that God would fulfill the promise of the Covenant He was in the process of making with Abram. It is at this juncture that Abram became the partaker of the blood and body of Jesus Christ, through the blessing of the eternal High Priest, Melchizedek. Abram drank all of this cup. This was the ratification of the everlasting Covenant (beriyth) of Grace, given Sovereignly by God to Abram and to all the redeemed who are of his seed, throughout all generations. This was the Covenant of promise of the Christ to come, which was only fulfilled when the promised seed came, that is when Jesus Christ was made manifest in the flesh.

Lot, through the lust of the flesh, was not able to appreciate this "cutting asunder of the soul and the Spirit" which was his inheritance as a believer, through the Covenant of Grace given to Abram. Lot once again made a poor choice, for he once again, chose to continue to live under the influence of the world system, in Sodom. We will see a little later in this chapter, the grievous consequences of this choice. Although Lot was a just man, justified and righteous before God, he hadn't awakened to the Spiritual blessing that had been given him through Abram.

And delivered just Lot, vexed with the filthy
conversation of the wicked:
(For that righteous man dwelling among them,
in seeing and hearing, vexed his righteous soul
from day to day with their unlawful deeds;)
(2 Peter 2:7,8)

In Genesis chapter fifteen we see a further confirmation of

the Covenant, God in His Divine Mercy and Sovereign love, was in the process of instilling into the heart of Abram.

After these things the word of the LORD came unto Abram in a vision, saying, Fear not, Abram: I am thy shield, and thy exceeding great reward. (Genesis 15:1)

The Word of the Lord came to Abram in a vision; The Spirit of the Lord assured Abram that He would give Abram all that He had promised, especially Abram's request for an heir to propagate his seed. The Lord Sovereignly assures Abram that He is the Rewarder of them that diligently seek Him. (Hebrews 11:6)

Here the Lord expresses one of His least understood gracious characteristics. The Lord gives! The Lord has sworn a Covenant with himself to give to mankind to the extent, that we as mere humans find it hard to comprehend, the manifold blessings of His goodness. The most difficult aspect of Christianity is to awaken to the truth, that all believers have graciously been given the gift of God's very own Holy Nature, if we would simply open our hearts to the leading of the Holy Spirit. God's heart purpose and deepest desire for man is, that believers would simply receive the fullness of the Covenanted blessings He has Sovereignly bestowed upon those who put their faith in Him. Any misguided attempt on man's part, to earn God's Holy Nature, is to be ignorant of His constant love and interest toward His creation. God created man that He might have someone with whom to share His very own Kingdom of righteousness. Any attempt by an individual to earn this gift of His Kingdom is to blaspheme and deny the very Sovereign gracious nature of God, and do despite to the Spirit of Grace. The only work God requires of the believer is to simply believe and understand more of His rewarding nature through His Word.

Labour not for the meat which perisheth, but for that meat which endureth unto everlasting life, which the Son of man shall give unto you: for him hath God the Father sealed.

Then said they unto him, What shall we do, that we might work the works of God?

Jesus answered and said unto them, <u>*This is the work of God, that ye believe on him whom he hath sent.*</u> (John 6:27-29)

Now, the Lord once again gives reassurance to Abram that the Covenant of promise which He swore to him, in the beginning, would become an experienced reality. Abram had been promised of the Lord, that he would make of him a great nation. However, the Lord had been testing Abram's faith throughout the years. As the result of Abram's faith in the Lord, and the promise of blessing not having been rescinded, the Lord was now willing to make manifest to Abram, the further blessing of an heir of his own seed.

And Abram said, Lord GOD, what wilt thou give me, seeing I go childless, and the steward of my house is this Eliezer of Damascus?

And Abram said, Behold, to me thou hast given no seed: and, lo, one born in my house is mine heir.

And, behold, the word of the LORD came unto him, saying, This shall not be thine heir; but he that shall come forth out of thine own bowels shall be thine heir.

And he brought him forth abroad, and said, Look now toward heaven, and tell the stars, if thou be able to number them: and he said unto him, So shall thy seed be. (Genesis 15:2-5)

The magnitude of the blessing which the Lord promised Abram, was probably more than he could comprehend at that time. To an old man who's wife had been barren all her child bearing years, the promise that he would be the father of many nations, seemed much too good to be true, and as unobtainable as being able to reach out and touch the stars themselves.

The Covenant of promise given to all believers through Abram, highlights the thought of God's loving nature. God is faithful to give each believer uncomprehensible blessings of His very own loving nature, if we simply ask in faith. It is only through faith in the accomplishments of the sprinkling of the blood of Christ, through which the Father rewards those who diligently seek His righteousness.

For this cause I bow my knees unto the Father of our Lord Jesus Christ,

Of whom the whole family in heaven and earth is named, That he would grant you, according to the riches of his glory, to be strengthened with might by his Spirit in the inner man; That Christ may dwell in your hearts by faith; that ye, being rooted and grounded in love, May be able to comprehend with all saints what is the breadth, and length, and depth, and height; And to know the love of Christ, which passeth knowledge, that ye might be filled with all the fulness of God.

Now unto him that is able to do exceeding abundantly above all that we ask or think, according to the power that worketh in us, Unto him be glory in the church by Christ Jesus throughout all ages, world without end. Amen.

(Ephesians 3:14-21)

One of the key verses of the Bible not only concerned Abraham, it concerns every believer today, for all believers ever since, are the seed of Abraham.

And he believed in the LORD; and he counted it to him for righteousness. (Genesis 15:6)

Although the righteousness of God with which God blessed Abram, occurred many, many years ago, it applies to everyone ever since, who believe that God gracefully justifies them through faith in the blood of Christ. Through faith in the blood of

Christ, all believers ever since Abram believed, have become the seed of Abraham and heirs of the promise of everlasting life, in God's righteous Kingdom. Also, justification through faith in the blood of Christ, applied to all believers from Adam and Eve onward, those to whom the witness of the blood of Able spoke, that of the perfect sacrifice of the blood of Christ to come.

The above verse again speaks of the incomprehensible goodness of God, for it was He that Sovereignly judged and declared Abram righteous. Once again, this points out the most difficult aspect of Christianity, which is to simply believe and receive the Glory of God's Holy Nature within our hearts. The Divine Nature of the Spirit of Jesus Christ mysteriously indwells all believers who hear the voice of the blood of Christ.

> *Simon Peter, a servant and an apostle of Jesus Christ, to them that have obtained like precious faith with us through the righteousness of God and our Saviour Jesus Christ:*
> *Grace and peace be multiplied unto you through the knowledge of God, and of Jesus our Lord,*
> *According as his divine power hath given unto us all things that pertain unto life and godliness, through the knowledge of him that hath called us to glory and virtue:*
> *Whereby are given unto us exceeding great and precious promises: <u>that by these ye might be partakers of the divine nature</u>, having escaped the corruption that is in the world through lust.*
> (2 Peter 1:1-4)

The question then is; if God declared Abram to be righteous, then how righteous did God judge him to be? In his flesh nature Abram had many faults, as is the nature of all men born of woman, but still God judged him to be Spiritually righteous. There can be no half measures, if God has declared believers to be His very own righteousness, then there cannot be any unrighteousness within the believer. God, who through faith in the blood of Christ, justifies and declares all believers to be His very own righteousness, also sanctifies and separates those believers from all unrighteousness. This truth is one of the prime principles of the oracles of God

There is a great gulf between those whom God has declared to be righteous, and those who still dwell in the unrighteous unredeemed sinful nature of the flesh. This applies today, even as it also is true throughout all eternity, future and past.

> *And it came to pass, that the beggar died, and was carried by the angels into Abraham's bosom: the rich man also died, and was buried;*
> *And in hell he lift up his eyes, being in torments, and seeth Abraham afar off, and Lazarus in his bosom.*
> *And he cried and said, Father Abraham, have mercy on me, and send Lazarus, that he may dip the tip of his finger in water, and cool my tongue; for I am tormented in this flame.*
> *But Abraham said, Son, remember that thou in thy lifetime receivedst thy good things, and likewise Lazarus evil things: but now he is comforted, and thou art tormented.*
> *<u>And beside all this, between us and you there is a great gulf fixed:</u> so that they which would pass from hence to you cannot; neither can they pass to us, that would come from thence.*
> (Luke 16:22-26)

Do we suppose, in unbelief, that God will lay anything to the charge of those whom He Himself has justified? Do we suppose God will condemn those whom He has declared righteous? The meaning of justification is to be declared God's righteousness.

> *What shall we then say to these things? If God be for us, who can be against us?*

He that spared not his own Son, but delivered him up for us all, how shall he not with him also freely give us all things? <u>Who shall lay any thing to the charge of God's elect? It is God that justifieth.</u> Who is he that condemneth? It is Christ that died, yea rather, that is risen again, who is even at the right hand of God, who also maketh intercession for us. (Romans 8:31-34)

Believers cannot be both the righteousness of God, and still be a little bit unrighteous.

Be not deceived: evil communications corrupt good manners.

<u>*Awake to righteousness, and sin not;*</u> *for some have not the knowledge of God: I speak this to your shame.* (1 Corinthians 15:33,34)

The baptism of the believer, is an individual outward testimony of an inward Spiritual truth. When the believer accepts the fact that faith in the blood of Christ is everything which God requires of him to be judged His righteousness, then at the same time God considers the old man of unrighteousness and sin and flesh to be dead. So then the ordinance, or sacrament of baptism, is symbolic of this separation of the two natures of man, righteousness and unrighteousness. Coincidentally, when believers are born of the Spirit of righteousness, they are, through the consecrating power of the Holy Spirit, divested of the old man of unrighteous flesh.

Being then made free from sin, ye became the servants of righteousness.

I speak after the manner of men because of the infirmity of your flesh: for as ye have yielded your members servants to uncleanness and to iniquity unto iniquity; even so now yield your members servants to righteousness unto holiness.

*For when ye were the servants of sin, ye were
free from righteousness.*

*What fruit had ye then in those things whereof ye
are now ashamed? for the end of those things is
death.*

*But now being made free from sin, and become
servants to God, ye have your fruit unto holiness,
and the end everlasting life.* (Romans 6:18-22)

Indeed, as the Scripture below clearly states, that if believers
do not fully accept that we have been given God's very own
Spirit of righteousness, and have been separated from the
unrighteousness of the flesh, we cannot fully consciously receive
the knowledge and assurance of the power of His resurrection,
which also indwells believers through the Holy Spirit.

*But what things were gain to me, those I counted
loss for Christ.*

*Yea doubtless, and I count all things but loss for
the excellency of the knowledge of Christ Jesus
my Lord: for whom I have suffered the loss of all
things, and do count them but dung, that I may
win Christ,*

*And be found in him, not having mine own
righteousness, which is of the law, but that which
is through the faith of Christ, the righteousness
which is of God by faith:*

*That I may know him, and the power of his
resurrection, and the fellowship of his sufferings,
being made conformable unto his death;*
(Philippians 3:7-10)

As is stated in 1 Corinthians 3:15 below, it is at the
judgement seat of Christ where believers will receive the reward
for their work in accepting God's indwelling righteousness. Here,
at the judgement seat of Christ, God's consuming fire will finally
separate and do away with the unfruitful works of the believers

unbelief. Through fire all believers will then become refined as pure precious gold.

Every man's work shall be made manifest: for the day shall declare it, because it shall be revealed by fire; and the fire shall try every man's work of what sort it is.

If any man's work abide which he hath built thereupon, he shall receive a reward.

If any man's work shall be burned, he shall suffer loss: but he himself shall be saved; yet so as by fire.

Know ye not that ye are the temple of God, and that the Spirit of God dwelleth in you?

(1 Corinthians 3:13-16)

We do not pretend to be able to judge whether or not God would remove His righteous Spirit from a carnal believer, we do not pretend to be able to judge who is going to heaven or not.

Brethren, my heart's desire and prayer to God for Israel is, that they might be saved.

For I bear them record that they have a zeal of God, but not according to knowledge.

For they being ignorant of God's righteousness, and going about to establish their own righteousness, have not submitted themselves unto the righteousness of God.

For Christ is the end of the law for righteousness to every one that believeth.

For Moses describeth the righteousness which is of the law, That the man which doeth those things shall live by them.

But the righteousness which is of faith speaketh on this wise, Say not in thine heart, Who shall ascend into heaven? (that is, to bring Christ down from above:)

*Or, Who shall descend into the deep? (that is, to
bring up Christ again from the dead.)*

(Romans 10:1-7)

In the Scriptures below, we will see once again a further
confirmation of the Covenant, which God in His all enveloping
love, gave to all believers through our Father Abraham.

*And he said unto him, I am the LORD that
brought thee out of Ur of the Chaldees, to give
thee this land to inherit it.*

*And he said, Lord GOD, whereby shall I know
that I shall inherit it?*

*And he said unto him, Take me an heifer of three
years old, and a she goat of three years old, and
a ram of three years old, and a turtledove, and a
young pigeon.*

*And he took unto him all these, and divided them
in the midst, and laid each piece one against
another: but the birds divided he not.*

*And when the fowls came down upon the
carcases, Abram drove them away.*

*And when the sun was going down, a deep sleep
fell upon Abram; and, lo, an horror of great
darkness fell upon him.*

*And he said unto Abram, Know of a surety that
thy seed shall be a stranger in a land that is not
theirs, and shall serve them; and they shall
afflict them four hundred years;*

*And also that nation, whom they shall serve, will
I judge: and afterward shall they come out with
great substance.*

*And thou shalt go to thy fathers in peace; thou
shalt be buried in a good old age.*

*But in the fourth generation they shall come
hither again: for the iniquity of the Amorites is*

not yet full.

And it came to pass, that, when the sun went down, and it was dark, behold a smoking furnace, and a burning lamp that passed between those pieces. (Genesis 15:7-17)

Through faith, we recognize that this highly visible impressive scene also represented a promise of a Spiritual truth which applies to all believers, who are the seed of Abraham. All who receive the blessing of the Spirit through the Covenant of Abraham, are come unto Spiritual Mount Zion, the city of the living God, and to the Heavenly Jerusalem. The smoking furnace, as depicted above, represents the judgement of condemnation that is promised to all who look for fulfilment in the present Spirit of the World system. The burning lamp represents God's judgement of righteousness which is imputed to all believers through the light of His Word, the Gospel. His Word is a lamp unto our feet.

The Scriptures above once again confirm God's promise to fulfill his Covenant to all believers, through Abram, represented by passing between the blood sacrifices of divided animals. The cutting and dividing (the meaning of the word Covenant) of the flesh and Spirit of the seed of Abraham, is represented by a smoking furnace, and a burning lamp passing between the divided pieces.

This dramatic representation of the division of the flesh and Spirit, of the separation of the Spirit of righteousness and unrighteousness, is another of the first principles of the oracles of God. Until believers, once again return to the knowledge of the first principles which God has spoken to all whom He has chosen as being separated unto Himself, believers will be feeding on milk and not on the satisfying strong meat of the Word of righteousness. This revelation of the sanctifying of believers unto Himself, through the promise of the High Priestly ministry of Christ, who's blood sacrifice was yet to be revealed on the cross, was confirmed by God to Abram through Christ's Old Testament forerunner, Melchizedek.

Though he were a Son, yet learned he obedience by the things which he suffered;

And being made perfect, he became the author of eternal salvation unto all them that obey him;

Called of God an high priest after the order of Melchisedec.

Of whom we have many things to say, and hard to be uttered, seeing ye are dull of hearing.

For when for the time ye ought to be teachers, ye have need that one teach you again which be the first principles of the oracles of God; and are become such as have need of milk, and not of strong meat.

For every one that useth milk is unskilful in the word of righteousness: for he is a babe.

But strong meat belongeth to them that are of full age, even those who by reason of use have their senses exercised to discern both good and evil.

(Hebrews 5:8-14)

It is this believers firm conviction that Christians will not have their faith in God fully confirmed, until they come to understand the primary significance of what God had in mind for us, when He revealed this scene of divided animals to Abram. The divided animals represented the shedding of blood that was necessary to separate and pronounce the judgement of death upon the believers old sin nature, while at the same time being unconditionally reunited with God, and being made alive in our new Holy Spirit nature. Without understanding this blood Covenant we cannot see the separation of our own Spiritual nature as having been completely sanctified and severed from our original sin nature. It was the sharp sword of the Spirit of the Word of God who passed between the divided flesh of the slain animals, thus representing the complete dividing and cutting off of the flesh of the believers original sin nature, from the Spirit nature of the new man of God who has been reborn from above.

> *For the word of God is quick, and powerful, and*
> *sharper than any twoedged sword, piercing even*
> *to the dividing asunder of soul and spirit, and of*
> *the joints and marrow, and is a discerner of the*
> *thoughts and intents of the heart.*
>
> (Hebrews 4:12)

The word of God creates a great gulf between the believers old nature and the believers new nature in Christ, who is born of the Holy Spirit. These two were never made to be reunited or so much as to touch each other again.

> *If so be that ye have heard him, and have been*
> *taught by him, as the truth is in Jesus:*
> *That ye put off concerning the former*
> *conversation the old man, which is corrupt*
> *according to the deceitful lusts;*
> *And be renewed in the spirit of your mind;*
> *And that ye put on the new man, which after God*
> *is created in righteousness and true holiness.*
>
> (Ephesians 4:21-24)

The smoking furnace represented the condemning judgement and separation of the flesh of the old unregenerated sinful nature of the natural man, born under the law of sin and death. The burning lamp represented the light of God's judgement of righteousness upon the new man born of the Spirit, by His grace.

Baptism is the present day New Covenant's depiction of this separation and divesting of the old man of the flesh, from off the newly resurrected man of the Spirit of the believers life in Christ. It is no longer the old man that lives within the heart of the believer, but it is the Spirit of Christ who lives within us, the hope of glory.

Hopefully we will be made aware, as we continue this study, of the significance of the dividing of the flesh and Spirit through

God's righteous judgement. The purpose of God's unconditional Covenants has been to provide for mankind just that, the means whereby we are enabled or encouraged, through belief in His Word, to allow the Holy Spirit to separate our old nature from a new God given nature. It is through faith in God's Covenant of promise given to Abraham, and subsequently to all believers who accept this promise, which exhorts believers to separate themselves from the guilt of the past. Only the blessing of Abraham, which comes to believers through the blessing of Melchisedec, frees us from the guilt of natural carnal law, as distinct from now living in the freedom of the new found Spirit of God's grace.

The word "Covenant," the foundational principle in the Old Testament, is a translation of the Hebrew word "beriyth," which means a dividing or cutting, in the sense of cutting a Covenant, or entering into a league made by passing or walking between two separated pieces of flesh. This word does not suggest that man had any active part in initiating this blessing, it is not a conditional agreement between God and man. It is a Sovereign pronouncement of God, it is He alone who establishes His will in the heart of believers. The word Covenant implies the cutting off a portion of the main body, as in circumcision or baptism, as in the example as stated above. In these instances the old original nature of the believer, with which we are born from our mother's womb, is separated from the new God given nature of becoming a new Spiritual being. Simply to believe and accept the "beriyth," or Covenant, of God's saving grace, separates the old man born with a sin nature from the new man led of the Spirit of God. There can be no cutting off of the flesh of the old man without the shedding of blood. Christ has shed and sprinkled his blood on mankind's behalf, therefore believers need not shed their own blood to be born of the Spirit from above, we just need to place our faith in the efficacy of Christ's blood on the Mercy Seat. The sin consciousness of the flesh is only separated from the believers

Spirit nature through faith in the advocacy of the sprinkled blood of Jesus Christ's High Priestly ministry, a High Priest forever in the order of Melchisedec.

For the word of God is quick, and powerful, and sharper than any two edged sword, piercing even to the dividing asunder of soul and spirit, and of the joints and marrow, and is a discerner of the thoughts and intents of the heart.

Neither is there any creature that is not manifest in his sight: but all things are naked and opened unto the eyes of him with whom we have to do.

Seeing then that we have a great high priest, that is passed into the heavens, Jesus the Son of God, let us hold fast our profession.

For we have not an high priest which cannot be touched with the feeling of our infirmities; but was in all points tempted like as we are, yet without sin.

Let us therefore come boldly unto the throne of grace, that we may obtain mercy, and find grace to help in time of need. (Hebrews 4:12-16)

Although the believer's sanctified righteous Spiritual nature has been completely severed from our original flesh nature, and has no fellowship with our old sin nature, we often times, through lack of faith, lose our conscious awareness of Gods perfect provision given to us through faith in the blood of Christ, and unwisely turn back to pamper our old nature. This is the constant battle in which all believers are engaged. Victory in this battle is only realized when we once again, through our Heavenly High Priest, boldly reenter and dwell in the knowledge of God's presence, within the Throne Room of Grace.

This human trait was also present in our progenitors, father Abram and mother Sarai. Whenever believers, throughout the ages, decided to exercise their own will, and not wait upon God's perfect will to lead them, they suffered the consequences of these lapses of faith. Sometimes these consequences were quite severe as we shall see in the lives of Abram and Sarai. Always, as with Abram and Sarai, and also with all believers throughout the ages, the results of these lapses of faith have eternal consequences. At the judgement seat of Christ believers will suffer loss for the worthless works which we have done, through labours of our natural will, in vain attempts to establish our own self righteousness.

> *For we are labourers together with God: ye are God's husbandry, ye are God's building.*
>
> *According to the grace of God which is given unto me, as a wise masterbuilder, I have laid the foundation, and another buildeth thereon. But let every man take heed how he buildeth thereupon. For other foundation can no man lay than that is laid, which is Jesus Christ.*
>
> *Now if any man build upon this foundation gold, silver, precious stones, wood, hay, stubble;*
>
> *Every man's work shall be made manifest: for the day shall declare it, because it shall be revealed by fire; and the fire shall try every man's work of what sort it is.*
>
> *If any man's work abide which he hath built thereupon, he shall receive a reward.*
>
> *If any man's work shall be burned, he shall suffer loss: but he himself shall be saved; yet so as by fire.* (1 Corinthians 3:9-15)

God who justifies and declares righteous all believers, does not condemn us for our lapses of faith, but we suffer the diminishing of this perfect unity through which God desires to remain continually in communion with His people. For example:

Abram and Sarai had waited for many years for God to fulfill His promise to them, that of a child through whom their seed would become innumerable as the stars of the heavens, as we saw in previous Scriptures. Abram had lived in the land of Canaan ten years and still had not seen God's promise of a son to himself and Sarai made manifest. It was at this time, at Sarai's suggestion, that Abram took Sarai's Egyptian handmaiden as a wife in the hope that through Hagar they might help God to fulfill His Covenant of the promised child to them.

> *Now Sarai Abram's wife bare him no children: and she had an handmaid, an Egyptian, whose name was Hagar.*
>
> *And Sarai said unto Abram, Behold now, the LORD hath restrained me from bearing: I pray thee, go in unto my maid; it may be that I may obtain children by her. And Abram hearkened to the voice of Sarai.*
>
> *And Sarai Abram's wife took Hagar her maid the Egyptian, after Abram had dwelt ten years in the land of Canaan, and gave her to her husband Abram to be his wife.*
>
> *And he went in unto Hagar, and she conceived: and when she saw that she had conceived, her mistress was despised in her eyes.*

(Genesis 16:1-4)

Note, that it was Sarai's suggestion and Abram's compliance that got them into this undesirable situation, similar to that which happened in the Garden of Eden with Eve and Adam. It was Eve who partook of the forbidden fruit, when tempted of the Devil, who in turn enticed Adam to partake of the same, through which the will of God was abrogated. All of mankind has suffered the consequences of this lack of faith ever since this fall of Adam and Eve. Sarai too, soon realized her mistake, and as a consequence suffered a temporary loss of guiltless communion with God and her husband Abram, and a permanent loss of fellowship with her handmaid Hagar, after Sarai realized that Hagar was pregnant of

Abram. There are eternal ramifications here that affected not only the principles involved, but the consequences of these lapses of faith impacted all of mankind ever since.

The seed of Ishmael fostered a nation that has divided all other nations ever since, as we shall see in the text below. This division between the unrighteous world system, as represented here by the offspring of Sarai's Egyptian handmaid, Ishmael, and the righteous seed of Isaac, began with Sari immediately after she realized that Hagar was pregnant by her husband Abram. Sarai despised the spirit of the flesh of the progenitor of the world system, which began while Ishmael was still in his mother Hagar's womb. So Abram gave permission to Sarai to cast the bondwoman and her unborn child out of their home and into the dessert.

> *But Abram said unto Sarai, Behold, thy maid is in thy hand; do to her as it pleaseth thee. And when Sarai dealt hardly with her, she fled from her face.* (Genesis 16:6)

Now the Lord had compassion upon Hagar and her unborn son, and He visited her in the desert. The Holy Spirit of the Lord appeared to Hagar as an angel of the Lord and said, "I will" multiply your seed exceedingly. Only God, who's will and Word alone is truth, is able to speak promises which bring nations into being.

> *And the angel of the LORD found her by a fountain of water in the wilderness, by the fountain in the way to Shur.*
> *And he said, Hagar, Sarai's maid, whence camest thou? and whither wilt thou go? And she said, I flee from the face of my mistress Sarai.*
> *And the angel of the LORD said unto her, Return to thy mistress, and submit thyself under her hands.*
> <u>*And the angel of the LORD said unto her, I will multiply thy seed exceedingly, that it shall not be*</u>

numbered for multitude.
And the angel of the LORD said unto her,
Behold, thou art with child, and shalt bear a son,
and shalt call his name Ishmael; because the
LORD hath heard thy affliction.
And he will be a wild man; his hand will be
against every man, and every man's hand
against him; and he shall dwell in the presence
of all his brethren. (Genesis 16:7-12)

In obedience to the angel of the Lord, Hagar returned to the house of her mistress Sarai, and just as the Lord had admonished her she became subservient to Sarai. However, she would be cast out once again by Abraham, as we shall see later on.

As the Lord promised Hagar, the seed of Ishmael and the nation of Islam has been a great nation down through the centuries, also as is the case today. However, as we see in verse twelve above, the Lord said that Ishmael would be a wild man, and that his seed and every other seed would be at odds with each other, also as it is today. Note that the Spirit of the Lord did not promise that it would be through the seed of Ishmael that the nations of the earth would be blessed, but rather that the seed of Ishmael would be a divisive factor throughout history.

Abram's most heart felt inward desire was that the Lord would give him a son, through which the nations of the earth would be blessed, as the Lord had promised. Although Abram in the past had temporary lapses of faith by yielding to the desires of his old flesh nature, he had not lost sight of the vision the Lord had promised him. Indeed Abram's lapses of faith occurred when he was trying to help God implement his promises.

Abram, having been declared righteous by God, has now become a completely new creation through faith in the promises God has made to him and his seed. The Spirit of the Lord Jehovah now makes another appearance to Abram, who further reveals the provisions of His Covenant, as attested in the scripture below, to once again reaffirm to him that he has been completely separated from his old nature.

> *And when Abram was ninety years old and nine,*
> *the LORD appeared to Abram, and said unto*
> *him, I am the Almighty God; <u>walk before me, and</u>*
> *<u>be thou perfect.</u>* (Genesis 17:1)

It has been thirteen long years since the birth of Ishmael, during which time Abram's faith in the promises of God were sorely tested. As a reward, and a further blessing for his continuing faith in a faithful God, the Lord appears again to Abram and declares him to be PERFECT. God now Sovereignly imputes to Abram His very own perfection, His very Divine Nature of righteousness and holiness. The knowledge of having been separated from his old unredeemed nature, and having been given God's very perfect nature, must have been to Abram, as character shaking as having been promised a son in his old age. God had promised Abram that He would work out His plan of salvation, through Abram and his seed, so effectively God had already given Abram all things pertaining to life and Godliness.

> *Grace and peace be multiplied unto you through*
> *the knowledge of God, and of Jesus our Lord,*
> *According as his divine power hath given unto us*
> *all things that pertain unto life and godliness,*
> *through the knowledge of him that hath called us*
> *to glory and virtue:*
> *Whereby are given unto us exceeding great and*
> *precious promises: that by these ye might be*
> *partakers of the divine nature, having escaped*
> *the corruption that is in the world through lust.*
> (2 Peter 1:2-4)

God, ever since has indwelt all believers, being the seed of Abraham, with His very own perfect nature, through faith in the blood of Christ. It is only when we try, like Abram, to improve upon the gift of the nature of Christ, which dwells in the heart of every believer, that we suffer the consequences of unbelief. Unless we as believers, simply accept that our bodies are temples of the Holy Ghost, unless we accept that God has already made His mystical Spiritual church the pure spotless bride of Christ, we deny the perfection of the Spirit of Christ within. Only the Spirit of God's perfect righteousness, who dwells within the heart of all believers, is anointed to do the works of righteousness, no one can do the works of righteousness through the flesh. From the beginning, through the Covenant God has given to all believers through Abraham this has been true, believers have been given all things pertaining to life and Godly perfection.

>*Let that therefore abide in you, which ye have heard from the beginning. If that which ye have heard from the beginning shall remain in you, ye also shall continue in the Son, and in the Father. And this is the promise that he hath promised us, even eternal life.*
>
>*These things have I written unto you concerning them that seduce you.*
>
>*But the anointing which ye have received of him abideth in you, and ye need not that any man teach you: but as the same anointing teacheth you of all things, and is truth, and is no lie, and even as it hath taught you, ye shall abide in him. And now, little children, abide in him; that, when he shall appear, we may have confidence, and not be ashamed before him at his coming.*
>
>*If ye know that he is righteous, ye know that every one that doeth righteousness is born of him.* (1 John 2:24-29)

When we, as believers, try to improve upon our God given perfect nature through our original flesh nature, it is only then that we become an offense to God.

In the Sermon on the Mount, Jesus tells New Testament believers, that the only way we are enabled to do the perfect righteous works of God, <u>is through the acceptance that He has perfected us in the Spirit of love, love which has it's origins in God.</u> God's perfect indwelling nature has separated us from our old sin nature.

> *Be ye therefore perfect, even as your Father*
> *which is in heaven is perfect.* (Matthew 5:48)

The perfection that was given to Abram by promise, and to New Covenant believers as his seed, was not conditional upon the works of the flesh. Simple belief through faith in the sprinkling of the atoning blood of Christ, on the Mercy Seat in heaven, is all that God requires of us to become partakers of His Divine Perfect Nature.

> *Now the God of peace, who brought again from*
> *the dead the great shepherd of the sheep with the*
> *blood of an eternal Covenant, (even) our Lord*
> *Jesus, make you perfect in every good thing to do*
> *his will, working in us that which is*
> *well-pleasing in his sight, through Jesus Christ;*
> *to whom (be) the glory for ever and ever. Amen.*
> (Hebrews 13:20-21)

It is grievous to the heart of the remnant, the recipients of the Covenant God made to believers through Abraham, that Bible expositors have been blinded by the natural law, and are not able to graciously accept the simple truth of God's perfect Spirit who dwells within the heart of the redeemed. The separation of the law of the flesh from God's unconditional everlasting Covenant of Grace, which sanctifies and makes Holy the believers God given righteous nature, has been hidden from the wise and the prudent. As Jesus testified, this is a very simple truth, flesh and Spirit are separate.

> *Jesus answered, Verily, verily, I say unto thee,*
> *Except a man be born of water and of the Spirit,*
> *he cannot enter into the kingdom of God.*

That which is born of the flesh is flesh; and that which is born of the Spirit is spirit. (John 3:5-6)

The words for "perfect" are correctly translated from original texts in the King James Version of the Bible, why then do theologians and expositors attempt to change their meaning? The word translated as "perfect" in Genesis 17:1 above means just that, perfect. "Perfect" does not mean relatively perfect or mature, it means having been given God's perfection and righteousness in the Spirit. I would ask; if God has declared believers to be His righteousness, how righteous then are justified believers? Are believers then not perfectly righteous? Is there any unrighteousness in God's righteousness?

Yea doubtless, and I count all things but loss for the excellency of the knowledge of Christ Jesus my Lord: for whom I have suffered the loss of all things, and do count them but dung, that I may win Christ,

And be found in him, not having mine own righteousness, which is of the law, but that which is through the faith of Christ, the righteousness which is of God by faith:

That I may know him, and the power of his resurrection, and the fellowship of his sufferings, being made conformable unto his death;
(Philippians 3:8-10)

A later chapter in this book further clarifies the meaning of the words translated in the King James Version of the Bible as "perfect".

This gift of God's perfection does not become a Spiritual reality to believers until they come to understand that our God is a God of Grace, and that from the beginning. The blessing of God's righteousness and perfection was given to Abraham 430 years before the law of the flesh, the ten commandments, were given to the children of Israel, through Moses. The ten commandments were imposed upon the Israelites by God, because they had ignored the everlasting Covenant of Grace given to them through Abraham. The law given to the children of Israel on Mount Sinai was designed to mirror their sinful nature, and convince them that they needed to once again embrace the everlasting Covenant God gave to believers through Abraham. The Abrahamic Covenant, not the ten commandments, was the Covenant through which they were brought up out of the land of Egypt. The law God imposed on them at Mount Sinai, was never designed to redeem, but only to bring sinners to their knees in repentance, to seek deliverance from their hopeless sinful unrighteous nature. Deliverance from the curse of unrighteousness, into the Kingdom of God's righteousness, only comes through the Covenant of Grace given to mankind through Father Abraham. This was true in the Old Testament as well as it is today in the New Covenant.

> *Even all nations shall say, Wherefore hath the LORD done thus unto this land? what meaneth the heat of this great anger?*
> *Then men shall say, <u>Because they have forsaken the Covenant of the LORD God of their fathers, which he made with them when he brought them forth out of the land of Egypt:</u>*
> *For they went and served other gods, and worshipped them, gods whom they knew not, and whom he had not given unto them:*
> *And the anger of the LORD was kindled against this land, to bring upon it all the curses that are written in this book:*
> *And the LORD rooted them out of their land in anger, and in wrath, and in great indignation, and cast them into another land, <u>as it is this day</u>.*
> (Deuteronomy 29:24-28)

Also, immediately prior to giving the law on Mount Sinai, God reminded the children of Israel of the Covenant through which they were delivered from the land of bondage. The Lord God was reminding them of the unconditional Covenant given them through Abraham, He was not referring to the conditional ten commandments He was about to impose upon them.

And God spoke all these words, saying,
I am the LORD thy God, which have brought
thee out of the land of Egypt, out of the house of
bondage. (Exodus 20:1,2)

When God spoke to the children of Israel, He identified Himself as the God who brought them out of the land of Egypt, through the everlasting Covenant He gives to all believers, the Covenant of Promise He made to the seed of Abraham. When He called Moses, God referred to Himself, His being, His nature, His glory, as the God of father Abraham and his seed, Isaac and Jacob. It wasn't the man Moses who delivered the children of Israel from bondage, God alone delivered them from the cruel furnace, and simply used Moses as the messenger.

And when forty years were expired, there
appeared to him in the wilderness of mount Sina
an angel of the Lord in a flame of fire in a bush.
When Moses saw it, he wondered at the sight:
and as he drew near to behold it, the voice of the
Lord came unto him,
Saying, I am the God of thy fathers, the God of
Abraham, and the God of Isaac, and the God of
Jacob. Then Moses trembled, and durst not
behold.
Then said the Lord to him, Put off thy shoes from
thy feet: for the place where thou standest is holy
ground.
I have seen, I have seen the affliction of my
people which is in Egypt, and I have heard their
groaning, and am come down to deliver them.
And now come, I will send thee into Egypt.
(Acts 7:30-34)

As we see in the above Scriptures as well as those below; New Testament believers are reminded that the everlasting Covenant, the Gospel of Grace, preached for us through Abraham, is still the Covenant which delivers us from the curse of the law, through faith in the sprinkling of the blood of Christ.

> *Even as Abraham believed God, and it was accounted to him for righteousness.*
>
> *Know ye therefore that they which are of faith, the same are the children of Abraham.*
>
> *And the scripture, foreseeing that God would justify the heathen through faith, <u>preached before the gospel unto Abraham</u>, saying, In thee shall all nations be blessed.*
>
> *So then they which be of faith are blessed with faithful Abraham.*
>
> *For as many as are of the works of the law are under the curse: for it is written, Cursed is every one that continueth not in all things which are written in the book of the law to do them.*
>
> *But that no man is justified by the law in the sight of God, it is evident: for, The just shall live by faith.*
>
> *And the law is not of faith: but, The man that doeth them shall live in them.*
>
> *<u>Christ hath redeemed us from the curse of the law</u>, being made a curse for us: for it is written, Cursed is every one that hangeth on a tree:*
>
> *<u>That the blessing of Abraham might come on the Gentiles through Jesus Christ; that we might receive the promise of the Spirit through faith.</u>*

(Galatians 3:6-14)

God's righteous perfection is not given to believers through the law of the Levitical priesthood. Righteous perfection is only imputed to those who have faith in the High Priestly ministry and the sprinkling of blood of the Lamb of the tribe of Judah, Jesus Christ, called of God to be a High Priest forever in the order (the same as) of Melchizedek.

If therefore perfection were by the Levitical priesthood, (for under it the people received the law,) what further need was there that another priest should rise after the order of Melchisedec, and not be called after the order of Aaron?

For the priesthood being changed, there is made of necessity a change also of the law.

For he of whom these things are spoken pertaineth to another tribe, of which no man gave attendance at the altar.

For it is evident that our Lord sprang out of Juda; of which tribe Moses spake nothing concerning priesthood.

And it is yet far more evident: for that after the similitude of Melchisedec there ariseth another priest,

Who is made, not after the law of a carnal commandment, but after the power of an endless life.

For he testifieth, Thou art a priest for ever after the order of Melchisedec.

For there is verily a disannulling of the commandment going before for the weakness and unprofitableness thereof.

For the law made nothing perfect, but the bringing in of a better hope did; by the which we draw nigh unto God.

(Hebrews 7:11-19)

Returning once again to Genesis the seventeenth chapter, where God is, through His will alone, pouring out further blessings upon our Spiritual Father Abraham.

> *And I will make my Covenant between me and*
> *thee, and will multiply thee exceedingly.*
> *And Abram fell on his face: and God talked with*
> *him, saying,*
> *As for me, behold, my Covenant is with thee, and*
> *thou shalt be a father of many nations.*
> (Genesis 17:2-4)

God simply wanted to freely and Sovereignly give to Abram this His Covenant of unconditional love. It was upon God's heart to further implement a Covenant through Abram, which would allow all future generations of mankind the opportunity to share with Him the righteousness of his Kingdom. The only requirement God made of Abram was to simply trust and have faith that God would fulfill His promise to mankind through him.

Abram was so overwhelmed by the presence of the Lord and the power of the Spirit of His goodness, that he fell upon his face in praise and worship. It was the power of the presence of the goodness of God that was about to make of he and his wife Sarai new creations. God was about to establish their new names in His Glory, through which He might impress upon them the meaning of their new Spirit led identity. It is still the same today, it is the goodness of God that leads men to repentance, it is not the law of sin and guilt that sanctifies believers.

> *Or despisest thou the riches of his goodness and*
> *forbearance and longsuffering; not knowing that*
> *the goodness of God leadeth thee to repentance?*
> (Romans 2:4)

The acceptance of God's righteousness makes of believers a new creation in Christ, and gives them a new identity, the identity of God's righteousness which comes through faith in the burning lamp of His Word. As portrayed to Abram, this lamp separates the indwelling righteousness of our identity in God's Kingdom, from the deadness of our old nature as symbolized by a smoking furnace, the furnace of Egypt, the world system.

For Zion's sake will I not hold my peace, and for Jerusalem's sake I will not rest, <u>until the righteousness thereof go forth as brightness, and the salvation thereof as a lamp that burneth.</u>

And the Gentiles shall see thy righteousness, and all kings thy glory: <u>and thou shalt be called by a new name, which the mouth of the LORD shall name.</u>

Thou shalt also be a crown of glory in the hand of the LORD, and a royal diadem in the hand of thy God. (Isaiah 62:1-3)

Although the above Scriptures are intended for Israel at the time of the Messiah's return, they also are intended for all believers who receive the Covenant of righteousness God gave to all believers, through Abraham, NOW.

All believers who understand that righteousness comes from the Throne of Grace, from the heavenly Jerusalem and Mount Zion, the city of the living God, and not from Mount Sinai have become pillars in the mystical body of Christ, His church, they are blessed with a new name and identity in Christ.

Him that overcometh will I make a pillar in the temple of my God, and he shall go no more out: and I will write upon him the name of my God, and the name of the city of my God, which is new Jerusalem, which cometh down out of heaven from my God: and I will write upon him my new name. (Revelation 3:12)

Back again to Genesis: God reaffirms His unconditional blessing to the newly renamed Abraham. God promises that He will Sovereignly, unconditionally and forever establish His Covenant of love and righteousness to all succeeding believing generations, through the seed of Abraham and Sarah.

And <u>I will</u> make thee exceeding fruitful, and <u>I will</u> make nations of thee, and kings shall come out of thee.

And I will establish my Covenant between me and thee and thy seed after thee in their generations for an everlasting Covenant, to be a God unto thee, and to thy seed after thee.

And I will give unto thee, and to thy seed after thee, the land wherein thou art a stranger, all the land of Canaan, for an everlasting possession; and I will be their God.

And God said unto Abraham, Thou shalt keep my Covenant therefore, thou, and thy seed after thee in their generations. (Genesis 17:6-9)

Circumcision now became a seal of the Covenant which God made to Abraham. The Covenant itself was unconditional, a gift from God. However, the acknowledgment and response to this blessing was to be a blood sacrifice, by circumcision, that would signify the birth of a new nature and name, given to believers in the sight of God, and the cutting off of the old nature.

This is my Covenant, which ye shall keep, between me and you and thy seed after thee; Every man child among you shall be circumcised.

And ye shall circumcise the flesh of your foreskin; and it shall be a token of the Covenant betwixt me and you.

And he that is eight days old shall be circumcised among you, every man child in your generations, he that is born in the house, or bought with money of any stranger, which is not of thy seed.

He that is born in thy house, and he that is bought with thy money, must needs be circumcised: and my Covenant shall be in your flesh for an everlasting Covenant.

And the uncircumcised man child whose flesh of

his foreskin is not circumcised, that soul shall be cut off from his people; he hath broken my Covenant. (Genesis 17:10-14)

The blood from the physical act of circumcision, was a type which foreshadowed the blood which Jesus Christ shed on the cross, also of his death and resurrection in a new glorified state. All Covenants of Grace, from the time of Adam and Eve onward, were ratified by God through the shedding of blood. Blood was very evident, and typified the redemptive blood of Christ, when the Spirit of God passed between the divided animals, as a smoking furnace and a burning lamp, at the time when God made promise to Abram. No man becomes a new creature in Christ without the acknowledgement that His blood was shed for us, as a means to ratify the promised New Covenant, and to do completely away with our old sin nature. Circumcision, in the Old Testament, was a type of baptism, which became a sign of the believers new nature, after Jesus made the one time perfect sacrifice on the cross.

Therefore we are buried with him by baptism into death: that like as Christ was raised up from the dead by the glory of the Father, even so we also should walk in newness of life.

For if we have been planted together in the likeness of his death, we shall be also in the likeness of his resurrection:

Knowing this, that our old man is crucified with him, that the body of sin might be destroyed, that henceforth we should not serve sin.

For he that is dead is freed from sin.

Now if we be dead with Christ, we believe that we shall also live with him:

Knowing that Christ being raised from the dead dieth no more; death hath no more dominion over him.

For in that he died, he died unto sin once: but in that he liveth, he liveth unto God.

Likewise reckon ye also yourselves to be dead indeed unto sin, but alive unto God through Jesus Christ our Lord.

Let not sin therefore reign in your mortal body, that ye should obey it in the lusts thereof. (Romans 6:4-12)

And again:

But ye are not in the flesh, but in the Spirit, if so be that the Spirit of God dwell in you. Now if any man have not the Spirit of Christ, he is none of his. And if Christ be in you, the body is dead because of sin; but the Spirit is life because of righteousness. (Romans 8:9,10)

The blood which Jesus shed on the cross spoke to all of mankind, throughout history, of His death and burial. Jesus faithfully came to earth to fulfill the Father's perfect will, which was to implant resurrection power and eternal life with Him in His Kingdom, into the Spirit of believing man. It was therefore necessary that Christ, the believers continual High Priest, sprinkle his very own blood on the Mercy Seat in Heaven, within the veil, after His death and resurrection, thus the completion of the Father's perfect will was accomplished.

God sent forth His only begotten son to be a propitiation for believers, this propitiation however, was not accomplished until Christ entered the Holy of Holies with his own blood. Only after Christ's resurrection, the promise of the perfect redemption of the seed of Abraham was made manifest, through the sprinkling of His blood on the Mercy Seat in Heaven. The sprinkling of the blood of Christ on the Mercy Seat redeemed, and freed from prison, all believers, both in the Old Testament as well as New Testament.

Whereupon neither the first testament was dedicated without blood.

For when Moses had spoken every precept to all the people according to the law, he took the blood of calves and of goats, with water, and scarlet wool, and hyssop, and sprinkled both the book, and all the people,

Saying, This is the blood of the testament which God hath enjoined unto you.

Moreover he sprinkled with blood both the tabernacle, and all the vessels of the ministry.

And almost all things are by the law purged with blood; and without shedding of blood is no remission.

<u>It was therefore necessary that the patterns of things in the heavens should be purified with these; but the heavenly things themselves with better sacrifices than these.</u>

For Christ is not entered into the holy places made with hands, which are the figures of the true; but into heaven itself, now to appear in the presence of God for us: (Hebrews 9:18-24)

When the promised Covenant to all believers through Abraham, was made manifest through the resurrection of Christ, and the blood of His perfect sacrifice was sprinkled on the Mercy Seat, all believers past, present and future were forever purged of the guilt of the conscience of conditional laws.

Neither by the blood of goats and calves, but by his own blood he entered in once into the holy place, having obtained eternal redemption for us.

For if the blood of bulls and of goats, and the ashes of an heifer sprinkling the unclean, sanctifieth to the purifying of the flesh:

How much more shall the blood of Christ, who through the eternal Spirit offered himself without

spot to God, purge your conscience from dead
works to serve the living God?

(Hebrews 9:12-14)

Faith in the blood of the cross speaks of the death of Jesus, the promised perfect sacrifice of the Old Testament, saves the believer from the cruel bondage of the present world system, and assures him of eternal life in heaven. Faith in the power of Christ's own sprinkled blood on the Mercy Seat, however, gives further ongoing salvation to the uttermost, speaks of the gift of God's total remission of sin and guilt, from the believers conscience. Faith in the sprinkling of Jesus' blood on the Mercy Seat allows believers to continually dwell in the heavenly holy city, the city of the living God, the heavenly Jerusalem.

For ye are not come unto the mount that might
be touched, and that burned with fire, nor unto
blackness, and darkness, and tempest...
But ye are come unto mount Sion, and unto the
city of the living God, the heavenly Jerusalem,
and to an innumerable company of angels,
To the general assembly and church of the
firstborn, which are written in heaven, and to
God the Judge of all, and to the spirits of just
men made perfect,
And to Jesus the mediator of the new Covenant,
and to the blood of sprinkling, that speaketh
better things than that of Abel.

(Hebrews 12;18, 22-24)

The blood of Abel, and all other Old Testament blood sacrifices to God, spoke to Old Testament believers of the promise of the blood of Jesus Christ yet to come, and of the salvation and grace which would follow. Faith in the sprinkled blood of Christ on the Mercy Seat, speaks of the New Covenant of Grace, and the blotting out and total freedom from the guilt of the believers past sinful and iniquitous nature. We see from the Scriptures above that faith in the sprinkling of Christ's mediating blood (propitiation) on the Mercy Seat, delivers believers from the guilt of the law of Mount Sinai and brings them to the very Throne Room of Grace in the heavenly Jerusalem and Mount Zion. This is the promise of the blessing of the New Covenant God made to all believers through the Covenant He made to us through Abraham. The blessing of God's continual ongoing salvation to the uttermost, and the perfect purging of the believers conscience from the guilt of the flesh, only comes about through Jesus Christ's mediation in the heavenly Jerusalem.

Circumcision in the Old Testament, then, spoke of the blood of the promised redeemer, and the cutting off of the old nature, in order that the new nature might be sanctified and completely removed from the contaminated nature of the old man of sin. New Testament baptism speaks of the fulfilment of the promise made to us through Abraham, and the death of the believers original old sin nature, and being raised again in the newness of everlasting life. The new nature of the believer cannot be mixed with the old sinful nature because God's Covenant "beriyth" completely separates the two, through the dividing asunder of the soul and the Spirit by the quick, powerful and sharp sword of the Word of God.

Back in Genesis again we see that Abram fathered a son after the flesh, Ishmael, through Sari's handmaiden Hagar, prior to having his named changed from Abram to Abraham and thereby receiving a new identity in God's very own perfection. Now having been separated from his old nature and given the new name Abraham, which means the father of a multitude, God also gave Sarai a new perfect identity, and changed her name to Sarah. The Lord instructs Abraham to no longer call his wife Sarai but Sarah, showing once again that the old nature of the redeemed should not even be mentioned in conjunction with the new. It is of interest to note that both Abram's and Sarai's names were changed by adding the fifth letter of the Jewish alphabet, which is similar to the letter "h", the number five being the number which denotes God's grace. Abraham and Sarah were now reborn of grace through faith.

Abram's first son, Ishmael, was born of the flesh, but now God promises both Abraham and Sarah that they would be blessed with a son whom they were to name Isaac, not born of the flesh but of the union of their newly separated and sanctified natures.

> *And God said unto Abraham, As for Sarai thy wife, thou shalt not call her <u>name Sarai, but Sarah shall her name be.</u>*
>
> *And I will bless her, and give thee a son also of her: yea, I will bless her, and she shall be a mother of nations; kings of people shall be of her.*
>
> *Then Abraham fell upon his face, and laughed, and said in his heart, Shall a child be born unto him that is an hundred years old? and shall Sarah, that is ninety years old, bear?*
>
> *And Abraham said unto God, O that Ishmael might live before thee!*
>
> *And God said, Sarah thy wife shall bear thee a son indeed; and thou shalt call his name Isaac: and I will establish my Covenant with him for an everlasting Covenant, and with his seed after him.* (Genesis 17:15-19)

Although Abraham and Sarah were sanctified, declared righteous and perfect before the Lord, there seems to be a bit of confusion here, along with a bit of lapse in their faith toward God. God had previously promised Abraham that the seed (sperm) of his own body would produce an heir, through whom there would be offspring that would be as numerous as the stars in the heavens. Indeed it was through Abraham's faith in this promise that Abraham was blessed with the Lord's very righteousness. It was Abraham and Sarah's deepest desire that the Lord fulfill His promise to them, by blessing them with a son who in turn would pass this blessing on to future generations. Now when God once again reaffirms this Covenant to Abraham that he and Sarah would be blessed with a child of their union, incredibly Abraham falls over laughing before God, in unbelief. Abraham even goes further, he suggests to God that Ishmael, the son born of the flesh of his old nature, become the heir of promise. God once again clarifies His promise to Abraham that he and Sarah will have a son in a year whom they must name Isaac. Abraham had a difficult time believing that with God nothing is impossible, especially restoring fertility to a couple where the husband was 100 years old and his wife 90.

Abraham was perfect and righteous and the Father of Faith through whom all the children of faith are blessed, yet he, like all believers, at times wavered. Even though Abraham's faith in the promises of God wavered from time to time, God did not condemn him nor remove His Covenant of promise and blessing from him. Although, as we will see in the scriptures below, God went up from Abraham for a while. Apparently even Abraham was not able to see the distinct separation of the fruits of the flesh from the fruits of the Spirit. Abraham did not seem to fully understand that, Ishmael born of the flesh, would continually be against he who would be born of the Holy Spirit, Isaac. God has, through His Sovereign will, totally separated these two natures.

> *And as for Ishmael, I have heard thee: Behold, I have blessed him, and will make him fruitful, and will multiply him exceedingly; twelve princes shall he beget, and I will make him a great nation.*
> *But my Covenant will I establish with Isaac, which Sarah shall bear unto thee at this set time in the next year.*
> *And he left off talking with him, and God went up from Abraham.* (Genesis 17:20-22)

This truth then is one of the first principles of the oracles of God, one of the foundational truths upon which His love

Covenant for mankind would be continually made manifest to all believers who would seek and receive the blessings of Abraham. This absolute distinction between Isaac of the Spirit and Ishmael of the flesh is one of the themes continued throughout the Bible, and is most clearly underlined, among other places, in the book of Galatians.

> *Tell me, ye that desire to be under the law, do ye not hear the law?*
>
> *For it is written, that Abraham had two sons, the one by a bondmaid, the other by a freewoman.*
>
> *But he who was of the bondwoman was born after the flesh; but he of the freewoman was by promise.*
>
> *Which things are an allegory: for these are the two Covenants; the one from the mount Sinai, which gendereth to bondage, which is Agar.*
>
> *For this Agar is mount Sinai in Arabia, and answereth to Jerusalem which now is, and is in bondage with her children.*
>
> *But Jerusalem which is above is free, which is the mother of us all.*
>
> *For it is written, Rejoice, thou barren that bearest not; break forth and cry, thou that travailest not: for the desolate hath many more children than she which hath an husband.*
>
> *Now we, brethren, as Isaac was, are the children of promise.*
>
> *But as then he that was born after the flesh persecuted him that was born after the Spirit, even so it is now.*
>
> *Nevertheless what saith the scripture? Cast out the bondwoman and her son: for the son of the bondwoman shall not be heir with the son of the freewoman.*

> *So then, brethren, we are not children of the*
> *bondwoman, but of the free.* (Galatians 4:21-31)

How can it be made more evident? Believers today who would attempt to receive their strength and blessing from the law, are as those who have not received the blessing of the Covenant God made with His children through Abraham, and are destined to spiritually remain at Mount Sinai, which is an allegory for those born of the bondwoman Hagar. The heavenly Jerusalem, upon the Spiritual Mount Zion, is the secret dwelling place of the remnant who accept the blessing of the Covenant God made to all believers through the Spiritual seed of Father Abraham. The believer cannot dwell in both places at once without deceiving himself. Believers cannot be free and still be in bondage at the same time, nor can we be under the Covenant of Grace and the law at the same time. If believers attempt to sustain themselves with one morsel of the law, as did Esau, then we sell our Covenanted birthright of grace, and forsake His merciful provision of dwelling with Him within the veil, in His Holy Mountain.

> *Looking diligently lest any man fail of the grace*
> *of God; lest any root of bitterness springing up*
> *trouble you, and thereby many be defiled;*
> *Lest there be any fornicator, or profane person,*
> *as Esau, who for one morsel of meat sold his*
> *birthright.*
> *For ye know how that afterward, when he would*
> *have inherited the blessing, he was rejected: for*
> *he found no place of repentance, though he*
> *sought it carefully with tears.*
> *For ye are not come unto the mount that might*
> *be touched, and that burned with fire, nor unto*
> *blackness, and darkness, and tempest,*
> *And the sound of a trumpet, and the voice of*
> *words; which voice they that heard intreated that*

the word should not be spoken to them any more:
(For they could not endure that which was
commanded, And if so much as a beast touch the
mountain, it shall be stoned, or thrust through
with a dart:
And so terrible was the sight, that Moses said, I
exceedingly fear and quake:)
But ye are come unto mount Sion, and unto the
city of the living God, the heavenly Jerusalem,
and to an innumerable company of angels,
To the general assembly and church of the
firstborn, which are written in heaven, and to
God the Judge of all, and to <u>the spirits of just</u>
<u>men made perfect,</u>
<u>And to Jesus the mediator of the new Covenant,</u>
<u>and to the blood of sprinkling, that speaketh</u>
<u>better things than that of Abel.</u>
(Hebrews 12:15-24)

Abraham now follows God's instructions and was circumcised, along with all the members of his household. Ishmael, who was born of the bondwoman Hagar, was also circumcised although he was now thirteen years old, thirteen being significant as it is the number of rebellion. God had instructed Abraham to have the male children born in his house, from then on, to be circumcised on the eighth day after their birth. This would be a sign of the Covenant which Isaac would receive after his birth. The number eight being the number which denotes resurrection or new beginning as does also baptism.

In Genesis chapter eighteen the Lord (Yahweh) appears again to Abraham, this time in the form of three men. Abraham addresses all three men, throughout the chapter, as though they were one entity, he bows down to them and addresses the three as "My Lord". One cannot help but speculate if these three men in some way represented the trinity.

And the LORD appeared unto him in the plains
of Mamre: and he sat in the tent door in the heat
of the day;
And he lift up his eyes and looked, and, lo, <u>three</u>
<u>men</u> stood by him: and when he saw them, he ran
to meet them from the tent door, and bowed
himself toward the ground,
And said, <u>My Lord,</u> if now I have found favour in
thy sight, pass not away, I pray thee, from thy
servant: (Genesis 18:1-3)

Abraham goes to great lengths to cater to their every need, he spares no effort nor reserves any of his resources to make them welcome and comfortable. Abraham asked Sarah to bake cakes for them while he had a young calf dressed. These men had come to further confirm to Abraham the Covenant and blessing, which God swore to give to all believers through Abraham, as his seed. They came to confirm God's promise that, through Abraham, Sarah would bare a child whom they were to name Isaac, even though they were well past the years of sexual fertility.

And they said unto him, Where is Sarah thy wife?
And he said, Behold, in the tent.
And he said, I will certainly return unto thee
according to the time of life; and, lo, Sarah thy
wife shall have a son. And Sarah heard it in the
tent door, which was behind him.
Now Abraham and Sarah were old and well
stricken in age; and it ceased to be with Sarah
after the manner of women.
<u>Therefore Sarah laughed within herself, saying,</u>
After I am waxed old shall I have pleasure, my
lord being old also?
And the LORD said unto Abraham, Wherefore
did Sarah laugh, saying, Shall I of a surety bear
a child, which am old?

*Is any thing too hard for the LORD? At the time
appointed I will return unto thee, according to
the time of life, and Sarah shall have a son.
Then Sarah denied, saying, I laughed not; for
she was afraid. And he said, Nay; but thou didst
laugh.* (Genesis 18:9-15)

Here again, we see an example of how the Lord's provision
of mercy and grace were made evident, in that He understands
and sets aside the unfaithfulness of faithful Sarah. In His grace,
God promises to give Abraham and Sarah the most precious
desire of their hearts, a child. In His mercy the Lord does not
condemn Sarah for unbelief, even though she laughed at the
thought of her being able to bear a child of Abraham, at this stage
of their lives. God does not condemn Sarah for her momentary
lack of faith, He even overlooks her attempt to cover up her lie,
when she denied having laughed.

God, through the provisions of His Covenants, is merciful
towards the momentary unrighteousness lapses of faith of those
He has declared to be His very own righteousness, as is stated in
the New Covenant;

*For I will be merciful to their unrighteousness,
and their sins and their iniquities will I
remember no more.* (Hebrews 8:12)

The three men of the Lord now direct Abraham's attention to
the great sin of the nearby cities of Sodom and Gomorrah. They
had come to further assure and sanctify Abraham of God's
Covenanted promise, that all future generations of believers
would come out of his loins. They had also come to reaffirm, to
Abraham, that it would only be the righteous whom God would
deliver from His wrath upon unregenerated flesh. This truth was
about to be graphically illustrated when God would destroy the
wicked cities of Sodom and Gomorrah, with brimstone and fire.

*And the men rose up from thence, and looked
toward Sodom: and Abraham went with them to*

bring them on the way...
And the men turned their faces from thence, and
went toward Sodom: but Abraham stood yet
before the LORD. (Genesis 18:16; 22)

Abraham interceded in prayer before the Lord, as a type of Christ, the High Priest of all righteous, asking that the wicked cities of Sodom and Gomorrah be spared from destruction, for the sake of the righteous believers who might be living in these cities. Abraham could not bare to think that God would destroy some of His own people, people whom He had declared to be righteous, in order to take vengeance upon the cities of the world system.

And Abraham drew near, and said, Wilt thou also
destroy the righteous with the wicked?
PerAdventure there be fifty righteous within the
city: wilt thou also destroy and not spare the
place for the fifty righteous that are therein?
That be far from thee to do after this manner, to
slay the righteous with the wicked: and that the
righteous should be as the wicked, that be far
from thee: Shall not the Judge of all the earth do
right? (Genesis 18:23-25)

Through intercession and bargaining with the Lord, Abraham became aware of the hard facts; that there were none righteous in Sodom and Gomorrah, except Lot and his family.

And turning the cities of Sodom and Gomorrha
into ashes condemned them with an overthrow,
making them an ensample unto those that after
should live ungodly;
And delivered just Lot, vexed with the filthy
conversation of the wicked:
(For that righteous man dwelling among them,
in seeing and hearing, vexed his righteous soul
from day to day with their unlawful deeds;)

The Lord knoweth how to deliver the godly out of temptations, and to reserve the unjust unto the day of judgment to be punished:
(2 Peter 2:6-9)

We shall see as this historical account of God's example of wrathful judgement upon the unrighteous world system continues, that there are two sides to every coin. In the case of those whom God has judged to be included in His very own righteous Kingdom, through rebirth and their faith in the power of the blood of Christ, there will be everlasting peace and joy with Him in eternity. The judgement of God's wrath is reserved for unbelievers, for the Devil and his angels, for those who have not recognized that their sinful natural birth is not of God's nature. God is not unfair, His hearts desire is that all of mankind would accept His offer of becoming a part of His righteous kingdom, through faith in the blood of Jesus Christ. Natural sinful unrighteous mankind, cannot be mixed with nor become a part of His Holy Nature, neither in this present world nor in the next. Heaven is the land of righteousness, totally separated from all unrighteousness.

The Lord is not slack concerning his promise, as some men count slackness; but is longsuffering to us-ward, not willing that any should perish, but that all should come to repentance.

But the day of the Lord will come as a thief in the night; in the which the heavens shall pass away with a great noise, and the elements shall melt with fervent heat, the earth also and the works that are therein shall be burned up.

Seeing then that all these things shall be dissolved, what manner of persons ought ye to be in all holy conversation and godliness,

Looking for and hasting unto the coming of the day of God, wherein the heavens being on fire shall be dissolved, and the elements shall melt with fervent heat?

Nevertheless we, according to his promise, look for new heavens and a new earth, wherein dwelleth righteousness. (2 Peter 3:9-13)

God being true to His Word, as we read in 2 Peter 2:9 above, warned and delivered righteous Lot from Sodom and Gomorrah prior to their destruction. The life style of righteous Lot and his family, prior to the Lord calling them out from among the horrible worldly conditions of Sodom and Gomorrah, was almost unimaginable. The present word sodomy, meaning anal intercourse, conveys to us the nature of some of the sexual sins that were a part of the culture of Sodom and Gomorrah. The Scriptures which reveal to us some of the horrible conditions that Lot chose to live in are recorded below.

When two of the angels of the Lord met Lot upon their entrance to Sodom and Gomorrah, he greeted them with the utmost reverence.

And there came two angels to Sodom at even; and Lot sat in the gate of Sodom: and Lot seeing them rose up to meet them; and he bowed himself with his face toward the ground;

And he said, Behold now, my lords, turn in, I pray you, into your servant's house, and tarry all night, and wash your feet, and ye shall rise up early, and go on your ways. And they said, Nay; but we will abide in the street all night.

And he pressed upon them greatly; and they turned in unto him, and entered into his house; and he made them a feast, and did bake unleavened bread, and they did eat.

(Genesis 19:1-3)

Unleavened bread was symbolic of the God given sinless nature of the redeemed, free from the fermentation process, which was also representative of the sin sickness of man's original natural nature. Here again, in this example of the differences between leavened and unleavened bread, is reflected the distinct separation of the righteous and the unrighteous natures of the redeemed, as opposed to the sinful natures of the unredeemed man. Unleavened bread has nothing in common with leavened bread, they are entirely separate and distinct. So it is with believers, our new redeemed nature of the Holy Spirit has nothing to do with our old dead sin nature of the flesh.

After a horrible scene, in which the citizens of Sodom and Gomorrah attempted to sodomize the messengers of the Lord, Lot was barely successful in being able to close the door of his house to the degenerate citizens of these cities. In Lot's attempt to protect the angels of the Lord, he offered to send his two virgin daughters outside that the mob might do what they willed with them.

And they called unto Lot, and said unto him, Where are the men which came in to thee this night? bring them out unto us, that we may know them.

And Lot went out at the door unto them, and shut the door after him,

And said, I pray you, brethren, do not so wickedly.

Behold now, I have two daughters which have not known man; let me, I pray you, bring them out unto you, and do ye to them as is good in your eyes: only unto these men do nothing; for therefore came they under the shadow of my roof. (Genesis 19:5-8)

I cannot, spiritually entirely understand the reasoning, or the Lord's purpose or intended message in this scene. It would seem, that the message here is that, to respond to the Holy nature of God we must at times be willing to sacrifice not only our own lives, but to consider the lives of our offspring as expendable. This is not a new thought in God's dealing with unregenerated man, for God gave His very own son to suffer death on the cruel cross for sinful man, that believers might be reconciled to Him. We shall also see further on in this chapter, that Abraham as well, was challenged of God to offer up his only son Isaac, in a test of his faith toward God. Likewise, we understand that Ishmael was removed from the blessing of Abraham. Although Abram was the father of Ishmael, Ishmael was considered of God as being excluded from the blessing, and was cast out of Abraham's house because his mother Hagar was of the world system.

The citizens of Sodom and Gomorrah knew, through the conviction of the Holy Spirit, that they were in trouble, for they recognized that the angels of the Lord had come to judge them guilty in their sinful life style. In order to deny and attempt to cover their guilty consciences, they determined to satisfy their lustful nature on Lot. The two angels however, brought Lot back inside his house, and were able to protect him by keeping the door closed. Not only were they able to protect Lot and his family, they struck those blind who were attempting to enter his home.

> *And they said, Stand back. And they said again,*
> *This one fellow came in to sojourn, and he will*
> *needs be a judge: now will we deal worse with*
> *thee, than with them. And they pressed sore upon*
> *the man, even Lot, and came near to break the*
> *door.*
> *But the men put forth their hand, and pulled Lot*
> *into the house to them, and shut to the door.*
> *And they smote the men that were at the door of*
> *the house with blindness, both small and great:*
> *so that they wearied themselves to find the door.*
> (Genesis 19:9-11)

Even after this incident, Lot was still reluctant to believe that the iniquitous cities of Sodom and Gomorrah would be destroyed, as the angels of the Lord had warned him. His two sons-in-law, along with his two married daughters, did not believe the warning, and as a result were doomed to be destroyed as the angels had prophesied.

The angels of the Lord, even had to awaken reluctant Lot the following morning, and physically lead him along with his wife and their two unmarried daughters, out of their home, prior to the destruction of the cities.

> *And when the morning arose, then the angels hastened Lot, saying, Arise, take thy wife, and thy two daughters, which are here; lest thou be consumed in the iniquity of the city.*
>
> *And while he lingered, the men laid hold upon his hand, and upon the hand of his wife, and upon the hand of his two daughters; the LORD being merciful unto him: and they brought him forth, and set him without the city.*

(Genesis 19:15,16)

In righteous Lot's reluctance to leave the doomed cities, and escape to the mountain of God, we see the power of the flesh to hinder the moving of the Holy Spirit. Over powering lust of the flesh, is the consequence of living a life style which deadens the conscience to the leading of the Lord's will. Although Lot and his family were the only righteous people in Sodom and Gomorrah, they suffered the resultant confusion of not being sensitive to the leading of the indwelling Holy Spirit. Lot refused to escape to the mountain of God, as the messengers of the Lord had instructed he and his family, but instead insisted that he would rather live in a smaller nearby city, of his own choice, called Zoar. The angel of the Spirit of the Lord gracefully allowed Lot to escape to this city, even though it meant a further loss of eternal rewards for him. Lot, for his own selfish purposes, willfully and foolishly took advantage of the Lord's goodness and grace. His heart had become calloused to the leading of the Holy Spirit, during the time he chose to live in the two wicked cities.

> *And it came to pass, when they had brought them forth abroad, that he said, Escape for thy life;*

look not behind thee, neither stay thou in all the plain; escape to the mountain, lest thou be consumed.

And Lot said unto them, Oh, not so, my Lord: Behold now, thy servant hath found grace in thy sight, and thou hast magnified thy mercy, which thou hast shewed unto me in saving my life; and I cannot escape to the mountain, lest some evil take me, and I die:

Behold now, this city is near to flee unto, and it is a little one: Oh, let me escape thither, (is it not a little one?) and my soul shall live.

And he said unto him, See, I have accepted thee concerning this thing also, that I will not overthrow this city, for the which thou hast spoken.

Haste thee, escape thither; for I cannot do any thing till thou be come thither. Therefore the name of the city was called Zoar.

(Genesis 19:17-22)

Lot failed to appreciate and incorporate in his life, the wisdom of Abraham, for Abraham looked for a Spiritual City, who's builder and maker was God. Abraham, through faith in God's Covenanted promise to him, was searching for the Holy Mountain of God, and the Spiritual City of Jerusalem. However, Lot unwisely chose to dwell in the smaller insignificant city of Zoar.

Now comes the destruction of Sodom and Gomorrah, the cities which represented the world system, the same as Egypt was representative of the unredeemed world system, at the time God used Moses to deliver the children of Israel. Here once again, in the example of Sodom and Gomorrah, we see this distinct division between those whom God has justified, or declared righteous, and those who have ignored the provisions of the Covenant God swore to believers through Abraham. This division will once again become abundantly manifest, on the day when the Lord appears in a cloud of glory, to receive His pure spotless bride, His church, to escape the wrath of the great tribulation. Also when the Lord returns to earth, and sets His feet upon Mount Zion, at His second Advent, He will terribly separate the unrepentant world system from His chosen righteous people, Israel.

And Abraham gat up early in the morning to the place where he stood before the LORD:
And he looked toward Sodom and Gomorrah, and toward all the land of the plain, and beheld, and, lo, the smoke of the country went up as the smoke of a furnace. (Genesis 19:27,28)

We will recall the first time Abraham saw the wrathful judgement of God, as a smoking furnace. It was at the time when a smoking furnace and a burning lamp passed between two pieces of separated animal carcases. This was shortly after his victory over the heathen tribes then living in Palestine. The burning lamp then represented the deliverance of the redeemed, the smoking furnace, then as now, represented the condemnation of unbelievers. Although Abraham saw the destruction of Sodom and Gomorrah, and the surrounding plain country as the smoke of a furnace, there was no burning lamp of God's deliverance evident this time. Only righteous Lot and his family escaped the overthrow.

Unfortunately however, Lot's wife was reluctant to leave her old way of life behind, instead she chose to look back on the doomed cities rather than to continue on with the remainder of her redeemed family, consequently she too was cut off from God's blessings.

Then the LORD rained upon Sodom and upon Gomorrah brimstone and fire from the LORD out of heaven;

*And he overthrew those cities, and all the plain,
and all the inhabitants of the cities, and that
which grew upon the ground.*

*But his wife looked back from behind him, and
she became a pillar of salt.* (Genesis 19:24-26)

The smoking furnace of God's wrathful judgement, is also referred to in other parts of the Bible, for example in Deuteronomy 4:20.

The small city of Zoar, in which Lot had chosen as a refuge, now became unsuitable for he and his two virgin daughters, so he took them to dwell with him in a mountain cave. The result of his choosing not to accept the guiding of the Holy Spirit, now came to fruition. Because there were no other men of whom they might bear children, Lot's two daughters, each in turn, caused Lot to become drunk, and in desperation seduced their father that they might bear children from his seed.

*And they made their father drink wine that night:
and the firstborn went in, and lay with her
father; and he perceived not when she lay down,
nor when she arose.*

*And it came to pass on the morrow, that the
firstborn said unto the younger, Behold, I lay
yesternight with my father: let us make him drink
wine this night also; and go thou in, and lie with
him, that we may preserve seed of our Father.*

*And they made their father drink wine that night
also: and the younger arose, and lay with him;
and he perceived not when she lay down, nor
when she arose.*

*Thus were both the daughters of Lot with child
by their father.*

*And the firstborn bare a son, and called his
name Moab: the same is the father of the
Moabites unto this day.*

*And the younger, she also bare a son, and called
his name Benammi: the same is the father of the
children of Ammon unto this day.*

(Genesis 19:33-38)

The two children which Lot's daughters gave birth to, of their
father's seed, became the progenitor of the Moabites, and the
other, the father of the Ammonites. Both the Moabites and the
Ammonites became wicked nations of the unredeemed, noted for
their incestuous and fleshly nature.

In conclusion we see that Lot, although he remained
righteous all his days before God, because of the pagan lifestyle
he chose to live, he became insensitive to a good degree, to the
leading of the Holy Spirit. Consequently, he suffered the loss of
most of the rewards of the righteousness promised to God's
people, through the Covenant He made for us through Abraham.

Abraham and Sarah too, from time to time, had lapses of
faith, and, from time to time, momentarily lost conscious contact
of the leading of the Holy Spirit. As is true of all of God's
redeemed, they eventually suffered the consequences of reverting
to their old nature of the flesh. Not only did Abraham and Sarah
have lapses of faith from time to time, but they, like most
believers, made the same mistake the second time.

Although Abraham and Sarah were children of the same
father they had different mothers, so they were both husband and
wife, as well as being brother and half sister.

*And Abraham said, Because I thought, Surely the
fear of God is not in this place; and they will slay
me for my wife's sake.*

*And yet indeed she is my sister; she is the
daughter of my father, but not the daughter of my
mother; and she became my wife.*

(Genesis 20:11,12)

As we saw above in Genesis chapter twelve, because
Abraham and Sarah were afraid of the ruling authorities, at the

time they journeyed to Egypt, they took what they thought to be, advantage of this situation and ended up in trouble because they subscribed to a half truth. They only mentioned to Pharaoh that they were brother and half sister, but neglected to tell him they also were husband and wife. Now we will see how they again, acting out of fear, tried to hide behind the same half truth as before. We will see how Abraham and Sarah again foolishly adulterated the truth, in an attempt to cover their fears.

> *And Abraham journeyed from thence toward the*
> *south country, and dwelled between Kadesh and*
> *Shur, and sojourned in Gerar.*

(Genesis 20:1)

After the destruction of Sodom and Gomorrah, Abraham and Sarah went south to Gerar, a city that had been established by the exiled Philistines. The name of the king of Gerar was Abimelech.

> *And Abraham said of Sarah his wife, She is my*
> *sister: and Abimelech king of Gerar sent, and*
> *took Sarah.*
> *But God came to Abimelech in a dream by night,*
> *and said to him, Behold, thou art but a dead*
> *man, for the woman which thou hast taken; for*
> *she is a man's wife.* (Genesis 20:2,3)

Abimelech, the king of a righteous nation, was led of the Holy Spirit, not to touch Abraham's wife and so escaped the wrath of God. Even though believers, like Abraham and Sarah, have a lapse of faith from time to time, the wrath of God is reserved for the unredeemed. There is no condemnation to those who walk in the Sprit, for the love of the Holy Spirit gracefully guides believers to live lives separated, through the sword of the Word, from the desires of the flesh.

> *But Abimelech had not come near her: and he*
> *said, Lord, wilt thou slay also a righteous*
> *nation?*
> *Said he not unto me, She is my sister? and she,*
> *even she herself said, He is my brother: in the*

integrity of my heart and innocency of my hands have I done this.

And God said unto him in a dream, Yea, I know that thou didst this in the integrity of thy heart; for I also withheld thee from sinning against me: therefore suffered I thee not to touch her.

Now therefore restore the man his wife; for he is a prophet, and he shall pray for thee, and thou shalt live: and if thou restore her not, know thou that thou shalt surely die, thou, and all that are thine.

(Genesis 20:4-7)

Not only did Abimelech restore Sarah to the bosom of her husband Abraham, but he gave his brother in the Lord further great riches, for Abimelech had the utmost respect for Abraham as a prophet of God.

And Abimelech took sheep, and oxen, and menservants, and womenservants, and gave them unto Abraham, and restored him Sarah his wife.

And Abimelech said, Behold, my land is before thee: dwell where it pleaseth thee.

And unto Sarah he said, Behold, I have given thy brother a thousand pieces of silver: behold, he is to thee a covering of the eyes, unto all that are with thee, and with all other: thus she was reproved.

So Abraham prayed unto God: and God healed Abimelech, and his wife, and his maidservants; and they bare children.

For the LORD had fast closed up all the wombs of the house of Abimelech, because of Sarah Abraham's wife. (Genesis 20:14-18)

Already Abimelech, and the people of his kingdom, had suffered the loss of the Lord's rewards, for He had made barren the women of his household when Abimelech took Sarah from

Abraham. However God restored these blessings when Abraham interceded on the behalf of Abimelech.

Adultery, both as we think of it in the flesh as well as in the spiritual realm, results in the dying of the soul. If believers, through unbelief, become involved in extra marital relations they suffer loss of Spiritual rewards. If believers adulterate the truth, through not preaching the entire Gospel in context, they suffer loss of Spiritual rewards, both in this present life, and also at the time when we all must appear before the judgement seat of Christ, to receive our eternal rewards.

> *For we must all appear before the judgment seat*
> *of Christ; that every one may receive the things*
> *done in his body, according to that he hath done,*
> *whether it be good or bad.* (2 Corinthians 5:10)

Believers, those who have accepted the Spirit of Jesus Christ as the corner stone of their lives, through faith in His blood, will suffer loss for useless works done through the will of their own flesh. However, believers will be saved from the wrath of God because it was He who declared the Spirit of Christ within us to be of His righteousness and perfection, when we were born of His Spirit from above. Even though useless works of the believers flesh will be burned, the believer himself will enter into God's rest, because the Holy Spirit continues to dwell in the heart of the righteous. It is through the believers inheritance, which is the unconditional Covenant (the dividing of the soul and flesh) which God swore to all believers, as being the seed of Abraham, that they have been declared righteous and perfect before God.

> *<u>For other foundation can no man lay than that is</u>*
> *<u>laid, which is Jesus Christ.</u>*
> *Now if any man build upon this foundation gold,*
> *silver, precious stones, wood, hay, stubble;*
> *Every man's work shall be made manifest: for*
> *the day shall declare it, because it shall be*
> *revealed by fire; and the fire shall try every*

man's work of what sort it is.
If any man's work abide which he hath built
thereupon, he shall receive a reward.
If any man's work shall be burned, he shall suffer
loss: but he himself shall be saved; yet so as by
fire.
Know ye not that ye are the temple of God, and
that the Spirit of God dwelleth in you?
(1 Corinthians 3:11-16)

Also, after restoring the fertility of the household of
Abimelech God, as promised, restored fertility to Abraham and
Sarah. The reward of their faith in the promise which God had
made to them regarding a child through whom Abraham's seed
would bless all men of God's will upon the earth, was about to
become manifest. Isaac, who's name means "laughing", was
about to be born.

And the LORD visited Sarah as he had said, and
the LORD did unto Sarah as he had spoken.
For Sarah conceived, and bare Abraham a son
in his old age, at the set time of which God had
spoken to him.
And Abraham called the name of his son that
was born unto him, whom Sarah bare to him,
Isaac.
And Abraham circumcised his son Isaac being
eight days old, as God had commanded him.
And Abraham was an hundred years old, when
his son Isaac was born unto him.
And Sarah said, God hath made me to laugh, so
that all that hear will laugh with me.
And she said, Who would have said unto
Abraham, that Sarah should have given children
suck? for I have born him a son in his old age.
And the child grew, and was weaned: and

*Abraham made a great feast the same day that
Isaac was weaned.* (Genesis 21:1-8)

God would have all believers share in the joy of the Lord and
laugh both inwardly and outwardly, as recipients of the fulfilling
of the Covenant God made with His people through Abraham and
Isaac. We can only speculate as to whether or not Abraham
realized that through his seed the Messiah, Jesus Christ, would be
born, but it seems very likely that he did. We wonder also if the
Lord revealed to Abraham that David, the promised deliverer and
King of Israel would be of his seed, as the very first verse in the
New Testament informs it's readers.

*The book of the generation of Jesus Christ, the
son of David, the son of Abraham.* (Matthew 1:1)

This verse is the connecting link, the umbilical cord, the
blood connection, the scarlet cord, which from the very
beginning was meant to join as one, all Old Testament believers
and those of the New Covenant or New Testament, as one in
Christ. The righteousness of God, for which all of mankind has
inwardly desired from the beginning of time, comes to believers
through the first principles which God has spoken from the
beginning, His oracles that formed the worlds. His oracles, His
Words from the beginning spoke the worlds into being.

*God, who at sundry times and in divers manners
spake in time past unto the fathers by the
prophets,
Hath in these last days spoken unto us by his
Son, whom he hath appointed heir of all things,
by whom also he made the worlds;*
(Hebrews 1:1,2)

Ever since the blessing of the Covenant God made with His
people through Abraham and Sarah, the righteousness of God
was passed on to His people through this union. The so called
Abrahamic Covenant has one central theme; faith in the efficacy
of the blood of Jesus Christ.

Hearken to me, ye that follow after righteousness, ye that seek the LORD: look unto the rock whence ye are hewn, and to the hole of the pit whence ye are digged.

Look unto Abraham your father, and unto Sarah that bare you: for I called him alone, and blessed him, and increased him.

For the LORD shall comfort Zion: he will comfort all her waste places; and he will make her wilderness like Eden, and her desert like the garden of the LORD; joy and gladness shall be found therein, thanksgiving, and the voice of melody.

Hearken unto me, my people; and give ear unto me, O my nation: for a law shall proceed from me, and I will make my judgment to rest for a light of the people.

My righteousness is near; my salvation is gone forth, and mine arms shall judge the people; the isles shall wait upon me, and on mine arm shall they trust.

Lift up your eyes to the heavens, and look upon the earth beneath: for the heavens shall vanish away like smoke, and the earth shall wax old like a garment, and they that dwell therein shall die in like manner: but my salvation shall be for ever, and my righteousness shall not be abolished.

Hearken unto me, ye that know righteousness, the people in whose heart is my law; fear ye not the reproach of men, neither be ye afraid of their revilings.

For the moth shall eat them up like a garment, and the worm shall eat them like wool: but my righteousness shall be for ever, and my salvation from generation to generation.

Awake, awake, put on strength, O arm of the LORD; awake, as in the ancient days, in the generations of old. Art thou not it that hath cut Rahab, and wounded the dragon?

Art thou not it which hath dried the sea, the waters of the great deep; that hath made the depths of the sea a way for the ransomed to pass over?

Therefore the redeemed of the LORD shall return, and come with singing unto Zion; and everlasting joy shall be upon their head: they shall obtain gladness and joy; and sorrow and mourning shall flee away.

(Isaiah 51:1-11)

If believers desire to receive the blessings of Abraham through Jesus Christ, we too, as did Abraham, in faith look for this city who's builder and maker is God. The Scriptures are the only guide through which believers are able to seek and find this city, the heavenly Jerusalem, and having found it coming with joy and singing to the Spiritual Heavenly Jerusalem on Mount Zion. This joyful experience of our inheritance, is meant for believers to Spiritually experience, NOW! As recorded earlier.

But that no man is justified by the law in the sight of God, it is evident: for, The just shall live by faith.

And the law is not of faith: but, The man that doeth them shall live in them.

Christ hath redeemed us from the curse of the law, being made a curse for us: for it is written, Cursed is every one that hangeth on a tree:

That the blessing of Abraham might come on the Gentiles through Jesus Christ; that we might receive the promise of the Spirit through faith.

(Galatians 3:11-14)

It is only when believers come to understand the goodness and mercy of God, through the Scriptures, that the Holy Spirit guides and opens our eyes to see God's Holy Nature from a proper perspective. Only when believers awaken to the truth that they have been given the very righteousness of God, through faith in what the blood of Christ has accomplished for us, that we begin to focus on His gifts and Covenant for us, rather than to continue to lament our own individual shortcomings and failures in the flesh.

This truth became evident to Abraham and Sarah after the birth of Isaac. It wasn't until Sarah began to rejoice in the gift of God's goodness, through the birth of Isaac, that she became aware of the futility of her and Abraham's past efforts in trying to accomplish God's will, through their own willful flesh, that of the birth of Ishmael. Only when Sarah saw that God was faithful to fulfill His Covenant of promise, that a child would be born to them of Abraham's seed, that she began to resent the seed of the flesh, Ishmael through Hagar.

Here again we shall see that which is born of the Spirit, Isaac, is totally and irrevocably separate from that which was of the flesh, Ishmael. This truth also is manifest in the heart of the believer, the Spirit of Christ and the righteousness of God who dwells within the heart of the believer has no connection with that of our natural birth in the flesh.

> *And Sarah saw the son of Hagar the Egyptian, which she had born unto Abraham, mocking.*
> *Wherefore she said unto Abraham, Cast out this bondwoman and her son: for the son of this bondwoman shall not be heir with my son, even with Isaac.*
> *And the thing was very grievous in Abraham's sight because of his son.*
> *And God said unto Abraham, Let it not be grievous in thy sight because of the lad, and*

because of thy bondwoman; in all that Sarah
hath said unto thee, hearken unto her voice; for
in Isaac shall thy seed be called.
And also of the son of the bondwoman will I
make a nation, because he is thy seed.
(Genesis 21:9-13)

Like all believers, Abraham found out that it is a difficult thing to let go of that which we seemed to have accomplished in the flesh. It is a difficult test of faith by which we allow the Holy Spirit to circumcise our hearts, and allow our flesh of unrighteousness to be separated from the new life, which the Lord gives us when we come to have faith in His blood and it's resurrection power. While our body remains the temple of the Holy Ghost, it is His Holy Spirit that guides the decisions of the flesh, if we listen to His leading.

As we see in verse 13 above, Ishmael was living proof that our legalistic flesh nature, although separated from the Spirit, will remain and continue to be a problem until it goes to the grave.

God had promised Abraham He would preserve the life of Ishmael and that He would make of Ishmael a great nation. God also underlined the fact that it was and still is through Isaac, that all the nations of the earth would be blessed. In Genesis 15:12, we see that God also had previously informed Hagar that Ishmael would be a wild man and that his hand would be against every man. This is confirmed in verse 20 and 21 of this chapter, where we see that Ishmael was to become an archer, a perpetual warrior, and as such he and the nations which he fostered would be against every man. Also in these verses we see that Ishmael's seed would be propagated through a wife of the Egyptian world system.

As we quoted before in Galatians, Isaac and Ishmael represent two different and opposing nations allegorized as two spiritual mountains. Isaac representing Mount Zion and the heavenly Jerusalem, the City of the Living God, and Ishmael represented

Mount Sinai in Egypt, the mountain of the law of the flesh.

My little children, of whom I travail in birth again until Christ be formed in you,

I desire to be present with you now, and to change my voice; for I stand in doubt of you.

Tell me, ye that desire to be under the law, do ye not hear the law?

For it is written, that Abraham had two sons, the one by a bondmaid, the other by a freewoman.

But he who was of the bondwoman was born after the flesh; but he of the freewoman was by promise.

Which things are an allegory: for these are the two Covenants; the one from the mount Sinai, which gendereth to bondage, which is Agar.

For this Agar is mount Sinai in Arabia, and answereth to Jerusalem which now is, and is in bondage with her children.

But Jerusalem which is above is free, which is the mother of us all.

For it is written, Rejoice, thou barren that bearest not; break forth and cry, thou that travailest not: for the desolate hath many more children than she which hath an husband.

Now we, brethren, as Isaac was, are the children of promise.

But as then he that was born after the flesh persecuted him that was born after the Spirit, even so it is now.

Nevertheless what saith the scripture? Cast out the bondwoman and her son: for the son of the bondwoman shall not be heir with the son of the freewoman.

So then, brethren, we are not children of the bondwoman, but of the free.

(Galatians 4:19-31)

These two mountains, one of the law and the other of the Spirit of Grace, are separated by many miles of desert, consequently the believer cannot be in both places at once. Believers are either led by the cruel letter of the law or are led through the Covenant and dispensation of grace. If for one moment believers think that we need to be under both we deceive ourselves.

This I say then, Walk in the Spirit, and ye shall not fulfil the lust of the flesh.

For the flesh lusteth against the Spirit, and the Spirit against the flesh: and these are contrary the one to the other: so that ye cannot do the things that ye would.

But if ye be led of the Spirit, ye are not under the law.

(Galatians 5:16-18)

Likewise the believer cannot enter the promised land and come to dwell on the Spiritual Mount Zion unless he first crosses the river Jordan. Only the Word of God is quick and powerful enough to Spiritually separate our desert experience, so that we may cross the river Jordan and enter into the gates of the Holy City, the Heavenly Jerusalem. The redeemed of the Lord will come with singing unto Zion only after accepting the blessing which is ours through the Covenant God made to us through Abraham.

Abraham and Sarah had waited many years, they had their faith in God tested in numerous ways before they came to realize the living proof of the rewards of their trust in the Lord, the birth of Isaac. They must have felt secure and sanctified in the knowledge that it was their faith in the goodness of God which gave them the hope that the Gospel which they had received of God, would continue to be preached to all nations through Isaac, the seed of their son of the Spirit.

It must have been a heart rending experience beyond comprehension, when God told Abraham that he must now offer up his only son Isaac, as a burnt offering unto the Lord. To Abraham and Sarah, Isaac had become the focal point of their lives ever since God made promise that He would give them a son of Abraham's seed. It seems almost inconceivable that after many years of faithfully waiting upon God to fulfill His promise to them, Abraham would then be asked to make a choice as to who he loved the most, God or his son Isaac. Abraham would be asked to clarify to God whom he loved most, Isaac who was God's gift to him, or God who was the giver of that gift. God was about to ask Abraham to demonstrate who he loved the most, God, or his only begotten son. In God the Father asking Abraham to sacrifice his only begotten son, God was using a literal physical example in order to portray a literal Spiritual truth. Isaac, in the flesh represented God's gift of physical viability to Abraham, a sense of being, a conduit through which would flow the substance that spoke of a greater everlasting cause. Isaac was an outward manifestation of an inner Spiritual truth. Abraham, through Isaac, now had reason to hope that his name, which means "a father of many nations" might become a reality. Abraham now had Isaac to "hold onto". God was about to demonstrate to Abraham that it is only by letting go of that which we desire to keep for ourselves that God willingly gives believers that which is of His eternal Kingdom. God was about to demonstrate, through the Covenant He has made to all believers through Abraham, that only in letting go of everything that He has given us in the flesh, and by letting go of everything that may be dear to us in the natural, are we given everything pertaining to life and Godliness in the Spiritual.

And it came to pass after these things, that God did tempt Abraham, and said unto him, Abraham: and he said, Behold, here I am.

And he said, Take now thy son, thine only son Isaac, whom thou lovest, and get thee into the land of Moriah; and offer him there for a burnt offering upon one of the mountains which I will tell thee of.

And Abraham rose up early in the morning, and saddled his ass, and took two of his young men with him, and Isaac his son, and clave the wood for the burnt offering, and rose up, and went unto the place of which God had told him.

Then on the third day Abraham lifted up his eyes, and saw the place afar off.

And Abraham said unto his young men, Abide ye here with the ass; and I and the lad will go yonder and worship, and come again to you,

And Abraham took the wood of the burnt offering, and laid it upon Isaac his son; and he took the fire in his hand, and a knife; and they went both of them together.

And Isaac spake unto Abraham his father, and said, My father: and he said, Here am I, my son.

And he said, Behold the fire and the wood: but where is the lamb for a burnt offering?

And Abraham said, My son, God will provide himself a lamb for a burnt offering: so they went both of them together.

And they came to the place which God had told him of; and Abraham built an altar there, and laid the wood in order, and bound Isaac his son, and laid him on the altar upon the wood.

And Abraham stretched forth his hand, and took the knife to slay his son.

And the angel of the LORD called unto him out of heaven, and said, Abraham, Abraham: and he said, Here am I.

And he said, Lay not thine hand upon the lad, neither do thou any thing unto him: for now I know that thou fearest God, seeing thou hast not withheld thy son, thine only son from me.

And Abraham lifted up his eyes, and looked, and behold behind him a ram caught in a thicket by his horns: and Abraham went and took the ram, and offered him up for a burnt offering in the stead of his son.

And Abraham called the name of that place Jehovah-jireh: as it is said to this day, In the mount of the LORD it shall be seen.

And the angel of the LORD called unto Abraham out of heaven the second time,

And said, By myself have I sworn, saith the LORD, for because thou hast done this thing, and hast not withheld thy son, thine only son:

That in blessing I will bless thee, and in multiplying I will multiply thy seed as the stars of the heaven, and as the sand which is upon the sea shore; and thy seed shall possess the gate of his enemies;

And in thy seed shall all the nations of the earth be blessed; because thou hast obeyed my voice.
(Genesis 22:1-18)

Once again we see demonstrated, in this further testing of Abraham's faith, that it is our belief and trust in the Spiritual aspects of life in Christ, which separates and gives us complete victory over the concerns of the flesh. As we see in verse 13 above, God graciously provided a ram for Abraham, a substitute sacrifice, so that the blood of Abraham's son need not be spilled. It is obvious that the ram which was caught in the thicket by his horns, was representative of our Lord Jesus Christ. This demonstration of God's gracious desire to provide a perfect vicarious blood sacrifice for all believers, demonstrates that all we hold dear in the flesh is totally inadequate to reveal the resurrection power made manifest to us, through faith in the blood of Jesus Christ.

By faith Abraham, when he was tried, offered up Isaac: and he that had received the promises offered up his only begotten son,
Of whom it was said, That in Isaac shall thy seed be called:
Accounting that God was able to raise him up, even from the dead; from whence also he received him in a figure. (Hebrews 11:17-19)

It is only when we as believers, as did Abraham, die to ourselves and come to realize that God our Father has provided the perfect sacrifice of Jesus Christ, that we receive the assurance of eternal resurrected life in the Spirit. In this instance, God also demonstrated to all believers, through Abraham's experience, that the sacrifice which we would offer of our own flesh is totally insignificant for there is only one acceptable sacrifice for sin, the Lamb which He has slain from the foundation of the world, Jesus Christ. Here again we see that the flesh and the Spirit are as totally separated from each other, as were the divided pieces of the animals which God passed through as a smoking furnace and a burning lamp, when He first made the everlasting Covenant to all believers through Abraham. Notice in Genesis 22:18 above, how God once more confirms to Abraham the Covenant of the blessing of righteousness He has given to all believers, as being the seed of Abraham.

We would once again remind all of this truth in the following Scriptures; all believers, as well as Jesus Christ, are the seed of Abraham and through this blessing we have become eligible recipients of the Covenant of Grace God made for us through Abraham. Although these Scriptures have been recently quoted above, they are worthy of being repeated once again.

Hearken to me, ye that follow after righteousness, ye that seek the LORD: look unto the rock whence ye are hewn, and to the hole of the pit whence ye are digged.

Look unto Abraham your father, and unto Sarah that bare you: for I called him alone, and blessed him, and increased him.

For the LORD shall comfort Zion: he will comfort all her waste places; and he will make her wilderness like Eden, and her desert like the garden of the LORD; joy and gladness shall be found therein, thanksgiving, and the voice of melody.

Hearken unto me, my people; and give ear unto me, O my nation: for a law shall proceed from me, and I will make my judgment to rest for a light of the people.

My righteousness is near; my salvation is gone forth, and mine arms shall judge the people; the isles shall wait upon me, and on mine arm shall they trust.

Lift up your eyes to the heavens, and look upon the earth beneath: for the heavens shall vanish away like smoke, and the earth shall wax old like a garment, and they that dwell therein shall die in like manner: but my salvation shall be for ever, and my righteousness shall not be abolished.

Hearken unto me, ye that know righteousness, the people in whose heart is my law; fear ye not the reproach of men, neither be ye afraid of their revilings.

For the moth shall eat them up like a garment, and the worm shall eat them like wool: but my righteousness shall be for ever, and my salvation from generation to generation.

Awake, awake, put on strength, O arm of the LORD; awake, as in the ancient days, in the generations of old. Art thou not it that hath cut Rahab, and wounded the dragon?

Art thou not it which hath dried the sea, the waters of the great deep; that hath made the depths of the sea a way for the ransomed to pass over?

Therefore the redeemed of the LORD shall return, and come with singing unto Zion; and everlasting joy shall be upon their head: they shall obtain gladness and joy; and sorrow and mourning shall flee away.

I, even I, am he that comforteth you: who art thou, that thou shouldest be afraid of a man that shall die, and of the son of man which shall be made as grass;

And forgettest the LORD thy maker, that hath stretched forth the heavens, and laid the foundations of the earth; and hast feared continually every day because of the fury of the oppressor, as if he were ready to destroy? and where is the fury of the oppressor?

(Isaiah 51:1-13)

Do we as believers focus solely on the gift of God's only begotten son, Jesus Christ, who is the author of our faith, or do we fully realize and give appropriate praise and glory to God the Father, for sending us His gift? Jesus, the gift of God, came to give us the glory of the Father through which we are united in one perfect body, the pure spotless bride of Christ, His church.

I would suggest, that to a large degree, the present day denominationally organized church has forgotten the unity and mystery of the trinity and has inordinately focussed on Jesus' <u>death</u> on the cross. One reason Jesus laid down His own life on the cross was to demonstrate the <u>resurrection</u> power of the Father's will, and to share with all believers the joy of His High Priestly ministry at the right hand of the Father.

> *Looking unto Jesus the author and finisher of our faith; <u>who for the joy that was set before him endured the cross, despising the shame, and is set down at the right hand of the throne of God.</u>*

(Hebrews 12:2)

We recognize that it is through the Father's Sovereign will that Jesus's blood would be offered as the only perfect sacrifice for sin, but for believers to fail to recognize that it was the Spirit of Father God's loving heart who initiated this redemptive process is to ignore the Giver of His gift to mankind, Jesus Christ. For God (the Father) so loved the world that He gave.....

> *For God so loved the world, that he gave his only begotten Son, that whosoever believeth in him should not perish, but have everlasting life.*
>
> *For God sent not his Son into the world to condemn the world; but that the world through him might be saved.*
>
> *He that believeth on him is not condemned: but he that believeth not is condemned already, because he hath not believed in the name of the only begotten Son of God.* (John 3:16-18)

If through faith in the blood of Jesus Christ we are given the gift of God's very own righteousness, why do believers often lose sight of the fact that Jesus came primarily to accomplish the Father's will, that He might glorify the Father, and that He also, in turn, came to give believers the Father's very glory?

> *Neither pray I for these alone, but for them also which shall believe on me through their word;*
>
> *That they all may be one; as thou, Father, art in*

me, and I in thee, that they also may be one in us: that the world may believe that thou hast sent me.

And the glory which thou gavest me I have given them; that they may be one, even as we are one: I in them, and thou in me, that they may be made perfect in one; and that the world may know that thou hast sent me, and hast loved them, as thou hast loved me.

Father, I will that they also, whom thou hast given me, be with me where I am; that they may behold my glory, which thou hast given me: for thou lovedst me before the foundation of the world. (John 17:20-24)

Jesus himself said there is only One that is good. As believers we recognize that Jesus and the Father are one, however Jesus in giving glory to the Father when he was admonishing the rich young ruler, said:

So He said to him, "Why do you call Me good? No one is good but One, that is, God. But if you want to enter into life, keep the commandments." (Matthew 19:17)

As we have seen from the above chapter, Abraham is pictured with various characteristics: a righteous man, with wholehearted commitment to God; a man of peace (in settling a boundary dispute with his nephew Lot), compassionate (he argues and bargains with God to spare the people of Sodom and Gomorrah), and hospitable (he welcomes three visiting angels); a quick-acting warrior (he rescues Lot and his family from a raiding party); and an unscrupulous liar to save his own skin (he passes off Sarah as his sister in fear of his own neck). He appears as both a man of great spiritual depth and strength, and also as a person with common human weaknesses and needs. In all this God continued faithfully to give Abraham all the fullness of His blessing. God viewed Abraham as a Spiritually perfect and righteous man, in spite of his lapses of faith. Through the Covenant God swore to Abraham, He included all future believers as the seed of Abraham and consequently of the same Spiritual dimension of righteousness, Holiness and perfection.

Therefore may we conclude through this study of the Covenant God gave to all believers through Abraham, that the Gospel (the good news of Jesus Christ) of Grace and righteousness through the High Priestly ministry of Christ, was preached to all Old Testament believers as well as to New Testament believers? In speaking of the children of Israel in the Old Testament, the writer of the book of Hebrews states:

> *Let us therefore fear, lest, a promise being left us*
> *of entering into his rest, any of you should seem*
> *to come short of it.*
>
> *For unto us was the gospel preached, as well as*
> *unto them: but the word preached did not profit*
> *them, not being mixed with faith in them that*
> *heard it.*
>
> *For we which have believed do enter into rest, as*
> *he said, As I have sworn in my wrath, if they*
> *shall enter into my rest: although the works were*
> *finished from the foundation of the world.*
> (Hebrews 4:1-3)

We see that salvation came to Old Testament believers through exactly the same Gospel and Holy Spirit which saves New Testament believers.

> *Receiving the end of your faith, even the*
> *salvation of your souls.*
>
> *Of which salvation the prophets have inquired*
> *and searched diligently, who prophesied of the*
> *grace that should come unto you:*
>
> *Searching what, or what manner of time the*
> *Spirit of Christ which was in them did signify,*
> *when it testified beforehand the sufferings of*

Christ, and the glory that should follow.

Unto whom it was revealed, that not unto themselves, but unto us they did minister the things, which are now reported unto you by them that have preached the gospel unto you with the Holy Ghost sent down from heaven; which things the angels desire to look into. (1 Peter 1:9-12)

We see that the fullness of the complete Gospel of Grace and righteousness through faith was, and is preached to all believers through the Covenant given us as the seed of Abraham.

He therefore that ministereth to you the Spirit, and worketh miracles among you, doeth he it by the works of the law, or by the hearing of faith?

Even as Abraham believed God, and it was accounted to him for righteousness.

Know ye therefore that they which are of faith, the same are the children of Abraham.

And the scripture, foreseeing that God would justify the heathen through faith, preached before the gospel unto Abraham, saying, In thee shall all nations be blessed.

So then they which be of faith are blessed with faithful Abraham.

(Galatians 3:5-9)

Do we see that the redemptive power of the blood and body of Jesus Christ, was and is revealed to both Old and New Testament believers, through the Holy Spirit, as the seed (sperma) of Abraham? Do we see that both in the Old and New Testaments that all believers were, and are justified (declared righteous by God) through faith?

But that no man is justified by the law in the sight of God, it is evident: for, The just shall live by faith.

And the law is not of faith: but, The man that

doeth them shall live in them.
Christ hath redeemed us from the curse of the
law, being made a curse for us: for it is written,
Cursed is every one that hangeth on a tree:
That the blessing of Abraham might come on the
Gentiles through Jesus Christ; that we might
receive the promise of the Spirit through faith.
Brethren, I speak after the manner of men;
Though it be but a man's Covenant, yet if it be
confirmed, no man disannulleth, or addeth
thereto.
Now to Abraham and his seed were the promises
made. He saith not, And to seeds, as of many; but
as of one, And to thy seed, which is Christ.
(Galatians 3:11-16)

Do we see that through faith in the blood and body of Jesus Christ, a High Priest forever in the order of Melchisedec, that in both Old and New Testaments, through the two immutable Covenants, believers were and are given access into the secret place of the Most High, to dwell in the very Holy of Holies.

For when God made promise to Abraham,
because he could swear by no greater, he sware
by himself,
Saying, Surely blessing I will bless thee, and
multiplying I will multiply thee.
And so, after he had patiently endured, he
obtained the promise.
For men verily swear by the greater: and an oath
for confirmation is to them an end of all strife.
Wherein God, willing more abundantly to shew
unto the heirs of promise the immutability of his
counsel, confirmed it by an oath:
That by two immutable things, in which it was
impossible for God to lie, we might have a strong

consolation, who have fled for refuge to lay hold
upon the hope set before us:
Which hope we have as an anchor of the soul,
both sure and stedfast, and which entereth into
that within the veil;
Whither the forerunner is for us entered, even
Jesus, made an high priest for ever after the
order of Melchisedec. (Hebrews 6:13-20)

Have we been given to understand that the Covenant given to Abraham, was confirmed by God through the pre-incarnate Christ, Melchizedec?

Now to Abraham and his seed were the promises
made. He saith not, And to seeds, as of many; but
as of one, And to thy seed, which is Christ.
And this I say, that the Covenant, that was
confirmed before of God in Christ, the law,
which was four hundred and thirty years after,
cannot disannul, that it should make the promise
of none effect.
For if the inheritance be of the law, it is no more
of promise: but God gave it to Abraham by
promise. (Galatians 3:16-18)

Do we see that Christ, our High Priest in the order of Melchisedec, who met Abraham with bread and wine, continually presents both Old Testament and New Testament believers in His very own righteous perfection, separate from our flesh nature, to the Father?

But this man, after he had offered one sacrifice
for sins for ever, sat down on the right hand of
God;
From henceforth expecting till his enemies be
made his footstool.
For by one offering he hath perfected for ever
them that are sanctified.

Whereof the Holy Ghost also is a witness to us:
for after that he had said before,
This is the Covenant that I will make with them
after those days, saith the Lord, I will put my
laws into their hearts, and in their minds will I
write them;
And their sins and iniquities will I remember no
more.
Now where remission of these is, there is no
more offering for sin.
Having therefore, brethren, boldness to enter
into the holiest by the blood of Jesus,
By a new and living way, which he hath
consecrated for us, through the veil, that is to
say, his flesh;
And having an high priest over the house of
God;
Let us draw near with a true heart in full
assurance of faith, having our hearts sprinkled
from an evil conscience, and our bodies washed
with pure water. (Hebrews 10:12-22)

Have we come to understand, in our Spirit man, that it is through our faith in the blood of the everlasting Covenant promised to Abraham and his seed, through which believers are enabled to do the perfect works of God?

Now the God of peace, that brought again from
the dead our Lord Jesus, that great shepherd of
the sheep, through the blood of the everlasting
Covenant,
Make you perfect in every good work to do his
will, working in you that which is wellpleasing in
his sight, through Jesus Christ; to whom be glory
for ever and ever. Amen. (Hebrews 13:20,21)

Do we see that the ministry of our High Priest, Jesus Christ in a pre-incarnate appearing to Abraham as Melchisedec, entirely cleansed both Old and New Testament believers from a guilty conscience through faith in the sprinkling of His blood on the Mercy Seat in Heaven?

But Christ being come an high priest of good things to come, by a greater and more perfect tabernacle, not made with hands, that is to say, not of this building;

Neither by the blood of goats and calves, but by his own blood he entered in once into the holy place, having obtained eternal redemption for us.

For if the blood of bulls and of goats, and the ashes of an heifer sprinkling the unclean, sanctifieth to the purifying of the flesh:

How much more shall the blood of Christ, who through the eternal Spirit offered himself without spot to God, purge your conscience from dead works to serve the living God?

And for this cause he is the mediator of the new testament, that by means of death, for the redemption of the transgressions that were under the first testament, they which are called might receive the promise of eternal inheritance.
(Hebrews 9:11-15)

Has it been revealed to our hearts that faith in the better New Covenant, which fulfilled the promise made to all believers through Abraham, mercifully removes the judgement of guilt upon our sins and iniquities from God's memory?

But now hath he obtained a more excellent ministry, by how much also he is the mediator of a better Covenant, which was established upon better promises.

For if that first Covenant had been faultless, then should no place have been sought for the second.

For finding fault with them, he saith, Behold, the

days come, saith the Lord, when I will make a
new Covenant with the house of Israel and with
the house of Judah:

Not according to the Covenant that I made with
their fathers in the day when I took them by the
hand to lead them out of the land of Egypt;
because they continued not in my Covenant, and
I regarded them not, saith the Lord.

For this is the Covenant that I will make with the
house of Israel after those days, <u>saith the Lord; I</u>
<u>will put my laws into their mind, and write them</u>
<u>in their hearts: and I will be to them a God, and</u>
<u>they shall be to me a people:</u>

And they shall not teach every man his
neighbour, and every man his brother, saying,
Know the Lord: for all shall know me, from the
least to the greatest.

<u>For I will be merciful to their unrighteousness,</u>
<u>and their sins and their iniquities will I</u>
<u>remember no more.</u>

In that he saith, A new Covenant, he hath made
the first old. Now that which decayeth and
waxeth old is ready to vanish away.

(Hebrews 8:6-13)

Has the Holy Spirit confirmed to our hearts that, <u>until</u> we as believers come to understand that Jesus Christ our High Priest in the order of Melchisedec, who ministered to Abraham with bread and wine, was a pre-incarnate appearing of Jesus Christ, that we are on Spiritual milk and not on satisfying meat?

Called of God an high priest after the order of
Melchisedec.

Of whom we have many things to say, and hard
to be uttered, seeing ye are dull of hearing.

For when for the time ye ought to be teachers, ye

*have need that one teach you again which be the
first principles of the oracles of God; and are
become such as have need of milk, and not of
strong meat.*

*For every one that useth milk is unskilful in the
word of righteousness: for he is a babe.*

*But strong meat belongeth to them that are of full
age, even those who by reason of use have their
senses exercised to discern both good and evil.*

(Hebrews 5:10-14)

It is this writers earnest prayer that all who have read this document, would be led of the Holy Spirit to come to the understanding, that all believers are truly the seed of Abraham, whether they be Jew or Gentile. Included in this fervent prayer is the desire that, through awakening to the love which is upon God the Father's heart in giving this Covenant to believers through Abraham, that all would understand they are continually presented to God in His very own righteousness, through faith in the blood of our High Priest, the Lord Jesus Christ.

*But what things were gain to me, those I counted
loss for Christ.*

*Yea doubtless, and I count all things but loss for
the excellency of the knowledge of Christ Jesus
my Lord: for whom I have suffered the loss of all
things, and do count them but dung, that I may
win Christ,*

*And be found in him, not having mine own
righteousness, which is of the law, but that which
is through the faith of Christ, the righteousness
which is of God by faith:*

*That I may know him, and the power of his
resurrection, and the fellowship of his sufferings,
being made conformable unto his death;*

(Philippians 3:7-10)

6

MELCHISEDEC
Pre-incarnate Appearance of Christ

Until the redeemed of the Lord come to realize the significance of Melchisedec and His role in church history, the present day institutional church will remain on Spiritual milk without having been fed of the meat of the knowledge of God's perfect righteousness. As we have been shown in the last chapter it was through the High Priestly ministry of Melchisedec, who through bread and wine, witnessed to Abraham the perfecting and resurrection power of the atoning blood and body of Jesus Christ. The doctrine of the atoning blood of Jesus Christ itself is not being clearly defined to the believing church today, only the awareness of this doctrine will awaken believers to experience the satisfaction which comes through partaking of the strong meat of God's perfect indwelling righteousness. In order that we might partake of the strong meat of the knowledge of righteousness, the writer of the book of Hebrews exhorts believers to recall the first principles which God spoke to His people, the foundational Covenants upon which His church has been built. The Scriptures confirmed this from the time He first placed Adam and Eve in the garden of Eden, through to ratification of the New Covenant through the blood of Christ.

Called of God an high priest after the order of Melchisedec.

Of whom we have many things to say, and hard to be uttered, seeing ye are dull of hearing.

For when for the time ye ought to be teachers, ye have need that one teach you again which [be] the first principles of the oracles of God; and are become such as have need of milk, and not of strong meat.

For every one that useth milk [is] unskilful in the word of righteousness: for he is a babe.

But strong meat belongeth to them that are of full age, [even] those who by reason of use have their senses exercised to discern both good and evil.

Therefore leaving the principles of the doctrine of Christ, let us go on unto perfection; not laying again the foundation of repentance from dead works, and of faith toward God,

(Hebrews 5:10-6:1)

The Scriptures above are exhorting the redeemed of the Lord to come to understand the Covenants He spoke to His creation from the beginning. In this chapter we are considering the Covenant of Promise which was ratified to all believers, through Abraham, by Melchisedec, four hundred and thirty years before the law of the ten commandments were imposed upon the unbelieving children of Israel, through Moses. The above Scriptures point out the prime importance of coming to the knowledge of the first principles of God's Covenants with mankind, and with what intent they were spoken.

Through the study of the Covenants, God reveals to believers what was on His heart at the time He made these Covenants. Through the study of these eight Covenants the Holy Spirit will show the open minded, God's historical provisions and intent for

His church. Looking at church history from the perspective of His Covenants, we will see that viewing church history from man's perspective, ignores the power of the Holy Spirit to lead and the blood of the Covenants to sanctify.

Likewise the <u>dull of hearing</u> cannot receive the Spiritual meat of the many things which the Holy Spirit, through the written Word, would reveal to our hearts regarding Melchisedec. How many of us have come to realize that when the Spirit and the Word say "of whom we have many things to say" He indeed means exactly what is written? The revelation of who Melchisedec was, and still is, will be shocking to Spiritual babes. There is little specific Scriptural reference to Melchisedec except in Genesis, Psalms and the book of Hebrews, however the office of the High Priest is referred to in many other of the Books of the Bible.

<u>Melchisedec was a pre-incarnate appearing of the Lord Jesus Christ.</u>

Accepting the blessing of Abraham brings into focus the unity of the two prime principles of the oracles of God, the Covenant God made to believers through Abraham and the New Covenant. These two immutable Covenants of Grace, were given to mankind through God's oath and made manifest through the blood of Christ, the believers High Priest in the order of Melchisedec. Only through the recognition of these Covenants of Grace is the believer given the boldness to enter through the rent veil of the Holy of Holies.

> *For when God made promise to Abraham, because he could swear by no greater, he sware by himself,*
> *Saying, <u>Surely blessing I will bless thee, and multiplying I will multiply thee.</u>*
> *And so, after he had patiently endured, he obtained the promise.*

For men verily swear by the greater: and an oath
for confirmation is to them an end of all strife.
Wherein God, willing more abundantly to shew
unto the heirs of promise the immutability of his
counsel, confirmed it by an oath:
That by two immutable things, in which it was
impossible for God to lie, we might have a strong
consolation, who have fled for refuge to lay hold
upon the hope set before us:
Which hope we have as an anchor of the soul,
both sure and stedfast, and which entereth into
that within the veil;
Whither the forerunner is for us entered, even
Jesus, made an high priest for ever after the
order of Melchisedec. (Hebrews 6:13-20)

It is our faith in the blood of these two Covenants which
gives believers the boldness to enter within the veil, into the
Heavenly Holy Place of God Most High. This thought, that of the
blood of Christ through his High Priestly ministry, uniting both
Old Covenant and New Covenant believers is also expressed in
the following Scriptures.

But Christ being come an high priest of good
things to come, by a greater and more perfect
tabernacle, not made with hands, that is to say,
not of this building;
Neither by the blood of goats and calves, but by
his own blood he entered in once into the holy
place, having obtained eternal redemption for us.
For if the blood of bulls and of goats, and the
ashes of an heifer sprinkling the unclean,
sanctifieth to the purifying of the flesh:
How much more shall the blood of Christ, who
through the eternal Spirit offered himself without
spot to God, purge your conscience from dead

works to serve the living God?

And for this cause he is the mediator of the new testament, that by means of death, for the redemption of the transgressions that were under the first testament, they which are called might receive the promise of eternal inheritance.
(Hebrews 9:11-15)

Melchisedec, when he met Abraham with bread and wine, did not shed his own blood, but he bore witness of the perfect sacrifice of the blood and body of Jesus Christ to come. Melchisedec was not the redeemer, but he was a witness of the redeemer to come, as was John the Baptist.

> *For this Melchisedec, king of Salem, priest of the most high God, who met Abraham returning from the slaughter of the kings, and blessed him;*
> *To whom also Abraham gave a tenth part of all; first being by interpretation King of righteousness, and after that also King of Salem, which is, King of peace;*
> (Hebrews 7:1,2)

In the Scriptures above we are given to understand that Melchisedec was priest of the Most High God (El Elyon), the King of Righteousness and the King of Peace. Who other than Christ is both priest of the Most High God, King of righteousness and also the King of peace? The Bible mentions many priests and kings, but other than Jesus Christ there are none that are both.

> *Without father, without mother, without descent, having neither beginning of days, nor end of life; but made like unto the Son of God; abideth a priest continually.* (Hebrews 7:3)

The Greek word "apator", interpreted here as "without father", makes a definitive statement. It does not infer that Melchisedec had no known genealogy, but states empathically that he had no genealogy. Some would suggest that what is meant here is that Melchisedec had no recorded genealogy, but this does not address the fact that he had neither "beginning of days nor end of life". Who other than Jesus Christ is an eternal priest and yet made like unto the Son of God? If Melchisedec was of human origin and priesthood he could not be as the scriptures say above; an eternal priest who abides continually. Speaking further of Melchisedec, the writer of the book of Hebrews exhorts believers.

> *Now consider how great this man [was], unto whom even the patriarch Abraham gave the tenth of the spoils.*
> *And verily they that are of the sons of Levi, who receive the office of the priesthood, have a commandment to take tithes of the people according to the law, that is, of their brethren, though they come out of the loins of Abraham:*
> *But he whose descent is not counted from them received tithes of Abraham, and blessed him that had the promises.*
> <u>*And without all contradiction the less is blessed of the better.*</u> (Hebrews 7:4-7)

As is underlined in the last verse above, Abram recognized Melchisedec as the High Priest of God, and so gave tithes of ten percent of all his possessions. Would Abram, who is the Father of all believers, give tithes to anyone other than to the Lord Himself?

> *And the king of Sodom went out to meet him after his return from the slaughter of Chedorlaomer, and of the kings that were with him, at the valley of Shaveh, which is the king's dale.*
> <u>*And Melchizedek king of Salem brought forth bread and wine: and he was the priest of the most high God.*</u>
> *And he blessed him, and said, Blessed be Abram*

of the most high God, possessor of heaven and earth:
And blessed be the most high God, which hath delivered thine enemies into thy hand. And he gave him tithes of all. (Genesis 14:17-20)

Through the witness and blessing of bread and wine, Abram came to recognize Melchisedec as being God's eternal High Priest, Jesus Christ. Abram recognized that it was not by his own power or might, but by the Spirit of the Lord, through faith in the blood and body of Christ, that his enemies, the evil Kings, were delivered into his hands. As recorded in the previous chapter, Abram was to learn later, it was through faith in the blood of Christ that God made Abram to be of His very own nature, perfect and righteous. Abram understood that Melchizedek was sent of God's grace to meet and anoint him, and that God's righteousness would not be imputed to him through an earthly priesthood. It is only through faith in the atoning blood of the High Priestly ministry of Christ, who was called of God to be a High Priest forever in the order of Melchizedek, that believers are enabled to come into the very presence of God, with the full assurance that they too, like Abram, have been declared perfect and righteous by God himself.

If therefore perfection were by the Levitical priesthood, (for under it the people received the law,) what further need [was there] that another priest should rise after the order of Melchisedec, and not be called after the order of Aaron?
For the priesthood being changed, there is made of necessity a change also of the law...
For he testifieth, Thou art a priest for ever after the order of Melchisedec. (Hebrews 7:11,12,17)

During the time of the Old Testament tabernacles, prior to the death and resurrection of Jesus Christ, only High priests of the lineage of Aaron were allowed to enter the Holy of Holies on the

Day of Atonement, once every year. Those of the Levitical priesthood only served the outer court and the tabernacle within the first veil, however they were never allowed to enter into the Holy of Holies, the dwelling place of the Spirit of the Lord, which was within the second veil.

> Now when these things were thus ordained, the priests went always into the first tabernacle, accomplishing the service of God.
>
> But into the second went the high priest alone once every year, not without blood, which he offered for himself, and for the errors of the people:
>
> The Holy Ghost this signifying, that the way into the holiest of all was not yet made manifest, while as the first tabernacle was yet standing:
>
> Which was a figure for the time then present, in which were offered both gifts and sacrifices, that could not make him that did the service perfect, as pertaining to the conscience;
>
> Which stood only in meats and drinks, and divers washings, and carnal ordinances, imposed on them until the time of reformation.

(Hebrews 9:6-10)

The function of the Levitical priesthood was to administer the law of carnal commandments and ordinances, while it was solely the function of the High Priests, in the lineage of Aaron, to make atonement once every year. He was ordained of God to sprinkle blood on the Mercy Seat, within the closed second veil, first for his own sins and then the sins of the people of the children of Israel. These temporary earthly tabernacles were a figure of the true tabernacle in heaven. These tabernacles were a testimony of the mercy and grace, a figure of the Throne of God from which perfect redemption flows.

> Receiving the end of your faith, even the salvation of your souls.

*Of which salvation the prophets have inquired
and searched diligently, who prophesied of the
grace that should come unto you:
Searching what, or what manner of time the
Spirit of Christ which was in them did signify,
when it testified beforehand the sufferings of
Christ, and the glory that should follow.
Unto whom it was revealed, that not unto
themselves, but unto us they did minister the
things, which are now reported unto you by them
that have preached the gospel unto you with the
Holy Ghost sent down from heaven; which things
the angels desire to look into.* (1 Peter 1:9-12)

Therefore, it is necessary, that when the everlasting heavenly
tabernacle was made accessible to believers, through the death
and resurrection of Jesus Christ, we must also be aware of the
truth that He is a High Priest in the order of Melchizedek. The
High Priestly ministry of Jesus Christ ushered in a new law of
grace which enables believers in the New Covenant to Spiritually
enter, through the rent veil, and even dwell in the Throne Room
of Grace, that is the Holy of Holies.

*Having therefore, brethren, boldness to enter
into the holiest by the blood of Jesus,
By a new and living way, which he hath
consecrated for us, through the veil, that is to
say, his flesh;
And having an high priest over the house of
God;
Let us draw near with a true heart in full
assurance of faith, having our hearts sprinkled
from an evil conscience, and our bodies washed
with pure water.* (Hebrews 10:19-22)

Prior to the veil in the heavenly tabernacle being torn from
top to bottom, Old Testament believers who had faith in the blood

of the promised Christ, waited in the bosom of Abraham until the promised redeemer should come.

The structure of the Old Testament tabernacles witnessed the Gospel of redemption to all who simply understood and believed that all the blood sacrifices which were offered up, spoke of the blood and body of Christ to come. The Gospel was preached to the children of Israel through the very presence of the tabernacles in their midst. However, they did not enter into God's rest because of their unbelief, the very same as those of us who today do not understand and believe the doctrine of the High Priestly ministry of Christ.

> *Let us therefore fear, lest, a promise being left us of entering into his rest, any of you should seem to come short of it.*
>
> *For unto us was the gospel preached, as well as unto them: but the word preached did not profit them, not being mixed with faith in them that heard it.*
>
> *For we which have believed do enter into rest, as he said, As I have sworn in my wrath, if they shall enter into my rest: although the works were finished from the foundation of the world.*
>
> *For he spake in a certain place of the seventh day on this wise, And God did rest the seventh day from all his works.*
>
> *And in this place again, If they shall enter into my rest.*
>
> *Seeing therefore it remaineth that some must enter therein, and they to whom it was first preached entered not in because of unbelief:*
>
> (Hebrews 4:1-6)

Believers throughout the ages who came to accept the promise of the perfecting power of the blood of the High Priestly ministry of Jesus Christ, within the second veil, also knew that they had been freed from the carnal commandments of the law of the flesh. The Holy Spirit opens the eyes and further glorifies the heart of those who were under the law, when they realize that the second veil has been opened, that we may boldly come to the Throne of Grace. The manifestation of our great High Priest in the order of Melchisedek confers, to both Old Testament and New Testament believers, the blessings of grace, separate from the law of sin and death, as we see in the Scriptures above as well as those below.

For the law of the Spirit of life in Christ Jesus hath made me free from the law of sin and death.

For what the law could not do, in that it was weak through the flesh, God sending his own Son in the likeness of sinful flesh, and for sin, condemned sin in the flesh:

That the righteousness of the law might be fulfilled in us, who walk not after the flesh, but after the Spirit. (Romans 8:2-4)

This does not mean that believers who hopelessly attempt to live by the law of the ten commandments lose their position of justification, but to the degree believers walk in the flesh of a carnal command, we are not able to be led of the Spirit of Grace.

O foolish Galatians, who hath bewitched you, that ye should not obey the truth, before whose eyes Jesus Christ hath been evidently set forth, crucified among you?

This only would I learn of you, Received ye the Spirit by the works of the law,
or by the hearing of faith?

Are ye so foolish? having begun in the Spirit, are ye now made perfect by the flesh?

Have ye suffered so many things in vain? if it be yet in vain.

He therefore that ministereth to you the Spirit, and worketh miracles among you, doeth he it by the works of the law, or by the hearing of faith?

Even as Abraham believed God, and it was accounted to him for righteousness.

Know ye therefore that they which are of faith, the same are the children of Abraham.

And the scripture, foreseeing that God would justify the heathen through faith, preached before the gospel unto Abraham, saying, In thee shall all nations be blessed.

So then they which be of faith are blessed with faithful Abraham.

For as many as are of the works of the law are under the curse: for it is written, Cursed is every one that continueth not in all things which are written in the book of the law to do them.

But that no man is justified by the law in the sight of God, it is evident: for, The just shall live by faith.

And the law is not of faith: but, The man that doeth them shall live in them.

Christ hath redeemed us from the curse of the law, being made a curse for us: for it is written, Cursed is every one that hangeth on a tree:

That the blessing of Abraham might come on the Gentiles through Jesus Christ; that we might receive the promise of the Spirit through faith.

(Galatians 3:1-14)

To the degree we adhere to the law of the Levitical priesthood, those who were not allowed to enter within the second veil, we cannot receive the blessings of the ratified promise made to Abraham through faith in the blood of Jesus Christ, our High Priest in the order of Melchisedec. The Levitical priesthood spoke of the undesirable, legal sacrifices, of religious ritual and death. The everlasting High Priestly ministry of Christ in the order of Melchisedec is founded upon the perfect sacrifice of the Lamb who was slain from the foundation of world. There was and still is a distinction between the efficacy of the two priesthood's. The knowledge of the law comes to us through the tribe of Levi, but the Priesthood in the order of Melchisedec comes through the tribe of Judah, which affords the believer the knowledge of revealed grace and righteousness.

> For he of whom these things are spoken pertaineth to another tribe, of which no man gave attendance at the altar.
>
> For it is evident that our Lord sprang out of Juda; of which tribe Moses spake nothing concerning priesthood.
>
> And it is yet far more evident: for that after the similitude of Melchisedec there ariseth another priest,
>
> Who is made, not after the law of a carnal commandment, but after the power of an endless life.
>
> For he testifieth, Thou art a priest for ever after the order of Melchisedec. (Hebrews 7:13-17)

And again:

> The LORD said unto my Lord, Sit thou at my right hand, until I make thine enemies thy footstool.
>
> The LORD shall send the rod of thy strength out of Zion: rule thou in the midst of thine enemies.
>
> Thy people [shall be] willing in the day of thy power, in the beauties of holiness from the womb of the morning: thou hast the dew of thy youth.
>
> The LORD hath sworn, and will not repent, Thou [art] a priest for ever after the order of Melchizedek. (Psalms 110:1-4)

As the word states in the Scriptures above; only through the Lion of the Tribe of Judah, within the heavenly Throne Room of

Grace, at the right hand of the Father, are believers enemies of the flesh and soul put under Christ's feet. <u>Only through faith in the perfecting power of the sprinkled blood of Christ on the Mercy Seat in Heaven are believers hearts purged of a guilty conscience.</u> The Levitical priesthood, through whom the people received the law of the commandments of the flesh, were prohibited from entering the Most Holy Place, because they were not ordained of God's grace to do so. Only knowledge and faith in the perfecting power of the blood of an eternal Priesthood in the order of Melchizedek, were High Priests ordained to annually ratify the Covenant God made to believers through Abraham. The same is true today, only the Lion of the tribe of Judah, the anointed one, has been ordained to make intercession for believers within the Holy Place.

> *If therefore perfection were by the Levitical priesthood, (for under it the people received the law,) what further need [was there] that another priest should rise after the order of Melchisedec, and not be called after the order of Aaron?*

(Hebrews 7:11)

To reiterate; The Covenant God made to believers through Abraham, was ratified by the blood of Christ, a High Priest forever in the order of Melchisedec. NOW, TODAY, since His death and resurrection, faith in His blood continually makes atonement for all believers, who receive the blessing of Abraham through faith.

> *Called of God an high priest after the order of Melchisedec.*
> <u>*Of whom we have many things to say, and hard to be uttered, seeing ye are dull of hearing.*</u>
> *For when for the time ye ought to be teachers, ye have need that one teach you again which [be] the first principles of the oracles of God; <u>and are become such as have need of milk, and not of</u>*

strong meat.

For every one that useth milk [is] unskilful in the word of righteousness: for he is a babe.

But strong meat belongeth to them that are of full age, [even] those who by reason of use have their senses exercised to discern both good and evil.

Therefore leaving the principles of the doctrine of Christ, let us go on unto perfection; not laying again the foundation of repentance from dead works, and of faith toward God,... (Hebrews 5:10-6:1)

The Covenant God made to all believers through Abraham is one of the first principles of the oracles of God. The Covenant God made to all Old Testament believers through Abraham was administered to Abraham by the eternal High Priest, Melchizedek.

Believers in the Old Testament received the anointing of righteous perfection through faith in the blood of the promised Eternal High Priest, Jesus Christ, a High Priest in the order of Melchisedec. New Testament believers will not be anointed to understand the provisions of the New Covenant until we see that Old Testament believers were saved from eternal damnation the same as we, that is through faith in the blood of Christ our High Priest in the order of Melchizedek.

In the Old Testament as well as in the New, God recorded in His Word that He would no longer remember the believers sin and iniquitous nature, if our faith remained in the Covenant of righteous perfection He promised to the seed of Abraham.

I, [even] I, [am] he that blotteth out thy transgressions for mine own sake, and will not remember thy sins. Put me in remembrance: let us plead together: declare thou, that thou mayest be justified. (Isaiah 43:25,26)

Christ is no longer on the cross of cruelty and shame but He is seated at the Throne of Grace, ever sprinkling His atoning blood, that He might present those who recognize His High Priestly Ministry, to the Father in His righteousness and perfection. Christ's present High Priestly Ministry fulfilled the promise made to Abraham through Melchizedek, thereby making it a very present reality. Unless believers realize that it is the sprinkling of Christ's blood on the Mercy Seat which does away with God's remembrance of our original nature of sin and iniquity, then we cannot receive the blessings of Abraham contained in the New Covenant as articulated below:

> *For I will be merciful to their unrighteousness, and their sins and their iniquities will I remember no more.*
>
> *In that he saith, A new [Covenant], he hath made the first old. Now that which decayeth and waxeth old [is] ready to vanish away.*

(Hebrews 8:12,13)

In the chapter on the New Covenant this provision of the present High Priestly mediating ministry of Jesus Christ, a High Priest forever in the order of Melchizedec will be expanded upon further.

7

MOSAIC COVENANT
The Torah, The Law of Grace

In order that the Gospel of Grace, which was preached to the children of Israel in the Old Testament, through Moses, be historically understood, it is highly recommended that the reader first read the entire book of Exodus. Before we look into the Spiritual aspects of the Tabernacle of Witness in the wilderness, it will be most beneficial if we first understand that the historical account of the Mosiac Covenant is one of the first principles of the oracles of God. In the reading of the book of Exodus we will come to understand that Moses, the writer of the Pentateuch, put much more emphasis on the Gospel of Grace preached through the structure of the tabernacle, than he did on the keeping of the law of the ten commandments. We will come to understand that both the Gospel of Grace and the law of the ten commandments are as relevant today as they were from the beginning. In the words of Jesus, in the Sermon on the Mount:

> *Think not that I am come to destroy the law, or the prophets: I am not come to destroy, but to fulfil.*
>
> *<u>For verily I say unto you, Till heaven and earth pass, one jot or one tittle shall in no wise pass</u>*

from the law, till all be fulfilled.

Whosoever therefore shall break one of these least commandments, and shall teach men so, he shall be called the least in the kingdom of heaven: but whosoever shall do and teach them, the same shall be called great in the kingdom of heaven.

For I say unto you, That except your righteousness shall exceed the righteousness of the scribes and Pharisees, ye shall in no case enter into the kingdom of heaven.

(Matthew 5:17-20)

As we see in the Scriptures above the law of the commandments given to the children of Israel, through Moses, on Mount Sinai, is as relevant today as it was the day God spoke it to them. It is also as true today as it was the day God spoke from Mount Sinai that righteousness does not come to believers through the law of the ten commandments. As we see in the Scriptures above, it did not give the Pharisees the required righteousness to enter into the Kingdom of Heaven, neither will it give today's believer the required righteousness to enter into the Kingdom of Heaven.

I do not frustrate the grace of God: for if righteousness come by the law, then Christ is dead in vain. (Galatians 2:21)

God's Righteousness only comes to believers by grace, through faith in the blood of the everlasting Covenant, as spoken and demonstrated to the children of Israel through the Tabernacle of Witness, which Moses was instructed to build in the wilderness.

The ten commandments make no mention of the redeeming blood of Jesus Christ, but the tabernacle of Moses which was a figure of the Heavenly Tabernacle, speaks of only one thing; the redeeming blood of Christ.

Then he said unto them, O fools, and slow of heart to believe all that the prophets have spoken:
Ought not Christ to have suffered these things, and to enter into his glory?
And beginning at Moses and all the prophets, he expounded unto them in all the scriptures the things concerning himself. (Luke 24:25-27)

The tabernacle of Moses was a physical representation of the Spiritual truth of eternal salvation, a promise to be fulfilled at the time of Jesus Christ's first Advent.

The birth of Moses was at a time when God's chosen people, the Jewish nation, where being severely suppressed by the Egyptian world system. This persecution by the world system, is typical of how Christianity flourishes in the face of individual hardship and political suppression. Surely God made a mockery of the world political system when He caused Moses to survive after his birth, at a time when other new born babes were being put to death by a decree of a fearful and politically motivated Pharaoh. The basket of bulrushes in which his mother placed him was a type of the Ark of the Covenant of the Lord. The pitch with which it was made water proof was representative of the love of God which seals the believer in His gentle care, and separates the believer from the waters of the Nile. The Nile, which the Egyptians worshipped, being representative of the spirit of the world political system. Note that in the Scriptures below, Moses chose to be separated from the treasures of Egypt, through faith in <u>Christ</u>. God demonstrating His Sovereign love and ability to work all things for good, arranged for Moses to have his own mother be appointed as his nurse maid. Moses grew in grace and prospered as a man, through the sponsorship of the Egyptian world system.

In the New Testament we read where Jesus Christ our intercessor, like Moses, an intercessor for the children of Israel, as an infant, was protected by his parents from the violent attempts to have him killed shortly after birth by the world political system of his time. Herod the cruel reigning King of Israel at the time of Jesus' birth learned through the wise men that Jesus was to be "King of the Jews" and out of jealousy sought to destroy him. After his birth, the Three Wise Men as well as Jesus' parents were warned of God to flee to Egypt in order to escape from the murderous intentions of Herod.

> *And being warned of God in a dream that they should not return to Herod, they departed into their own country another way.*
>
> *And when they were departed, behold, the angel of the Lord appeareth to Joseph in a dream, saying, Arise, and take the young child and his mother, and flee into Egypt, and be thou there until I bring thee word: for Herod will seek the young child to destroy him.* (Matthew 2:12,13)

Like Moses, Jesus was called to return to his people, after the death of Herod, to deliver his people from the condemnation of the world system, as was prophesied in the Old Testament.

> *But when Herod was dead, behold, an angel of the Lord appeareth in a dream to Joseph in Egypt, Saying, Arise, and take the young child and his mother, and go into the land of Israel: for they are dead which sought the young child's life.* *(Matthew 2:19,20)*

All believers who are born of the Spirit of God, through faith in the blood of Christ to continually cleanse from all sin, are delivered and separated from prime dependence upon the present day world religious and political system. It is impossible for unbelievers to comprehend this separation and sanctification from the predominate influence of the world system. The original sinful Adamic nature of the natural birth, with which we are brought into the world by our parents, is only of fleshly carnal nature and cannot be recognized by God as being of His Holy Nature. In order to escape the inheritance of natural death through natural birth, all who would inherit eternal life must be born from above, and be instilled with the Holy Spirit of God. Only those who are reborn of a Sovereign righteous nature, through faith in the blood of Christ, are enabled to be recognized by God, as heirs in His present and promised righteous Kingdom. There are no alternatives or exceptions, as we see in the Scriptures below.

> *For God so loved the world, that he gave his only begotten Son, that whosoever believeth in him should not perish, but have everlasting life.*
>
> *For God sent not his Son into the world to condemn the world; but that the world through him might be saved.*
>
> *He that believeth on him is not condemned: but he that believeth not is condemned already, because he hath not believed in the name of the only begotten Son of God.* (John 3:16-18)

When Moses, out of compassion for his fellow Hebrews, murdered the Egyptian who was beating them, he was in effect demonstrating the rejection of his royal Egyptian adoption and upbringing in favour of his Hebrew heritage. He had demonstrated his decision as to where his loyalties lay. He chose to suffer the affliction of his Hebrew brothers rather than live in a dead end world system. Although he was now guilty as a murderer, that aspect of his old life, that is his heritage under the Egyptian world system, was separated from his new nature as a faithful child of God. God chose the murderer Moses to condemn the world system. Moses esteemed the reproaches of CHRIST to be greater riches than all the riches of the Egyptian world system. Obviously Moses foresaw Christ as the coming saviour.

> *By faith Moses, when he was come to years, refused to be called the son of Pharaoh's*

daughter;
Choosing rather to suffer affliction with the
people of God, than to enjoy the pleasures of sin
for a season;
Esteeming the reproach of Christ greater riches
than the treasures in Egypt: for he had respect
unto the recompence of the reward.
(Hebrews 11:24-26)

Christ also left His home in glory to come to a sin filled world to redeem His people. Jesus set aside his royal robes to do the Father's will, in order that He might lead God's children out of the cruel bondage of the world system, and free us from the bondage of our natural flesh lineage. Like Moses, in order to demonstrate to His Father and the world where his loyalties lay, He destroyed or killed him that had the power of death, that is the devil. Through faith in the demonstration of God's resurrection power over His death on the cross, Christ frees believers from the power of the world system, Satan's dominion.

Forasmuch then as the children are partakers of
flesh and blood, he also himself likewise took
part of the same; that through death he might
destroy him that had the power of death, that is,
the devil;
And deliver them who through fear of death were
all their lifetime subject to bondage.
For verily he took not on him the nature of
angels; but he took on him the seed of Abraham.
Wherefore in all things it behoved him to be
made like unto his brethren, that he might be a
merciful and faithful high priest in things
pertaining to God, to make reconciliation for the
sins of the people.
For in that he himself hath suffered being
tempted, he is able to succour them that are
tempted. (Hebrews 2:14-18)

Although Jesus led a perfect sinless life and was born without Adam's sinful nature, but of the seed of Abraham, God the Father made Jesus on the cross to become as the vilest of sinners, even the sin of murder, on our behalf. The Father made Jesus Christ to be the essence of sin in order that He might lead the believer out of the world system into the promised land of His Kingdom.

> *Therefore if any man be in Christ, he is a new creature: old things are passed away; behold, all things are become new.*
>
> *And all things are of God, who hath reconciled us to himself by Jesus Christ, and hath given to us the ministry of reconciliation;*
>
> *To wit, that God was in Christ, reconciling the world unto himself, not imputing their trespasses unto them; and hath committed unto us the word of reconciliation.*
>
> *Now then we are ambassadors for Christ, as though God did beseech you by us: we pray you in Christ's stead, be ye reconciled to God.*
>
> *For he hath made him to be sin for us, who knew no sin; that we might be made the righteousness of God in him.*
>
> *We then, as workers together with him, beseech you also that ye receive not the grace of God in vain.* (2 Corinthians 5:17-6:1)

And again in the Old Testament:

> *Yet it pleased the LORD to bruise him; he hath put him to grief: when thou shalt make his soul an offering for sin, he shall see his seed, he shall prolong his days, and the pleasure of the LORD shall prosper in his hand.*
>
> *He shall see of the travail of his soul, and shall be satisfied: by his knowledge shall my righteous servant justify many; for he shall bear their iniquities.*

Therefore will I divide him a portion with the great, and he shall divide the spoil with the strong; because he hath poured out his soul unto death: and he was numbered with the transgressors; and he bare the sin of many, and made intercession for the transgressors.
(Isaiah 53:10-12)

We see from the Scriptures above that all believers, whether in Old Testament or New Testament times, were delivered and separated, from the world system and eternal death, through faith in the Lamb who was slain from the foundation of the world. Old Testament believers, like Moses and those that remained faithful of the children of Israel, looked forward in faith to the manifestation of God's promised righteousness, that is, Jesus Christ's first Advent. New Testament believers look back two thousand years to the glory of the cross, to the resurrection and ascension of Jesus Christ. Old Testament and New Testament believers then were saved in the same way, by grace through faith in the blood of Christ.

God still blesses believers in the very same way today! Those whom God chooses are spiritually separated from a corrupt world system, sanctified and glorified as eternal members of His Heavenly Kingdom, although we are still living as strangers and sojourners on this earth. He enables the believer to see that His righteousness is more to be desired than the things of this world. The gift of His righteousness is the strength of the Spirit of Christ within the believer, who gives him the assurance and strength of life for today, and confidence in the promise of eternal life with God.

In practice then, all we who have the God given gift of human life need do is believe in the blood of our faithful deliverer, Jesus Christ. Faith in His blood alone frees believers from the fear of death and bondage and delivers us from a condemned world system, into His Kingdom of everlasting life.

After Moses denied his identity with Pharaoh's people and accepted his Jewish heritage, which was symbolic of acknowledging his need for redemption through faith in Christ, he was led of the Spirit to leave Egypt, that he might be tried of God on the back side of the desert, for forty years. It was here in the desert that God removed from Moses all the adverse effects and allegiance to the corrupt world system, and instilled in him the power of faith in Christ.

> By faith Moses, when he was come to years, refused to be called the son of Pharaoh's daughter;
>
> Choosing rather to suffer affliction with the people of God, than to enjoy the pleasures of sin for a season;
>
> Esteeming the reproach of Christ greater riches than the treasures in Egypt: for he had respect unto the recompence of the reward.
>
> (Hebrews 11:24-26)

Jesus also, like Moses, was tested and suffered in the wilderness of the desert for forty days, after He had been baptized by John the Baptist.

> Then was Jesus led up of the Spirit into the wilderness to be tempted of the devil.
>
> And when he had fasted forty days and forty nights, he was afterward an hungred.
>
> (Matthew 4:1,2)

Again like Moses, Jesus Christ came to free His people from the cruel bondage of the world system, from the need to fear death through faith in His blood.

> Forasmuch then as the children are partakers of flesh and blood, he also himself likewise took part of the same; that through death he might destroy him that had the power of death, that is, the devil;

> *And deliver them who through fear of death were*
> *all their lifetime subject to bondage.*
> *For verily he took not on him the nature of*
> *angels; but he took on him the seed of Abraham.*
> (Hebrews 2:14-16)

Jesus was on probation as was Moses? Yes. Jesus too learned obedience by the things which He suffered, for He took on Him the natural human seed of Abraham.

> *Who in the days of his flesh, when he had offered*
> *up prayers and supplications with strong crying*
> *and tears unto him that was able to save him*
> *from death, and was heard in that he feared;*
> *Though he were a Son, yet learned he obedience*
> *by the things which he suffered;*
> *And being made perfect, he became the author of*
> *eternal salvation unto all them that obey him;*
> *Called of God an high priest after the order of*
> *Melchisedec.* (Hebrews 5:7-10)

It was in the desert that Jesus demonstrated and confirmed the power of God's Word that He had learned of the Father from a child up. God had prepared Him for the ministry He was about to embark on and had instilled and fostered in Him the power of the Word to overcome the temptations of Satan, and the world system. Each time Jesus was tempted of the devil to abandon His mission of redemption to a lost world, He rebuked Satan with the Word of God.

> *And when the tempter came to him, he said, If*
> *thou be the Son of God, command that these*
> *stones be made bread.*
> *But he answered and said, It is written, Man*
> *shall not live by bread alone, but by every word*
> *that proceedeth out of the mouth of God.*
> (Matthew 4:3,4)

Also like Moses and Jesus, after new believers are saved and delivered out of the bondage of the world system, they are often tempted of Satan to revert to walking in the old nature of the flesh.

And Jesus, when he was baptized, went up straightway out of the water: and, lo, the heavens were opened unto him, and he saw the Spirit of God descending like a dove, and lighting upon him:
And lo a voice from heaven, saying, This is my beloved Son, in whom I am well pleased.
(Matthew 3:16,17)

And:

Then was Jesus led up of the Spirit into the wilderness to be tempted of the devil.
And when he had fasted forty days and forty nights, he was afterward an hungred.
And when the tempter came to him, he said, If thou be the Son of God, command that these stones be made bread.
But he answered and said, It is written, Man shall not live by bread alone, but by every word that proceedeth out of the mouth of God.

(Matthew 4:1-4)

After having his faith tested and being Spiritually strengthened of God in the wilderness, Elohim, the almighty God, appeared to Moses on Mount Horeb, the mountain of God, as a fire in a bush that was not consumed. It was here that Moses learned that the Word of God is a consuming fire. The fire of the Word of God consumes the believers desire to be identified with the world and the desires of the flesh, and walking in the shoes and paths of a lost world system. When Moses approached the burning bush he was instructed to take off his shoes, with which he walked the earth, and instead revere that provision of God's Grace which allows believers to walk on Holy Ground. The bush that was not consumed represents the righteous judgements of God, which burns off the useless works of man's original fallen nature. God's fire of His Word does not consume but preserves the soul, that it may be made a fit dwelling place for the Spirit of Holiness.

> *Now if any man build upon this foundation gold, silver, precious stones, wood, hay, stubble;*
> *Every man's work shall be made manifest: for the day shall declare it, because it shall be revealed by fire; and the fire shall try every man's work of what sort it is.*
> *If any man's work abide which he hath built thereupon, he shall receive a reward.*
> *If any man's work shall be burned, he shall suffer loss: but he himself shall be saved; yet so as by fire.*
> *Know ye not that ye are the temple of God, and that the Spirit of God dwelleth in you?*
> (1 Corinthians 3:12-16)

It was here at the burning bush, which was not consumed, that Moses learned of the Gospel of Grace. Elohim introduced Himself as the God of his Spiritual Father Abraham. It is through faith in the first and everlasting Covenant of Promise that God made with Abraham, through which all believers are united by grace.

> *Christ hath redeemed us from the curse of the law, being made a curse for us: for it is written, Cursed is every one that hangeth on a tree:*
> *That the blessing of Abraham might come on the Gentiles through Jesus Christ; that we might receive the promise of the Spirit through faith.*
> (Galatians 3:13,14)

All believers are the spiritual seed of Abraham.

> *Therefore it is of faith, that it might be by grace; to the end the promise might be sure to all the*

seed; not to that only which is of the law, but to that also which is of the faith of Abraham; who is the father of us all,

(Romans 4:16)

It was here at the burning bush, after his wilderness experience, where the Lord anointed Moses to be the minister and deliverer of His people. God remembered His Covenant He had made with the father of all believing nations, Abraham, and with Abraham's seed Isaac and Jacob, and was about to deliver His chosen people through Moses' leadership.

Now Moses kept the flock of Jethro his father in law, the priest of Midian: and he led the flock to the backside of the desert, and came to the mountain of God, even to Horeb.

And the angel of the LORD appeared unto him in a flame of fire out of the midst of a bush: and he looked, and, behold, the bush burned with fire, and the bush was not consumed.

And Moses said, I will now turn aside, and see this great sight, why the bush is not burnt.

And when the LORD saw that he turned aside to see, God called unto him out of the midst of the bush, and said, Moses, Moses. And he said, Here am I.

And he said, Draw not nigh hither: put off thy shoes from off thy feet, for the place whereon thou standest is holy ground.

Moreover he said, I am the God of thy father, the God of Abraham, the God of Isaac, and the God of Jacob. And Moses hid his face; for he was afraid to look upon God.

And the LORD said, I have surely seen the affliction of my people which are in Egypt, and have heard their cry by reason of their

taskmasters; for I know their sorrows;
And I am come down to deliver them out of the
hand of the Egyptians, and to bring them up out
of that land unto a good land and a large, unto a
land flowing with milk and honey;
(Exodus 3:1-8)

The Covenant of Promise, which God had Sovereignly sworn to His people, through Abraham, and now made known to their intercessor Moses, was the Sovereign Covenant which would enable the children of Israel to escape the cruel bondage of the Egyptian world system. Likewise, Jesus was baptised by the forerunner John the Baptist, and was anointed of the Holy Spirit of God's super natural power, to bring believers into the promised land of the New Covenant, which God had promised to Abraham and his seed.

And as they departed, Jesus began to say unto
the multitudes concerning John, What went ye
out into the wilderness to see? A reed shaken
with the wind?
But what went ye out for to see? A man clothed
in soft raiment? behold, they that wear soft
clothing are in kings' houses.
But what went ye out for to see? A prophet? yea,
I say unto you, and more than a prophet.
For this is he, of whom it is written, Behold, I
send my messenger before thy face, which shall
prepare thy way before thee.
Verily I say unto you, Among them that are born
of women there hath not risen a greater than
John the Baptist: notwithstanding he that is least
in the kingdom of heaven is greater than he.
And from the days of John the Baptist until now
the kingdom of heaven suffereth violence, and
the violent take it by force.

For all the prophets and the law prophesied until John. (Matthew 11:7-13)

All the law and every prophet, from the time of Adam onward, spoke of Christ's coming Advent. At His appearing he confirmed, as we read in the Sermon on the Mount, that all Old Testament prophesies spoke of Him.

Think not that I am come to destroy the law, or the prophets: I am not come to destroy, but to fulfil.

For verily I say unto you, Till heaven and earth pass, one jot or one tittle shall in no wise pass from the law, till all be fulfilled.

(Matthew 5:17,18)

The believer, like Moses and Jesus, becomes more acutely aware of the power of the Word to deliver from the bondage of the flesh, after having been tried in a Spiritual desert. For it is only through faith in the Word that new believers are given a new life in Christ, however, until we are tested with a desert experience we have a natural tendency to revert back to our own resources and ignore the power of the Word of God. It is only when the believer has life experiences that expose him to the inadequacy of his own being and will power, only when we have lost total dependence upon self, only when we see that there is nothing in the world system that is eternal, are we open to receive the Word of God as a gift of eternal life in the Spirit.

As we see from the Scripturally recorded early history of Moses, the Lord is well aware of the problems which his people encounter in a unbelieving secular society. He is Sovereignly compassionate toward his chosen people, and willing to deliver, through very definitive and miraculous means. Moses's recognition of, and consequentially Spiritual motivational experience, to the Covenant making God of Abraham, Isaac and Jacob, demonstrates this very distinct separation between secular natural unregenerated man, and Spirit born believers in the

Gospel. The burning bush experience, which Moses encountered, demonstrated the consuming power of the fire of God's Word to separate and burn off the dross of the humanitarian system of the world, and afford the necessary salvation power to leave the believer Spiritually cleansed and intact.

After the believer, like Moses, recognizes that he is the Spiritual seed and heir of the promise God made to Abraham, he is often tested by God on the back side of a Spiritual desert. A desert experience builds character and individuality, for God would build us each as individuals, according to our understanding of Biblical doctrine and anointing through the knowledge of His Word. This testing strengthens the believer to be separated, and resistant to the influence of a secular society, humbly dependent upon the leading of God's perfect will through his Word.

> *Let that therefore abide in you, which ye have heard from the beginning. If that which ye have heard from the beginning shall remain in you, ye also shall continue in the Son, and in the Father.*
> *And this is the promise that he hath promised us, [even] eternal life.*
> *These [things] have I written unto you concerning them that seduce you.*
> *But the anointing which ye have received of him abideth in you, and ye need not that any man teach you: but as the same anointing teacheth you of all things, and is truth, and is no lie, and even as it hath taught you, ye shall abide in him.*
> (1 John 2:24-27)

As was Moses' experience, the believer today may feel totally inadequate to stare down the authoritative representatives of the world system, we may feel tongue tied when it comes to verbally describing and affirming this gulf between the redeemed and the natural man. However it is to the degree that the believer accepts his own natural inadequacy, that he is able to allow the Holy Spirit to intercede and give him the confidence to express his identity in Jesus Christ. It is only as the believer accepts that God has made him the recipient of His perfect will that the believer comes to understand who he is in Christ. It was true in the days of Moses, as it is true today, it is the Lord who is willing to lead, deliver and instill the confidence necessary to put down the world system, through the promise and fulfilment of the Abrahamic Covenant. In instilling Moses with the confidence of the Spirit, and the strength to confront Pharaoh, God once again reassures Moses, by reminding him of the Covenant He made with Abraham, Isaac and Jacob. The everlasting Covenant given to believers through Abraham, preceded the law of the ten commandments. The giving of the ten commandments did not do away with the promise of the Abrahamic Covenant.

> *Then the LORD said unto Moses, Now shalt thou see what I will do to Pharaoh: for with a strong hand shall he let them go, and with a strong hand shall he drive them out of his land.*
>
> *And God spake unto Moses, and said unto him, I [am] the LORD:*
>
> *And I appeared unto Abraham, unto Isaac, and unto Jacob, by [the name of] God Almighty, but by my name JEHOVAH was I not known to them.*
>
> *And I have also <u>established my Covenant</u> with them, to give them the land of Canaan, the land of their pilgrimage, wherein they were strangers.*
>
> *And I have also heard the groaning of the children of Israel, whom the Egyptians keep in bondage; and I have remembered my Covenant.*
>
> *Wherefore say unto the children of Israel, I [am] the LORD, and I will bring you out from under the burdens of the Egyptians, and I will rid you out of their bondage, and I will redeem you with a stretched out arm, and with great judgments:*

And I will take you to me for a people, and I will be to you a God: and ye shall know that I [am] the LORD your God, which bringeth you out from under the burdens of the Egyptians.

And I will bring you in unto the land, concerning the <u>which I did swear to give it to Abraham, to Isaac, and to Jacob; and I will give it you for an heritage: I [am] the LORD.</u> (Exodus 6:1-8)

In verse three of the above Scripture, God makes known to Moses, that although the children of Israel were aware of the Covenant He made to them through Abraham, Isaac and Jacob, they had not come to realize the significance of the name of God Almighty. (El Shaddai, the all sufficient one). Included in the name of the Almighty God is the aspect of the Lord as Jehovah, the Saviour, the promised Messiah, THE LORD OUR RIGHTEOUSNESS, the perfecting of the Lord. Although the children of Israel had not learned to appreciate the Lord as redeemer, Abraham himself had much earlier, been made aware of His redeeming grace by which God had declared him righteous.

And when Abram was ninety years old and nine, the LORD appeared to Abram, and said unto him, I [am] the Almighty God; walk before me, and be thou perfect.

And I will make my Covenant between me and thee, and will multiply thee exceedingly.

And Abram fell on his face: and God talked with him, saying,

As for me, behold, my Covenant [is] with thee, <u>and thou shalt be a father of many nations.</u>

For what saith the scripture? <u>Abraham believed God, and it was counted unto him for righteousness.</u> (Genesis 17:1-4)

King David also testified in the Old Testament book of the

Psalms of God's redeeming grace and declaration of righteousness given to those who, at the time of David, had faith in redeeming blood.

> *Now to him that worketh is the reward not reckoned of grace, but of debt.*
>
> *But to him that worketh not, but believeth on him that justifieth the ungodly, his faith is counted for righteousness.*
>
> *Even as David also describeth the blessedness of the man, unto whom God imputeth righteousness without works,*
>
> *[Saying], Blessed [are] they whose iniquities are forgiven, and whose sins are covered.*
>
> *Blessed [is] the man to whom the Lord will not impute sin.* (Romans 3:4-8)

As we saw from reading the historical account of the Mosaic Covenant in the book of Exodus, Moses now demonstrates to Pharaoh the Glory and power of God through the numerous plagues He said He would bring upon the Egyptian nation. However, God hardened Pharaoh's heart, and the plagues although severe, did not persuade Pharaoh that he should let the Hebrews leave Egypt. It was only when these plagues were climaxed by the death of all the first born sons of the Egyptians, did Pharaoh relent, and agree to allow the Hebrews to leave Egypt.

> *But the LORD hardened Pharaoh's heart, and he would not let them go.*
>
> *And Pharaoh said unto him, Get thee from me, take heed to thyself, see my face no more; for in that day thou seest my face thou shalt die.*
>
> *And Moses said, Thou hast spoken well, I will see thy face again no more.*
>
> *And the LORD said unto Moses, Yet will I bring one plague more upon Pharaoh, and upon*

Egypt; afterwards he will let you go hence: when he shall let you go, he shall surely thrust you out hence altogether.

(Exodus 10:27-11:1)

The first born of the children of Israel, however, were spared from the power of the death angel (Satan) to take their lives, because they were of the Lord's chosen and not of the Egyptian world system. It was through the sprinkling of the blood of a sacrificial lamb upon their doorposts, according to the Lord's instructions to Moses and the children, that they were separated and protected from the death angel's ability to even touch them. They were also instructed to eat of the Passover Lamb (The body of Christ.)

And they shall take of the blood, and strike it on the two side posts and on the upper door post of the houses, wherein they shall eat it....

And thus shall ye eat it; with your loins girded, your shoes on your feet, and your staff in your hand; and ye shall eat it in haste: it is the LORD's passover.

For I will pass through the land of Egypt this night, and will smite all the firstborn in the land of Egypt, both man and beast; and against all the gods of Egypt I will execute judgment: I am the LORD.

And the blood shall be to you for a token upon the houses where ye are: <u>*and when I see the blood, I will pass over you, and the plague shall not be upon you to destroy you, when I smite the land of Egypt.*</u>

And this day shall be unto you for a memorial; and ye shall keep it a feast to the LORD throughout your generations; <u>*ye shall keep it a feast by an ordinance for ever.*</u>

(Exodus 12:7; 11-14)

In the above Scriptures we see that the Passover Lamb was to be eaten as an acceptance of the believers complete identity with Jesus Christ, the blood was a testament of having been given His very nature, His DNA if you will. The believers life is in the faithfulness of the blood of Jesus Christ, and Jesus Christ is the same yesterday, today and forever. Although God initiated the ordinance of the Passover, the slaying of the animal sacrifices were only meant to be an outward representation of the Spiritual truth of the Lamb of God, who was predestined to be slain upon the Cross of Calvary in the future. The animal sacrifices in the Old Testament had no power to deliver, but faith in the blood of the Lamb, of which the sacrifices of animals prophesied, gave believers all power to be delivered from all unrighteousness.

Here we see the ordinance of the Passover initiated, an ordinance that was to be an everlasting memorial, as it is this day. The first Passover was a physical representation of the preaching of Gospel truth. This Gospel truth was made manifest when God sent His only begotten son, Jesus Christ, to offer His body and blood, which ushered in the New Covenant. He not only is the believers present salvation, seated at the right hand of the Father, but the efficacy of His blood has delivered us from all unrighteousness, not only in the present earth age, but He also will be our salvation throughout eternity. It was as true then, as it is true today, faith in the blood of Christ prevents the Evil One from having the ability to even touch God's chosen people.

We know that whosoever is born of God sinneth
not; but he that is begotten of God keepeth
himself, and that wicked one toucheth him not.
(1 John 5:18)

If we cannot appreciate that it was the pre-incarnate blood and body of Jesus Christ as being the sacrificial Lamb in this instance, I would then ask how could the blood of a mere four footed animal have delivered the children from the death angel? Jesus Christ is the Lamb of God who was slain from the foundation of the world.

> *And it was given unto him to make war with the saints, and to overcome them: and power was given him over all kindreds, and tongues, and nations.*
>
> *And all that dwell upon the earth shall worship him, whose names are not <u>written in the book of life of the Lamb slain from the foundation of the world.</u>* (Revelation 13:7,8)

Also:

> *Jesus Christ the same yesterday, and to day, and for ever.* (Hebrews 13:8)

And:

> *Jesus answered, If I honour myself, my honour is nothing: it is my Father that honoureth me; of whom ye say, that he is your God:*
>
> *Yet ye have not known him; but I know him: and if I should say, I know him not, I shall be a liar like unto you: but I know him, and keep his saying.*
>
> *Your father Abraham rejoiced to see my day: and he saw [it], and was glad.*
>
> *Then said the Jews unto him, Thou art not yet fifty years old, and hast thou seen Abraham?*
>
> *<u>Jesus said unto them, Verily, verily, I say unto you, Before Abraham was, I am.</u>* (John 8:54-58)

Moses had no trouble in understanding that the blood of the first Passover, was a pre-incarnate manifestation of the efficacy of the sprinkling of the blood of the promised Christ. He had every confidence that the blood of the Passover had greater power than the Death Angel and the King of Egypt combined. Moses had full knowledge of Jesus Christ's presence at the time of the coming out of Egypt of the children of Israel, for he chose to follow the promised Christ rather become a part of the world system.

Choosing rather to suffer affliction with the people of God, than to enjoy the pleasures of sin for a season;

Esteeming the reproach of Christ greater riches than the treasures in Egypt: for he had respect unto the recompence of the reward.

By faith he forsook Egypt, not fearing the wrath of the king: for he endured, as seeing him who is invisible.

Through faith he kept the passover, and the sprinkling of blood, lest he that destroyed the firstborn should touch them.

(Hebrews 11:25-28)

Although the promise of the sprinkling of the blood of Christ on the Mercy Seat in Heaven, was only to be made manifest after the crucifixion and resurrection of Christ, never the less, God saved all Old Testament believers to the uttermost, those who had faith in the promised blood of Christ. The promise of the perfect blood sacrifice to deliver His people was not new to the children of Israel, God's Sovereign giving of the Abrahamic Covenant had made the promise of deliverance and resurrection power, through faith in the blood of Christ, to all Abraham's seed 400 years earlier.

But now they desire a better country, that is, an heavenly: wherefore God is not ashamed to be called their God: for he hath prepared for them a city.

By faith Abraham, when he was tried, offered up Isaac: and he that had received the promises offered up his only begotten son,

Of whom it was said, That in Isaac shall thy seed be called:

Accounting that God was able to raise him up, even from the dead; from whence also he received him in a figure. (Hebrews 11:16-19)

As we saw in the reading of the historical account of the coming out of the children of Israel in the book of Exodus; after having been asked to leave Egypt, after all the first born sons of the Egyptian children were slain by the Lord, the Israelite's progress was halted as they came to the Red Sea. The Spirit of the Lord who was in the pillar of a cloud, led them by day as well as being in the pillar of fire, with which He led them by night. These pillars of cloud and fire were not only a provision of the Lord's mercy and grace, the Lord was Himself present within the pillars. The Spirit of the Lord led them day and night even as His Holy Spirit leads believers by day and night today, in this present age and dispensation. This was no lesser Spirit of God than indwells believers today, for He is the same yesterday, today and forever. This Sovereign direction was provided for by God's Grace and His Grace alone.

And the LORD went before them by day in a pillar of a cloud, to lead them the way; and by night in a pillar of fire, to give them light; to go by day and night:

He took not away the pillar of the cloud by day, nor the pillar of fire by night, from before the people. (Exodus 13:21,22)

The Lord had deliberately lead them into this blind alley at the shores of the Red Sea, in order that He might demonstrate His mighty power to deliver and save his people, dividing them from the power of the world system. In the meantime the Pharaoh had changed his mind and was in hot pursuit of the Israelites, he and his army were on a mission to bring the Hebrews back to Egypt once again, in order to put them under bondage as slaves to the world system.

And the angel of God, which went before the camp of Israel, removed and went behind them; and the pillar of the cloud went from before their

face, and stood behind them:
And it came between the camp of the Egyptians
and the camp of Israel; and it was a cloud and
darkness to them, but it gave light by night to
these: so that the one came not near the other all
the night.
(Exodus 14:19,20)

Here we see a clear picture of how the Lord separates and divides the unredeemed from His Kingdom, while at the same time He brings His chosen into unity with Him. The Egyptians saw the Lords protecting pillar as fearful dark judgement upon them, but the chosen of God sees His guiding presence as a light of grace and mercy. Once again, we see this portrayal of a smoking furnace and a burning lamp, a confirmation of God's Covenant to the children of Israel, the same symbol which confirmed His Covenant with Abraham and his seed. We saw previously how the Lord miraculously intervened to completely destroy the entire Egyptian army, and once again, protect Moses and the children from destruction, enabling them to continue on their journey towards the promised land of the Lord's peace.

Now, At the crossing of the Red Sea we see the salvation of the Lord made manifest, by faith, as Moses lifts up his rod, which was representative of the righteous judgements of the Lord. He stretched his hand over the Red Sea and the Lord caused it to part, which allowed the Israelites to pass through on dry ground.

And Moses said unto the people, Fear ye not,
stand still, and see the salvation of the LORD,
which he will shew to you to day: for the
Egyptians whom ye have seen to day, ye shall see
them again no more for ever.
The LORD shall fight for you, and ye shall hold
your peace. (Exodus 14:13,14)

And:

And Moses stretched out his hand over the sea;

and the LORD caused the sea to go back by a strong east wind all that night, and made the sea dry land, and the waters were divided.

And the children of Israel went into the midst of the sea upon the dry ground: and the waters were a wall unto them on their right hand, and on their left. (Exodus 14:21,22)

Prior to being parted the waters of the Red Sea represented certain death to the children of Israel, here again Moses demonstrates his faith in the Word of the Lord, as he did throughout the entire time of his leading of God's people. It is important that believers come to understand that the salvation and deliverance of God's people is only possible after we have been completely Spiritually separated from unbelievers. By keeping His people from certain death, God separates them unto Himself. The children of Israel, once having been separated from the bondage and sin of the world system, Egypt, through faith in the sprinkling of the blood of Christ, are now eligible for water baptism. Baptism representing the outward physical testimony of an internal Spiritual transformation. In this case, the children, by passing through the water of the Red Sea, having their old identity with sinful Egypt left at the bottom of the sea, the baptismal tank, emerge on the other side renewed in the leading of the Spirit of God's Promise.

And the Egyptians pursued, and went in after them to the midst of the sea, even all Pharaoh's horses, his chariots, and his horsemen.

And it came to pass, that in the morning watch the <u>LORD looked unto the host of the Egyptians through the pillar of fire and of the cloud,</u> and troubled the host of the Egyptians,

And took off their chariot wheels, that they drave them heavily: so that the Egyptians said, Let us flee from the face of Israel; for the LORD fighteth for them against the Egyptians.

And the LORD said unto Moses, Stretch out thine hand over the sea, that the waters may come again upon the Egyptians, upon their chariots, and upon their horsemen.

And Moses stretched forth his hand over the sea, and the sea returned to his strength when the morning appeared; and the Egyptians fled against it; and the LORD overthrew the Egyptians in the midst of the sea.

And the waters returned, and covered the chariots, and the horsemen,

and all the host of Pharaoh that came into the sea after them; there remained not so much as one of them.

But the children of Israel walked upon dry land in the midst of the sea; and the waters were a wall unto them on their right hand, and on their left.

Thus the LORD saved Israel that day out of the hand of the Egyptians; and Israel saw the Egyptians dead upon the sea shore.

And Israel saw that great work which the LORD did upon the Egyptians: and the people feared the LORD, and believed the LORD, and his servant Moses.   (Exodus 14:23-31)

Also, in terms of the message of the Gospel as contained in the testimony of the tabernacle of Moses, baptism represents the believers eligibility to enter through the first and second veil of the tabernacle. The Levites, the sons of Aaron, once having obtained the blood of the sacrificed offering, which was killed in the courtyard outside of the veil, now wash and cleanse themselves at the laver, prior to entering through the first veil to accomplish the service of God.

Thou shalt also make a laver of brass, and his foot also of brass, to wash withal: and thou shalt put it between the tabernacle of the congregation and the altar, and thou shalt put water therein.
For Aaron and his sons shall wash their hands and their feet thereat:
When they go into the tabernacle of the congregation, they shall wash with water, that they die not; or when they come near to the altar to minister, to burn offering made by fire unto the LORD:
So they shall wash their hands and their feet, that they die not: and it shall be a statute for ever to them, even to him and to his seed throughout their generations. (Exodus 30:18-21)

This also was the message that Jesus gave to his disciples when He washed their feet after the feast of the Passover. Although they had initially confessed their love for their Saviour, they did not fully understand that this confession of their faith in Him, had thoroughly cleansed and separated them from their old sinful nature. They did not understand that now, having been thoroughly cleansed through faith in the blood of the Passover, they need now only to have their feet be washed. The necessity of having only their feet washed, was a token of cleansing necessary for the sins of the flesh, which they unintentionally committed, after having been saved through faith. Jesus, in a demonstration of God's Sovereign love, took the initiative here to show them the nature of His present High Priestly ministry at the right hand of the Father. He demonstrated here that faith in the sprinkling of His efficacious blood on the Mercy Seat, would continually cleanse the believers feet from all unrighteousness.

He riseth from supper, and laid aside his garments; and took a towel, and girded himself.
After that he poureth water into a bason, and

*began to wash the disciples' feet, and to wipe
them with the towel wherewith he was girded.*

*Then cometh he to Simon Peter: and Peter saith
unto him, Lord, dost thou wash my feet?*

*Jesus answered and said unto him, What I do
thou knowest not now; but thou shalt know
hereafter.*

*Peter saith unto him, Thou shalt never wash my
feet. Jesus answered him, If I wash thee not, thou
hast no part with me.*

*Simon Peter saith unto him, Lord, not my feet
only, but also my hands and my head.*

*Jesus saith to him, <u>He that is washed needeth not
save to wash his feet, but is clean every whit</u>: and
ye are clean, but not all.*

*For he knew who should betray him; therefore
said he, Ye are not all clean.* (John 13:4-11)

Just as the believer today, the children of Israel now being
cleansed by the washing of the Word, represented by passing
through the Red Sea, and being separated from their old nature
and identity, are now eligible to travel further towards the
promised land by faith, and sing the song of the blood redeemed.

*Then sang Moses and the children of Israel this
song unto the LORD, and spake, saying, I will
sing unto the LORD, for he hath triumphed
gloriously: the horse and his rider hath he
thrown into the sea.*

*The LORD is my strength and song, and he is
become my salvation: he is my God, and I will
prepare him an habitation; my father's God, and
I will exalt him.*

*The LORD is a man of war: the LORD is his
name.*

Pharaoh's chariots and his host hath he cast into

the sea: his chosen captains also are drowned in
the Red sea.
The depths have covered them: they sank into the
bottom as a stone.
Thy right hand, O LORD, is become glorious in
power: thy right hand, O LORD, hath dashed in
pieces the enemy. (Exodus 15:1-6)

After having been baptised by the waters of the Red Sea, the children of Israel now enter the wilderness and soon quickly forget the grace which God had bestowed upon them, in delivering them from the hand of Pharaoh.

After journeying in the dessert for only three days and three nights, they came upon water, however it was too bitter to drink. Through Moses' prayerful intercession the Lord told him to cast a tree into the water, and the water then became sweet. The tree was a representation of the cross of Jesus Christ, yet to be revealed, which makes the Water of the Word sweet and palatable.

For the preaching of the cross is to them that
perish foolishness; but unto us which are saved
it is the power of God. (1 Corinthians 1:18)

Had this visible demonstration of purification not represented a Spiritual truth then the Lord would not have sanctified the incident by proclaiming it to be made a statute and an ordinance. It is through belief in the efficacy of the blood which Jesus shed on the cross that heals believers from the disease of death that is the destiny of the unbelieving world system, typified by Egypt. It is only through faith in the blood of Christ by which believers are enabled to do that which is right(eous) in God's sight.

And he cried unto the LORD; and the LORD
shewed him a tree, which when he had cast into
the waters, the waters were made sweet: there he
made for them a statute and an ordinance, and

there he proved them,
And said, If thou wilt diligently hearken to the
voice of the LORD thy God, and wilt do that
which is right in his sight, and wilt give ear to his
commandments, and keep all his statutes, I will
put none of these diseases upon thee, which I
have brought upon the Egyptians: for I am the
LORD that healeth thee. (Exodus 15:25,26)

After two and one half months in the desert, the Israelites now having lost faith in God's ability to sustain them physically, they began to murmur against Moses and Aaron. The children, once again, had lost their faith in God's ability to deliver them, and they expressed their desire to return to their previous state of bondage and slavery with the unredeemed in Egypt. They were complaining that there was not enough bread to eat to satisfy their hunger.

And the whole congregation of the children of
Israel murmured against Moses and Aaron in the
wilderness:
And the children of Israel said unto them, Would
to God we had died by the hand of the LORD in
the land of Egypt, when we sat by the flesh pots,
and when we did eat bread to the full; for ye
have brought us forth into this wilderness, to kill
this whole assembly with hunger.
(Exodus 16:2,3)

After being tried of God, they who had begun their Spiritual journey through the desert, soon forgot the Spirit of the Abrahamic Covenant through which God had delivered them. God reminded them of this when He revealed the law to them, later upon Mount Sinai.

And God spake all these words, saying,
I am the LORD thy God, which have brought
thee out of the land of Egypt, out of the house of
bondage. (Exodus 20:1,2)

The Israelites, who had just recently witnessed the healing power of the symbol of the cross, which sweetened the waters of Marah, now reverted to searching for fulfilment within their old nature. They were the forerunners of the foolish Galatians who, having begun through the working of the Spirit, now looked to their flesh for further salvation. They had begun their Christian journey in the Spirit of the Covenant God gave to all believers through Abraham. Simply by not acknowledging that they were the seed of Abraham, they by default, have reverted to the self righteous works of the flesh.

> *O foolish Galatians, who hath bewitched you, that ye should not obey the truth, before whose eyes Jesus Christ hath been evidently set forth, crucified among you?*
>
> *This only would I learn of you, Received ye the Spirit by the works of the law, or by the hearing of faith?*
>
> *Are ye so foolish? having begun in the Spirit, are ye now made perfect by the flesh?*
>
> *Have ye suffered so many things in vain? if it be yet in vain.*
>
> *He therefore that ministereth to you the Spirit, and worketh miracles among you, doeth he it by the works of the law, or by the hearing of faith?*
>
> *Even as Abraham believed God, and it was accounted to him for righteousness.*
>
> *Know ye therefore that they which are of faith, the same are the children of Abraham.*
>
> *And the scripture, foreseeing that God would justify the heathen through faith, preached before the gospel unto Abraham, saying, In thee shall all nations be blessed.*
>
> *So then they which be of faith are blessed with faithful Abraham.* (Galatians 3:1-9)

In spite of more murmuring against the Lord, He gracefully promises to provide them with manna from heaven as their daily bread, along with explicit instructions however, which were designed by God as a test of their willingness to obey His voice.

Then said the LORD unto Moses, Behold, I will rain bread from heaven for you; and the people shall go out and gather a certain rate every day, that I may prove them, whether they will walk in my law, or no. (Exodus 16:4)

The Israelites were instructed to gather enough manna each day to satisfy their needs for that day, but on the sixth day they were told to gather enough to do them for the next two days, so that they might observe the seventh day as the day of Sabbath rest. Even in this simple matter some were disobedient.

And it came to pass, [that] there went out [some] of the people on the seventh day for to gather, and they found none.

And the LORD said unto Moses, How long refuse ye to keep my commandments and my laws? (Exodus 16:27,28)

Here is another visible demonstration of a Spiritual truth. Just as the children were to work and gather their food six days, which the Lord made available for them, believers as well, are to rest on the seventh day in order that the Sabbath be kept Holy unto the Lord. The provision of the seventh day for bodily rest was not designed by God as a law to restrict our pleasure and freedom, but was given as a gift as a means to provide health, rest and sanity for the human body. The Sabbath was designed of God for a time to rejoice in the gift of the Spirit of life in Christ, and to express our gratitude for the hope and assurance of eternal life.

This manna was a physical representation of the Spiritual bread of the Word of God. Although it was given through Moses, it was not given from Moses, but from the Heavenly Father. This bread of the Word was made evident to believers when His Son Jesus Christ, Emmanuel, came to dwell among men.

*Our fathers did eat manna in the desert; as it is
written, He gave them bread from heaven to eat.
Then Jesus said unto them, Verily, verily, I say
unto you, Moses gave you not that bread from
heaven; but my Father giveth you the true bread
from heaven.*

*For the bread of God is he which cometh down
from heaven, and giveth life unto the world.*

*Then said they unto him, Lord, evermore give us
this bread.*

*And Jesus said unto them, I am the bread of life:
he that cometh to me shall never hunger; and he
that believeth on me shall never thirst.*

(John 6:31-35)

The Gospel of the bread of life, the Gospel of Grace through
faith in Christ's redeeming blood, was preached to the Israelites
thousands of years before the cross of Christ was made evident.
The Lord showed His mighty power to deliver them through their
faith in the sprinkling of blood upon their doorpost at the time
they were brought out of Egypt. Also the Lord preached to them
the Gospel of Grace through His continual presence with them
since being delivered from Egypt, for He was ever present in the
pillar of fire and the cloud which led them.

Jesus, Himself, pointed out to the two disciples who walked
with Him on the Emmaus road, that Moses spoke of Him.
Actually Jesus called them foolish for not having understood the
Gospel that was preached through Moses and the prophets.

*Then he said unto them, O fools, and slow of
heart to believe all that the prophets have
spoken:*

*Ought not Christ to have suffered these things,
and to enter into his glory?*

*And beginning at Moses and all the prophets, he
expounded unto them in all the scriptures the
things concerning himself.* (Luke 24:25-27)

The unconditional promise which God made to all believers in the Abrahamic Covenant, affirmed through Moses, was the Gospel of Grace which primarily, in the beginning, applied to the children of Israel. This Gospel is the same Gospel of Grace whereby all believers, whether Jew or Gentile, are saved today. The promise which God made to Abraham and his seed, 400 years before the children were released from Egyptian bondage, was made manifest with the appearing of the Lord Jesus Christ. All believers are Abraham's seed. Not only are believers the physical seed of Abraham, but we are Abraham's seed through the Spirit as well. This promise of the deliverance of Abraham's seed was made by God ever since God made promise to Abraham as recorded in the Scriptures below:

And when the sun was going down, a deep sleep fell upon Abram; and, lo, an horror of great darkness fell upon him.

And he said unto Abram, Know of a surety that thy seed shall be a stranger in a land that is not theirs, and shall serve them; and they shall afflict them four hundred years;

And also that nation, whom they shall serve, will I judge: and afterward shall they come out with great substance. (Genesis 15:12-14)

This message of the Gospel of Grace, and of the Covenant He had made with them through Abraham, was clearly passed on to the children of Israel, by Moses when "I AM THAT I AM" appeared to Moses in the burning bush, and anointed him to deliver this message of deliverance to the Israelites. One of God's very names is "the God of Abraham, the God of Isaac, and the God of Jacob", a memorial forever to all generations.

And God said moreover unto Moses, Thus shalt thou say unto the children of Israel, The LORD God of your fathers, <u>the God of Abraham, the God of Isaac, and the God of Jacob, hath sent me</u>

*unto you: this is my name for ever, and this is my
memorial unto all generations.* (Exodus 3:15)

Even though they murmured in the wilderness, and some
disobeyed and failed the test which God had set before them, God
continued to supply them with the necessary daily bread for the
forty years of their wandering in the wilderness. The Lord gave
instructions to Aaron, through Moses, that he was to lay up a
measure of manna in a golden pot, and to put in under the Mercy
Seat in the Ark of the Covenant. Aaron was to put it within the
Ark of the Covenant, as a testimony to all future generations, that
God had gracefully supplied all their needs of the flesh and of the
Spirit throughout the entire forty years of the wilderness journey.

> *And Moses said, This is the thing which the
> LORD commandeth, Fill an omer of it to be kept
> for your generations; that they may see the bread
> wherewith I have fed you in the wilderness, when
> I brought you forth from the land of Egypt.*
>
> *And Moses said unto Aaron, Take a pot, and put
> an omer full of manna therein, and lay it up
> before the LORD, to be kept for your
> generations.*
>
> *As the LORD commanded Moses, so Aaron laid
> it up before the Testimony, to be kept.*
>
> *And the children of Israel did eat manna forty
> years, until they came to a land inhabited; they
> did eat manna, until they came unto the borders
> of the land of Canaan.* (Exodus 16:32-35)

As they continued their journey, the chosen people of God
came from the Wilderness of Sin to a place called Rephidim.
Here, once again they were confronted with another test of
having no water to drink. So, true to form, forgetting that the
Lord had gracefully supplied all their needs throughout their
wilderness journey in the past, they began to blame Moses for
bringing them out of the house of bondage, Egypt. Moses made

them aware that they had no issue with him personally, and that their lack of faith in the Lord's ability to sustain them was a direct offense to the Lord.

> *And all the congregation of the children of Israel journeyed from the wilderness of Sin, after their journeys, according to the commandment of the LORD, and pitched in Rephidim: and there was no water for the people to drink.*
>
> *Wherefore the people did chide with Moses, and said, Give us water that we may drink. And Moses said unto them, Why chide ye with me? wherefore do ye tempt the LORD?*
>
> *And the people thirsted there for water; and the people murmured against Moses, and said, Wherefore is this that thou hast brought us up out of Egypt, to kill us and our children and our cattle with thirst?*
>
> *And Moses cried unto the LORD, saying, What shall I do unto this people? they be almost ready to stone me.*
>
> *And the LORD said unto Moses, Go on before the people, and take with thee of the elders of Israel; and thy rod, wherewith thou smotest the river, take in thine hand, and go.*
>
> *Behold, I will stand before thee there upon the rock in Horeb; and thou shalt smite the rock, and there shall come water out of it, that the people may drink. And Moses did so in the sight of the elders of Israel.*
>
> *And he called the name of the place Massah, and Meribah, because of the chiding of the children of Israel, and because they tempted the LORD, saying, Is the LORD among us, or not?*
>
> (Exodus 17:1-7)

Here again in the Scriptures above, we see another dynamic physical manifestation of a Spiritual truth. Jesus Christ was that Rock from which the water flowed, and the water was the meat of the Word and the Spirit of God, not only figuratively but literally as well. The water which comes from the believers Rock, Christ Jesus, is to quench the thirst of those believers who thirst after the righteousness of God.

> *Moreover, brethren, I would not that ye should be ignorant, how that all our fathers were under the cloud, and all passed through the sea;*
> *And were all baptized unto Moses in the cloud and in the sea;*
> *And did all eat the same spiritual meat;*
> <u>*And did all drink the same spiritual drink: for they drank of that spiritual Rock that followed them: and that Rock was Christ.*</u>
> *But with many of them God was not well pleased: for they were overthrown in the wilderness.*
> *Now these things were our examples, to the intent we should not lust after evil things, as they also lusted.* (1 Corinthians 10:1-6)

How much plainer can the Word of God make it! It was Jesus Christ who led the children of Israel throughout their wilderness journey, and if they were led of Jesus Christ then they were led by the washing of the water of the Word through the Holy Spirit of God! Why, then, is the Old Testament not understood for what it truly is, a Gospel of Grace? Why do the vast majority of Biblical teachers portray the prime message of the Old Testament to be a testimony of the cruel letter of the law? As long as believers consider the Old Testament to be a conditional letter of the "law", then they sadly remain under the law, for they are blinded to the Gospel of Grace as revealed in the Old Testament.

> *And not as Moses, which put a vail over his face, that the children of Israel could not stedfastly*

look to the end of that which is abolished:
But their minds were blinded: <u>*for until this day*</u>
<u>*remaineth the same vail untaken away in the*</u>
<u>*reading of the old testament; which vail is done*</u>
<u>*away in Christ.*</u>
<u>*But even unto this day, when Moses is read, the*</u>
<u>*vail is upon their heart.*</u>
Nevertheless when it shall turn to the Lord, the
vail shall be taken away.
Now the Lord is that Spirit: and where the Spirit
of the Lord is, there is liberty.
But we all, with open face beholding as in a
glass the glory of the Lord, are changed into the
same image from glory to glory, even as by the
Spirit of the Lord. (2 Corinthians 3:13-18)

The rod with which Moses was instructed to smite the rock that gushed out an abundance of water, was representative of the same rod of God's righteous judgement, with which He smote His Son upon the cross. In the Old Testament we read that it pleased the Lord, for His own sake, to bruise His Son on the cross, in order that every believer might be reconciled to Him.

Yet it pleased the LORD to bruise him; he hath
put him to grief:
when thou shalt make his soul an offering for sin,
he shall see his seed, he shall prolong his days,
and the pleasure of the LORD shall prosper in
his hand.
He shall see of the travail of his soul, and shall
be satisfied: by his knowledge shall my righteous
servant justify many; for he shall bear their
iniquities. (Isaiah 53:10-11)

The water which came from the rock that Moses smote here at Rephidim, revealed the same Gospel message of redemption through blood, which God proclaimed when He allowed His Son to go through the travail of His soul on the cruel cross.

> *Wherefore say unto the children of Israel, I am
> the LORD, and I will bring you out from under
> the burdens of the Egyptians, and I will rid you
> out of their bondage, and I will redeem you with
> a stretched out arm, and with great judgments:*
> (Exodus 6:6)

Also:

> *And he saved them from the hand of him that
> hated them, and redeemed them from the hand of
> the enemy.*
> *And the waters covered their enemies: there was
> not one of them left.*
> *Then believed they his words; they sang his
> praise.*
> *They soon forgat his works; they waited not for
> his counsel:*
> *But lusted exceedingly in the wilderness, and
> tempted God in the desert.*
> *And he gave them their request; but sent
> leanness into their soul.*
> (Psalms 106:10-15)

The entire chapter of Psalms 106 is a vivid portrayal of the lessons to be learned, for present day believers, from the negative responses of the children of Israel and their blindness to God's Grace, while being tempted in their desert wanderings. Their lack of faith became evident when they asked "Is the Lord among us or not?"

How often do we, as believers, doubt if the Lord is continually with us as we journey through life? Have we ever doubted that God is ever present and that He continually sustains us? There is a lesson in grace, for New Testament believers, to be learned here from the Old Testament writings and the desert wanderings of the children of Israel.

There is yet another Scriptural reference given of Moses'

smiting Christ, the Rock, as recorded in the book of Numbers, later on in their journey to the promised land. We will look into the Gospel message of this Scripture as we follow the children towards their destination, the land of Canaan. As is often the case when God's people receive the water of the Word that comes from our Rock, Christ Jesus, we are challenged to stand fast and proclaim our new found Spiritual freedom to an unbelieving world. So it was with the children of Israel again in this instance.

As the children of Israel continue on their journey towards the land which God promised to the seed of Abraham, they now abruptly come up against another test of their faith, this time having to do with the unbelieving children of the flesh, the anti-Spiritual tribe of the Amalekites.

Then came Amalek, and fought with Israel in Rephidim. (Exodus 17:8)

Apparently it was quite a brief encounter that Moses and the Israelites had with the Amalekites. The conflict was resolved quickly when, Moses accepting his role as mediator and high priest with the sceptre of the rod of God's righteous judgements in his hand, demonstrated once again the power of God's Spirit to save.

And Moses said unto Joshua, Choose us out men, and go out, fight with Amalek: to morrow I will stand on the top of the hill with the rod of God in mine hand. (Exodus 17:9)

While Aaron and Hur supported Moses' hand with the rod of the Lord in it, Joshua and the Israelites prevailed in their fight against the Amalekites, until they were defeated. Through the sceptre of the rod of God's righteousness in Moses' hand, God poured out His righteous judgement of wrath against the unbelieving Amalekites in favour of His chosen people, Israel. After their victory over the Amalekites, Moses, in gratitude to the Lord, built an altar and offered up a blood sacrifice of praise to Jehovah-nissi, the Lord who is our banner. The Lord Jehovah has gracefully given His banner to all believers to lead and inspire them in resisting those of the flesh nature, against those who would hinder our progress towards our Spiritual promised land of the Heavenly Jerusalem on Mount Zion.

And Joshua discomfited Amalek and his people with the edge of the sword.

And the LORD said unto Moses, Write this for a memorial in a book, and rehearse it in the ears of Joshua: for I will utterly put out the remembrance of Amalek from under heaven.

And Moses built an altar, and called the name of it Jehovah-nissi: (Exodus 17:13,14)

The same Lord Jehovah-nissi, is also, today, in the New Testament era, the Spirit led believers banner and source of strength to overcome our enemy, our own old nature of the flesh.

This I say then, Walk in the Spirit, and ye shall not fulfil the lust of the flesh.

For the flesh lusteth against the Spirit, and the Spirit against the flesh: and these are contrary the one to the other: so that ye cannot do the things that ye would.

But if ye be led of the Spirit, ye are not under the law.

(Galatians 5:16-18)

This rod which the Lord instructed Moses to take up, in the children's fight against the forces of the world system, was representative of the sceptre of the High Priestly ministry of Christ, through which God demonstrated His power to them several times previously in their wilderness journey. The power of this rod of God's Word, which was Moses' identity as God's chosen man of power to deliver, was typified when He had asked Moses to cast it on the ground and it became a serpent, and was once again restored to a rod when he picked it up by the tail as the Lord had commanded. This miracle was also to confirm and clarify that Moses was sent to deliver the children through the power of the Covenant He made with Abraham, Isaac and Jacob.

This miracle was also a prophecy of how Jesus Christ would be sent to a lost world, by the will of the Father, after having set aside the sceptre of His High Priestly ministry at the right hand of Glory. On the cross Jesus was made to be cast down upon the earth and become the sin of the flesh for us. Natural man's sin nature upon the cross was represented by the serpent which is a symbol of Satan.

> *And as Moses lifted up the serpent in the*
> *wilderness, even so must the Son of man be lifted*
> *up:* John 3:14

However, when Moses picked up the serpent by the tail and his rod once again became his sceptre, it was foretelling of Christ's resurrection and joyous returning to the right hand of The Father in glory. Never again would Jesus Christ be representative of the believers sin nature, but His regained sceptre of the power of God's Kingdom will be forever the assurance of our righteous standing in Christ, at the right hand of the Father.

This rod with which Moses led the Israelites, was also representative of God's wonder working power to save, separate and baptise, at the time the Red Sea was parted so that the children of Israel might cross to the other side on dry ground. This sceptre, was a symbol of God's righteous judgement which separated his chosen people from the influence of the Egyptian, global world system.

> *And the LORD said unto Moses, Wherefore*
> *criest thou unto me? speak unto the children of*
> *Israel, that they go forward:*
> *But lift thou up thy rod, and stretch out thine*
> *hand over the sea, and divide it: and the children*
> *of Israel shall go on dry ground through the*
> *midst of the sea.* (Exodus 14:15,16)

Here again we see that the Lord's salvation is a divisive force, separating the natural flesh nature from the gift of the freedom in the Spirit. In this case the Lord's salvation power divided the flesh of the world system, as represented by the nation of Egypt, from the Spirit of the redeemed as represented by Moses and the believers who were among the children of Israel.

The rod of Moses was also instrumental in the first instance of him smitting the rock in the wilderness, as referenced in Exodus 17:5,6 where he drew water from the rock in order that the thirst of his people might be quenched. The smitting of the Rock was a prophecy of how Jesus Christ would be smitten for our transgressions, in order that believers might be reconciled to God through faith in the water of His Word.

> *Surely he hath borne our griefs, and carried our*
> *sorrows: yet we did esteem him stricken, smitten*
> *of God, and afflicted.*
> *But he was wounded for our transgressions, he*
> *was bruised for our iniquities: the chastisement*
> *of our peace was upon him; and with his stripes*
> *we are healed.* (Isaiah 53:4,5)

The apostle Paul recognized that the promise of the Spirit of Christ, and the Spirit of baptism was present in the Old Testament. We all know that Jesus Christ is the same yesterday, today and forever and that He was the Lamb slain from the foundation of the world. The same, is true, both in the Old and in the New Testament. As previously quoted.

> *Moreover, brethren, I would not that ye should*
> *be ignorant, how that all our fathers were under*
> *the cloud, and all passed through the sea;*
> *And were all baptized unto Moses in the cloud*
> *and in the sea;*
> *And did all eat the same spiritual meat;*
> *And did all drink the same spiritual drink: for*
> *they drank of that spiritual Rock that followed*
> *them: and that Rock was Christ.*
> (1 Corinthians 10:1-4)

Baptism is a physical representation and testimony of an inner Spiritual new birth, another portrayal of the separation of the believers old sin nature being cut off from the new nature of the Spirit of life in Christ. First comes the inner gift of a new birth through faith in the blood Jesus Christ has shed for us, only then does the experience of baptism have any true meaning. First comes the gift of righteousness and the believers new position in Christ, only then follows the experience of living out that new life through faith in Christ's blood, separated from the previous experience of life in the carnal nature of the flesh.

Moses also used the rod of the Lord in error, when he smote the rock in Kadesh twice, instead of speaking to it as the Lord had instructed he and Aaron, at the time when the children once again thirsted on their journey. The rock which he struck earlier in Horeb is translated from a Hebrew word which means a smaller rock, a rocky ledge or boulder, as described in Exodus 17:6. This Rock was representative of Christ upon the cross prior to his death and resurrection. The rock which Moses struck here at Kadesh is translated from a Hebrew word in Numbers 20:11, which means a mighty rock, a fortress. This larger Rock represented Christ in his resurrection power and return to Glory having once suffered on the cross.

> *And the LORD spake unto Moses, saying,*
> *Take the rod, and gather thou the assembly together, thou, and Aaron thy brother, and speak ye unto the rock before their eyes; and it shall give forth his water, and thou shalt bring forth to them water out of the rock: so thou shalt give the congregation and their beasts drink.*
> *And Moses took the rod from before the LORD, as he commanded him.*
> *And Moses and Aaron gathered the congregation together before the rock, and he said unto them, Hear now, ye rebels; must we fetch you water out of this rock?*

And Moses lifted up his hand, and with his rod he smote the rock twice: and the water came out abundantly, and the congregation drank, and their beasts also.

And the LORD spoke unto Moses and Aaron, Because ye believed me not, to sanctify me in the eyes of the children of Israel, therefore ye shall not bring this congregation into the land which I have given them.

This is the water of Meribah; because the children of Israel strove with the LORD, and he was sanctified in them. (Numbers 20:7-13)

Obviously Moses and Aaron had displeased the Lord through their own lack of trust and faith by what they had done. The striking of the Rock twice had much deeper Spiritual implications than a mere momentary lapse of faith. The Spiritual message here is quite clear, Jesus Christ was stricken and smitten only once upon the cross as depicted in striking the Rock once at Horeb. By striking the Rock here at Kadesh twice, and not simply speaking to it as instructed by the Lord, Moses and Aaron were demonstrating their lack of appreciation for what the Lord would accomplish, when He would be made manifest on the cross. The lowly small Rock, which Moses struck at Horeb, was a depiction of the lowly estate Jesus Christ was asked of God to endure, during the time of His Passion on the Cross. What Moses and Aaron were portraying by striking the Rock of the Fortress twice at Kadesh, was in effect asking the Lord our Rock, our Fortress, to be crucified the second time. The gift of God's righteousness is granted to unbelievers, only after we simply accept that Jesus Christ has been smitten once of the Father's rod, and that He died for our sins at Calvary, and that we also believe that God raised Him from the dead. However, after Christ has been resurrected and ascended to the right hand of the Father, believers are only asked to accept their righteous position in God through faith in the blood of Christ, not to look back again to the cross for the forgiveness of sin. For those of us who accept our God given righteous position, through faith in the blood of our High Priest, we like Moses and Aaron, would be asking our Rock to be struck the second time, and would be ignoring the provisions of Christ's High priestly ministry. The promised land of rest in Christ, is here in the secret place of the Most High, within the second veil where our High Priest continually makes intercession for us, and presents believers to the Father in His righteousness, according to God's will.

It was for this momentary lapse of faith and self exaltation that both Moses and Aaron were denied entrance into the promised land. Crossing the river Jordan into the promised land, is representative of the access given to believers to the secret place of the Most High, through the rent veil of the Tabernacle in Heaven.

> *And the LORD said unto Moses, Get thee up into this mount Abarim, and see the land which I have given unto the children of Israel.*
>
> *And when thou hast seen it, thou also shalt be gathered unto thy people, as Aaron thy brother was gathered.*
>
> *For ye rebelled against my commandment in the desert of Zin, in the strife of the congregation, to sanctify me at the water before their eyes: that is the water of Meribah in Kadesh in the wilderness of Zin.*

(Numbers 27:12-14)

If present day believers do not have faith in the blood of Christ to believe that God's memory of our sins and iniquities were set aside at the cross, represented by the striking of the rock at Horeb, then each time we ask God to remove that which has already been removed, we crucify Jesus yet another time, represented by the striking of the rock at Kadesh twice. If our basic understanding of what Jesus Christ has accomplished for us upon the cross, does not first and foremost consider Him to be our ever present advocate and High Priest at the right hand of the Father, then we should examine our understanding of what we consider God's purpose was in sending Him to the cross in the first place. It is here at the Throne of Grace where Christ, our High priest forever in the order of Meclchisedec, continually presents believers in His righteousness to the Father.

> *For it is impossible for those who were once enlightened, and have tasted of the heavenly gift, and were made partakers of the Holy Ghost,*
> *And have tasted the good word of God, and the powers of the world to come,*
> *If they shall fall away, to renew them again unto repentance; seeing they crucify to themselves the Son of God afresh, and put him to an open shame.* (Hebrews 6:4-6)

Hezekiah considered cross worship, going back to the cross a second time, to be a major problem during his reign as King of Judah. Hezekiah was a king of Israel who did right in the sight of the Lord, and governed Israel according to all that David his father did before him. Hezekiah recognized that believers were worshipping the brazen serpent that God had instructed Moses to erect in the wilderness, that all who looked upon it were healed of the bites of serpents, the works of the devil. This brazen serpent erected on a pole, was representative of Christ on the cross, who was made to be the sin of the Serpent for us.

> *And as Moses lifted up the serpent in the wilderness, even so must the Son of man be lifted up:*
> *That whosoever believeth in him should not perish, but have eternal life.*
> *For God so loved the world, that he gave his only begotten Son, that whosoever believeth in him should not perish, but have everlasting life.*
> (John 3:14-16)

Because they continued to look on this Serpent in the wilderness, after they had been healed and their sin atoned for, Hezekiah had the serpent destroyed. Hezekiah made sure that the children of Israel were to understand that Jesus Christ would not remain on the cross, but after His resurrection, He would ascend to the right hand of the Father.

He removed the high places, and brake the images, and cut down the groves, and brake in pieces the brasen serpent that Moses had made: for unto those days the children of Israel did burn incense to it: and he called it Nehushtan.

(2 Kings 18:4)

If believers do not fully accept that we have been made partakers of His Divine Nature, as is written in 2 Peter 1:4, then we have forgotten that Jesus Christ was once crucified and that His blood, sprinkled on the Mercy Seat in Heaven, purged believers once and for all time and eternity, from our inherited sin nature.

But he that lacketh these things is blind, and cannot see afar off, and hath forgotten that he was purged from his old sins. (2 Peter 1:9)

The next major event in the journey of the children of Israel which we will consider, is the imposing of the ten commandments upon the tablets of stone, and then also the giving of the ordinances of the Law of Grace as depicted in the building of the tabernacle. The conditional law of the ten commandments and the giving of the unconditional Gospel of Grace, as witnessed through the tabernacle which God instructed Moses to have built, was at the time the children of Israel came to Mount Sinai.

In the third month, when the children of Israel were gone forth out of the land of Egypt, the same day came they into the wilderness of Sinai. For they were departed from Rephidim, and

> *were come to the desert of Sinai, and had pitched*
> *in the wilderness; and there Israel camped*
> *before the mount.* (Exodus 19:1,2)

We see in Exodus 19 that the conditional ten commandments were not imposed upon the children of Israel, until they were first proposed to them by God, through Moses. First we see that Moses was instructed to remind them of the everlasting Covenant of Abraham, by which He had brought them up out of the land of Egypt.

> *And Moses went up unto God, and the LORD*
> *called unto him out of the mountain, saying,*
> *Thus shalt thou say to the house of Jacob, and*
> *tell the children of Israel;*
> *Ye have seen what I did unto the Egyptians, and*
> *how I bare you on eagles' wings, and brought*
> *you unto myself.* (Exodus 19:3,4)

When God swore by Himself and gave the unconditional Covenant of Grace to Abraham, He did not ask Abraham to sware or make an oath in response, as He does here with the ten commandments, or the Covenant God made to all believers through Abraham, would have not been given through God's Grace. Here on Mount Sinai He asks the children to sware an oath and return to Him with their response.

> *And Moses came and called for the elders of the*
> *people, and laid before their faces all these*
> *words which the LORD commanded him.*
> *And all the people answered together, and said,*
> *All that the LORD hath spoken we will do. And*
> *Moses returned the words of the people unto the*
> *LORD.* (Exodus 19:7,8)

The conditional ten commandments did not in any way do away with the benefits to believers of the unconditional Abrahamic Covenant, nor is the suggestion made here that the ten commandments would or could justify or make anyone righteous. The ten commandments were not imposed for the benefit of those who live by faith, but they were added because of the transgressions of unbelieving Israel, who did not believe and accept the original Covenant God graciously gave to all believers through His Covenant He swore by Himself, to Abraham. Had the children of Israel believed in the Grace of God made known to them through His unconditional Covenant which He swore to all believers through Abraham, there would have been no need for the conditional Covenant of the law, to be made through Moses. The same is true today; if believers live in God's Grace given them as being the singular seed of Abraham, then the entire law of all of God's commandments has been gracefully fulfilled in Christ.

> *And this I say, that the Covenant, that was confirmed before of God in Christ, the law, which was four hundred and thirty years after, cannot disannul, that it should make the promise of none effect.*
>
> *For if the inheritance be of the law, it is no more of promise: but God gave it to Abraham by promise.*
>
> *Wherefore then serveth the law? It was added because of transgressions, till the seed should come to whom the promise was made; and it was ordained by angels in the hand of a mediator.*
>
> *Now a mediator is not a mediator of one, but God is one.*
>
> *Is the law then against the promises of God? God forbid: for if there had been a law given which could have given life, verily righteousness should have been by the law.*
>
> *But the scripture hath concluded all under sin, that the promise by faith of Jesus Christ might be given to them that believe.*

(Galatians 3:17-22)

When God spoke the ten commandments upon Mount Sinai, it was a terrible and fearful sight, in direct contrast to the law of Grace, which was revealed to Abraham 430 years earlier. The Covenant God swore to all believers through Abraham, promised to bring faithful believers to Mount Zion, the Heavenly City of the living God, in the promised land. Mount Sinai and Mount Zion are separated by miles of desert, as is the Covenant of Grace and the Covenant of the law.

Prior to the Lord speaking to the children of Israel from Mount Sinai which was covered by a thick cloud and the smoke and fire of the wrathful judgement of the Lord. God was not revealing Himself as a merciful approachable God, such as the children had experienced through His many acts of compassion in the past, He was revealing Himself as an unapproachable God to the guilt filled unbelieving children of Israel.

> *And Moses brought forth the people out of the camp to meet with God; and they stood at the nether part of the mount.*
> *And mount Sinai was altogether on a smoke, because the LORD descended upon it in fire: and the smoke thereof ascended as the smoke of a furnace, and the whole mount quaked greatly.*
> (Exodus 19:17,18)

Here again, we see the ascending smoke of the furnace of condemnation, as God spoke the ten commandments. We saw this same symbol, as witnessed by Abraham, after the destruction of Sodom and Gomorrah. There was no burning lamp here at Mount Sinai, which is representative of God's Grace, as at the time when the Lord swore His Covenant to Abraham. This incident did not speak of the dividing asunder of the soul and the Spirit, through belief in the Word of God, as did the Covenant made to believers through Abraham. This smoking furnace, spoke of the condemnation of the flesh, through the law, to unbelievers. This terrible sight was a warning, an exhortation to the children of Israel, to remember the Covenant He made to them through Abraham, the Covenant through which they were brought up out of the land of Egypt. This same principle is still true today. The ten commandments are not a guide upon which moral principles are to be established, they are a reminder that all believers are freed from the curse of the law through faith in the blood of Christ, the New Covenant, the fulfilment of the Covenant of Promise He gave to all believers as the seed of Abraham.

> *And God spake all these words, saying,*
> *I am the LORD thy God, which have brought*
> *thee out of the land of Egypt, out of the house of*
> *bondage.* (Exodus 20:1,2)

Thank God, believers need never again return to this mountain of wrath and smoke, after having come to see that it is God's intent to bring believers to the Heavenly Mountain of the redeemed, Mount Zion and the Heavenly City of Jerusalem, through faith in the sprinkling of the perfecting blood of Jesus Christ.

> *For ye are not come unto the mount that might*
> *be touched, and that burned with fire, nor unto*
> *blackness, and darkness, and tempest,*
> *And the sound of a trumpet, and the voice of*
> *words; which voice they that heard intreated that*
> *the word should not be spoken to them any more:*
> *(For they could not endure that which was*
> *commanded, And if so much as a beast touch the*
> *mountain, it shall be stoned, or thrust through*
> *with a dart:*
> *And so terrible was the sight, that Moses said, I*
> *exceedingly fear and quake:)*
> *But ye are come unto mount Sion, and unto the*
> *city of the living God, the heavenly Jerusalem,*
> *and to an innumerable company of angels,*

> *To the general assembly and church of the*
> *firstborn, which are written in heaven, and to*
> *God the Judge of all, and to the spirits of just*
> *men made perfect,*
> *And to Jesus the mediator of the new Covenant,*
> *and to the blood of sprinkling, that speaketh*
> *better things than that of Abel.*
> (Hebrews 12:18-24)

The purpose of the ten commandments then is to generate fear in the hearts of those who would attempt to touch the blackness of Mount Sinai, the mountain of the law of sin and death, while at the same time remind believers to steadily look toward the mountain of the living God, Mount Zion.

> *And all the people saw the thunderings, and the*
> *lightnings, and the noise of the trumpet, and the*
> *mountain smoking: and when the people saw it,*
> *they removed, and stood afar off.*
> *And they said unto Moses, Speak thou with us,*
> *and we will hear: but let not God speak with us,*
> *lest we die.*
> *And Moses said unto the people, Fear not: for*
> *God is come to prove you, and that his fear may*
> *be before your faces, that ye sin not.*
> (Exodus 20:18-20)

Although God mentions His mercy in the giving of the ten commandments, it is reserved for those who love Him and keep His commandments, the only way possible... which is: through faith in the blood of Christ. There is no provision for redemption through faith in Christ's blood mentioned in the ten commandments themselves. However, God emphasis the importance of blood sacrifices, separate from the law, when He, immediately after speaking the ten commandments, instructs Moses to offer up blood sacrifices, to confirm his own faith in redemptive blood.

An altar of earth thou shalt make unto me, and
shalt sacrifice thereon thy burnt offerings, and
thy peace offerings, thy sheep, and thine oxen: in
all places where I record my name I will come
unto thee, and I will bless thee.
(Exodus 20:24,25)

The purpose of the ten commandments, is clearly stated in the Scriptures below; the law was not given for believers whom God has already justified through faith in the blood of Christ, that is, those whom God has already declared to be righteous. The law was made to bring the unbeliever to the awareness of his Spiritual depravity, and the need for the unredeemed man to awaken to the gift of God's righteousness, the only way in which it is possible to fulfill the demands of the law.

Now the end of the commandment is charity out
of a pure heart, and of a good conscience, and of
faith unfeigned:
From which some having swerved have turned
aside unto vain jangling;
Desiring to be teachers of the law;
understanding neither what they say, nor
whereof they affirm.
But we know that the law is good, if a man use it
lawfully;
Knowing this, that the law is not made for a
righteous man, but for the lawless and
disobedient, for the ungodly and for sinners, for
unholy and profane, for murderers of fathers and
murderers of mothers, for manslayers,
(1 Timothy 1:5-9)

Exodus 21 begins the laws of social behaviour, which like the ten commandments, can only be kept as believers are led by the Spirit of Christ. The keeping of these laws are designed to be an outward visible manifestation of an inward Spiritual conviction and motivation. That is, if we believers are led of the Spirit of Grace, we will not desire to fulfill the lusts of the carnal flesh. If we trust the indwelling Spirit of Christ, then He leads us in the paths of righteousness through His Word.

Because these laws are only fulfilled through faith in the Gospel of Grace, for this reason we will go directly to the building of the tabernacle in the wilderness, in an attempt to show how, it too was a physical representation of the Gospel of Grace. The tabernacle of Moses in the wilderness was a meticulously perfect replica of God's Heavenly Tabernacle.

> *Now of the things which we have spoken this is the sum: We have such an high priest, who is set on the right hand of the throne of the Majesty in the heavens;*
>
> *A minister of the sanctuary, and of the true tabernacle, which the Lord pitched, and not man.*
>
> *For every high priest is ordained to offer gifts and sacrifices: wherefore it is of necessity that this man have somewhat also to offer.*
>
> *For if he were on earth, he should not be a priest, seeing that there are priests that offer gifts according to the law:*
>
> *Who serve unto the example and shadow of heavenly things, as Moses was admonished of God when he was about to make the tabernacle: for, See, saith he, that thou make all things according to the pattern shewed to thee in the mount.* (Hebrews 8:1-5)

The blood sacrifices of animals could never take away sin, but they were to be offered to continually remind people that the future manifestation of the perfect sacrifice of our High Priest, Jesus Christ, would do just that, once for all. The singular purpose of the Tabernacle of Witness in the wilderness was to witness to all who would believe, of redemption through the faithfulness of the blood of the High Priestly ministry of Christ, and of the gift of the Glory of God bestowed upon all who accept the fullness of His righteous Kingdom. The book of Hebrews speaks of the purpose of the earthly tabernacle.

Which was a figure for the time then present, in which were offered both gifts and sacrifices, that could not make him that did the service perfect, as pertaining to the conscience;

Which stood only in meats and drinks, and divers washings, and carnal ordinances, imposed on them until the time of reformation.

But Christ being come an high priest of good things to come, by a greater and more perfect tabernacle, not made with hands, that is to say, not of this building; (Hebrews 9:9-11)

The Tabernacle in the Wilderness, and all subsequent tabernacles were a figure for the time then present, of the Heavenly Tabernacle. Although these earthly tabernacles were made by the hands of men, the Holy Spirit literally dwelt in the Mosaic tabernacle. It was this dwelling of God's presence and glory which spoke of the Gospel of Jesus Christ. God's presence in the tabernacle of Moses was a guide to the children of Israel, throughout their wilderness journey, not the ten commandments.

Then a cloud covered the tent of the congregation, and the glory of the LORD filled the tabernacle.

And Moses was not able to enter into the tent of the congregation, because the cloud abode thereon, and the glory of the LORD filled the tabernacle.

And when the cloud was taken up from over the tabernacle, the children of Israel went onward in all their journeys:

But if the cloud were not taken up, then they journeyed not till the day that it was taken up.

For the cloud of the LORD was upon the tabernacle by day, and fire was on it by night, in the sight of all the house of Israel, throughout all their journeys. (Exodus 40:34-38)

Although the priests were ordained to enter through the opened first veil to daily service the tabernacle, as the Lord commanded, only the High Priest was allowed to go beyond the closed second veil, and that on the annual day of atonement. The second veil of the tabernacle, the access to the Throne Room of Grace, was rent from top to bottom only after Christ offered up the perfect sacrifice of His spotless blood. Even today, access into the Holy of Holies, is only granted to those who have faith in the sprinkled blood of the High Priestly ministry of Christ, to continually present believers in His perfection and righteousness, to the Father.

Now when these things were thus ordained, the priests went always into the first tabernacle, accomplishing the service of God.

But into the second went the high priest alone once every year, not without blood, which he offered for himself, and for the errors of the people:

The Holy Ghost thus signifying, that the way into the holiest of all was not yet made manifest, while as the first tabernacle was yet standing: (Hebrews 9:6-8)

Jesus Christ came to do away with the visible tabernacle made of hands, when He offered up the promised perfect sacrifice of His own blood. Ever since, believers have now become the mystical earthly tabernacle of His Spirit, not made with hands, but of the will of God.

Know ye not that ye are the temple of God, and that the Spirit of God dwelleth in you?

If any man defile the temple of God, him shall God destroy; for the temple of God is holy, which temple ye are. (1 Corinthians 3:16,17)

And again:

For we know that if our earthly house of this tabernacle were dissolved, we have a building of God, an house not made with hands, eternal in the heavens.

For in this we groan, earnestly desiring to be clothed upon with our house which is from heaven:

If so be that being clothed we shall not be found naked.

For we that are in this tabernacle do groan, being burdened: not for that we would be unclothed, but clothed upon, that mortality might be swallowed up of life. (2 Corinthians 5:1-4)

Prior to Moses' ascent onto Mount Sinai, to receive the tables of stone and instructions regarding the building of the Tabernacle of the Witness of the Gospel, he was first instructed of the Lord to build an altar and offer a blood sacrifice, through which he confirmed to God his faith in the blood of the promised redeemer. Moses also appointed representatives of each of the twelve tribes of Israel to offer sacrifices to the Lord. Moses then, taking on the role of high priest, sprinkles with the blood of those sacrifices, first the Altar, then the Book of the Covenant and lastly all the people.

And Moses came and told the people all the words of the LORD, and all the judgments: and all the people answered with one voice, and said, All the words which the LORD hath said will we do.

And Moses wrote all the words of the LORD, and rose up early in the morning, and builded an

*altar under the hill, and twelve pillars,
according to the twelve tribes of Israel.*

*And he sent young men of the children of Israel,
which offered burnt offerings, and sacrificed
peace offerings of oxen unto the LORD.*

*And Moses took half of the blood, and put it in
basons; and half of the blood he sprinkled on the
altar.*

*And he took the book of the Covenant, and read
in the audience of the people: and they said, All
that the LORD hath said will we do, and be
obedient.*

<u>*And Moses took the blood, and sprinkled it on
the people, and said, Behold the blood of the
Covenant, which the LORD hath made with you
concerning all these words.*</u> (Exodus 24:3-8)

Moses read to all the people from the Book of the Covenant which God made to all believers through Abraham, before ascending Mount Sinai. The word "Covenant" here, as in most instances in the Old Testament where the word occurs, is a translation of the Hebrew word "beriyth" and refers to the passing between two pieces of flesh, as was the unconditional Covenant which God gave to Abram, when the Lord confirmed His Covenant with him in the passing between two pieces of flesh by a smoking furnace and a burning lamp. The ten commandments themselves speak nothing of redeeming blood nor of a blood Covenant.

So the Book of the Covenant from which Moses read to the people of Israel must have included reference to the Abrahamic Covenant. The Covenant God made to us through Abraham as recorded below.

*And he brought him forth abroad, and said, Look
now toward heaven, and tell the stars, if thou be
able to number them: and he said unto him,
So shall thy seed be.*

And he believed in the LORD; and he counted it to him for righteousness.

And he said unto him, I am the LORD that brought thee out of Ur of the Chaldees, to give thee this land to inherit it.

And he said, Lord GOD, whereby shall I know that I shall inherit it?

And he said unto him, Take me an heifer of three years old, and a she goat of three years old, and a ram of three years old, and a turtledove, and a young pigeon.

And he took unto him all these, and divided them in the midst, and laid each piece one against another: but the birds divided he not.

And when the fowls came down upon the carcases, Abram drove them away.

And when the sun was going down, a deep sleep fell upon Abram; and, lo, an horror of great darkness fell upon him.

And he said unto Abram, Know of a surety that thy seed shall be a stranger in a land that is not theirs, and shall serve them; and they shall afflict them four hundred years;

And also that nation, whom they shall serve, will I judge: and afterward shall they come out with great substance.

And thou shalt go to thy fathers in peace; thou shalt be buried in a good old age.

But in the fourth generation they shall come hither again: for the iniquity of the Amorites is not yet full.

<u>And it came to pass, that, when the sun went down, and it was dark, behold a smoking furnace, and a burning lamp that passed</u>

between those pieces.
In the same day the LORD made a Covenant
with Abram, saying, Unto thy seed have I given
this land, from the river of Egypt unto the great
river, the river Euphrates: (Genesis 15:5-18)

The Book of Hebrews confirms how this incident spoke of the blood of Jesus Christ as being the only power that is able to cleanse, purge and put into remission the sin nature of unregenerate man.

Whereupon neither the first testament was
dedicated without blood.
For when Moses had spoken every precept to all
the people according to the law, he took the
blood of calves and of goats, with water, and
scarlet wool, and hyssop, and sprinkled both the
book, and all the people,
Saying, This is the blood of the testament which
God hath enjoined unto you.
Moreover he sprinkled with blood both the
tabernacle, and all the vessels of the ministry.
And almost all things are by the law purged with
blood; and without shedding of blood is no
remission.
It was therefore necessary that the patterns of
things in the heavens should be purified with
these; but the heavenly things themselves with
better sacrifices than these. (Hebrews 9:18-23)

The first Testament or Covenant which is referred to here does not refer to the Sinaic revelation of the law of the ten commandments, but of the first and everlasting Covenant God made with Abram. If the ten commandments of themselves, were able to purge or make a sinner righteous, then Jesus Christ died in vain. Not only that, but the first and everlasting Abrahamic Covenant was given by God 430 years before the ten commandments, and the ten commandments in no way abrogated or overturned God's original oath and Covenant of blessing to Abraham and all his seed. The law is a curse, Christ died to deliver believers from that curse.

> *Christ hath redeemed us from the curse of the law, being made a curse for us: for it is written, Cursed is every one that hangeth on a tree:*
> *That the blessing of Abraham might come on the Gentiles through Jesus Christ; that we might receive the promise of the Spirit through faith.*
> *Brethren, I speak after the manner of men; Though it be but a man's Covenant, yet if it be confirmed, no man disannulleth, or addeth thereto.*
> *Now to Abraham and his seed were the promises made. He saith not, And to seeds, as of many; but as of one, And to thy seed, which is Christ.*
> *And this I say, that the Covenant, that was confirmed before of God in Christ, the law, which was four hundred and thirty years after, cannot disannul, that it should make the promise of none effect.*
> *For if the inheritance be of the law, it is no more of promise: but God gave it to Abraham by promise.*
> *Wherefore then serveth the law? It was added because of transgressions, till the seed should come to whom the promise was made; and it was ordained by angels in the hand of a mediator.*
> *Now a mediator is not a mediator of one, but God is one.*
> *Is the law then against the promises of God? God forbid: for if there had been a law given which could have given life, verily righteousness should have been by the law.* (Galatians 3:14-21)

All believers are the seed of Abraham, not the seed of Moses. However, Moses' ministry testified of the blood of Jesus Christ to come, this was confirmed by Jesus, the CHRIST, Himself to some of His disciples on the Emmaus road, after his resurrection.

> *Then he said unto them, O fools, and slow of heart to believe all that the prophets have spoken:*
> *Ought not Christ to have suffered these things, and to enter into his glory?*
> *And beginning at Moses and all the prophets, he expounded unto them in all the scriptures the things concerning himself.* (Luke 24:25-27)

It is heart breaking that Moses is often considered, by believers and unbelievers alike, to be the giver of the ten commandments; God alone spoke the ten commandments, Moses was only the faithful intercessor between God and the children of Israel. God imposed the ten commandments as a warning to the unbelieving children of Israel that they were continually, through unbelief, transgressing the Covenant God gave to all believer through Abraham. The ten commandments which are often referred to as the Mosaic Covenant, in reality, had nothing to do with Moses as a person, but they were meant to convict the rebelling nation of Israel on Mount Sinai, and all unbelievers since, of the guilt of unbelief. When we refer to the Mosaic Covenant we should remember that it includes all of the five books of the Torah. The law of Moses, as it is most often referred to in the Bible, includes the entire Torah not simply the ten commandments alone. If we consider the Sinaic Covenant as being only the giving of the ten commandments, then we ignore the Gospel of Grace as testified to in the rest of the Torah, and the Gospel revealed to us in the building of the tabernacle. The life of Moses was a continual witness of the Gospel of Grace, and a constant reminder to the children of Israel that redemption came only through faith in the God who identified Himself to Moses as the God of Abraham, Isaac and Jacob.

> *And when the LORD saw that he turned aside to*
> *see, God called unto him out of the midst of the*
> *bush, and said, Moses, Moses. And he said, Here*
> *am I.*
> *And he said, Draw not nigh hither: put off thy*
> *shoes from off thy feet, for the place whereon*
> *thou standest is holy ground.*
> *Moreover he said, I am the God of thy father, the*
> *God of Abraham, the God of Isaac, and the God*
> *of Jacob. And Moses hid his face; for he was*
> *afraid to look upon God.* (Exodus 3:4-6)

Prior to his death Moses, as a legacy, taught the children of Israel and all future generations of believers, the song of the glorious perfecting power of the doctrine of Jesus Christ, the believers Rock.

> *Give ear, O ye heavens, and I will speak; and*
> *hear, O earth, the words of my mouth.*
> *My doctrine shall drop as the rain, my speech*
> *shall distil as the dew, as the small rain upon the*
> *tender herb, and as the showers upon the grass:*
> *Because I will publish the name of the LORD:*
> *ascribe ye greatness unto our God.*
> *He is the Rock, his work is perfect: for all his*
> *ways are judgment: a God of truth and without*
> *iniquity, just and right is he.*
> (Deuteronomy 32:1-4)

The Tabernacle

Moses was asked of God to ascend the Mountain of Sinai to receive the promised tables of stone, which would have the ten commandments written upon them by the finger of God, and also to receive instructions as to the building of the tabernacle. The purpose of the tabernacle was to be a constant proclamation of the Gospel of Christ and a continual reminder of the promise of His perfect blood sacrifice to come. The Shekinah Glory of God came to fill the finished tabernacle and covered the tent of the congregation. When the cloud of the Glory of the Lord moved, it was to guide the children on their way by day, the Glory of the Lord above the tabernacle also became a fire to guide them by night.

> *And he reared up the court round about the tabernacle and the altar, and set up the hanging of the court gate. So Moses finished the work.*
>
> *Then a cloud covered the tent of the congregation, and the glory of the LORD filled the tabernacle.*
>
> *And Moses was not able to enter into the tent of the congregation, because the cloud abode thereon, and the glory of the LORD filled the tabernacle.*
>
> *And when the cloud was taken up from over the tabernacle, the children of Israel went onward in all their journeys:*
>
> *But if the cloud were not taken up, then they journeyed not till the day that it was taken up.*
>
> *For the cloud of the LORD was upon the tabernacle by day, and fire was on it by night, in the sight of all the house of Israel, throughout all their journeys.* (Exodus 40:33-38)

And now:

> *And the LORD said unto Moses, Come up to me into the mount, and be there: and I will give thee tables of stone, and a law, and commandments which I have written; that thou mayest teach them.* (Exodus 24:12)

If the ten commandments were able to be kept without the knowledge of God's Covenanted Grace, then God would not have revealed to Moses the means whereby that Grace would be bestowed, that is, if the ten commandments were meant to be a means of salvation, then God would not have made provision to reveal His Sovereign Grace through the figure of the tabernacle. The tabernacle of Moses was representative of the Gospel of Grace to the children of Israel, and became the dwelling place of God's Glory. When Jesus came and established a new and better mystical Tabernacle, not made with hands, he revealed and made manifest forever the Covenant of Grace, and confirmed the everlasting promise of his perfecting High Priestly intercession.

> *Now of the things which we have spoken this is the sum: We have such an high priest, who is set on the right hand of the throne of the Majesty in the heavens;*
>
> *A minister of the sanctuary, and of the true tabernacle, which the Lord pitched, and not man.* (Hebrews 8:1,2)

The tables of stone upon which the ten commandments were written, were not meant to stand on their own as a Gospel, but were included within the overall message of the tabernacle. The two tablets of stone upon which the ten commandments were written, were to be placed within the Ark of the Covenant, under the Mercy Seat, upon which the promised blood of Christ was to be sprinkled, as Moses reminds everyone in the Scriptures below.

> *At that time the LORD said unto me, Hew thee two tables of stone like unto the first, and come up unto me into the mount, and make thee an ark of wood.*
>
> *And I will write on the tables the words that were in the first tables which thou brakest, <u>and thou shalt put them in the ark.</u>*
>
> *And I made an ark of shittim wood, and hewed two tables of stone like unto the first, and went up into the mount, having the two tables in mine*

hand.

And he wrote on the tables, according to the first writing, the ten commandments, which the LORD spake unto you in the mount out of the midst of the fire in the day of the assembly: and the LORD gave them unto me.

And I turned myself and came down from the mount, and put the tables in the ark which I had made; and there they be, as the LORD commanded me. (Deuteronomy 10:1-5)

More on this later in the section on the Contents of the Ark.

In the Book of the Exodus there are six chapters devoted to the instructions of the building of the tabernacle, and almost as a footnote in chapter thirty one, and in one verse only, there is mention made of the importance of the tables of stone. The Gospel of Grace, included in the Tabernacle of Witness, was of much more import than simply the ten commandments alone.

And he gave unto Moses, when he had made an end of communing with him upon mount Sinai, two tables of testimony, tables of stone, written with the finger of God. (Exodus 31:18)

Materials of the Tabernacle

All the materials for the building of the tabernacle were to be provided for by donations of those of the children who, had a willing heart. Only the proceeds which come from a willing heart, are acceptable for the continual building of the Temple of God, which indwells all believers.

And the LORD spake unto Moses, saying,

Speak unto the children of Israel, that they bring me an offering: of every man that giveth it willingly with his heart ye shall take my offering.

And:

> *And let them make me a sanctuary; that I may dwell among them.*
>
> *According to all that I shew thee, after the pattern of the tabernacle, and the pattern of all the instruments thereof, even so shall ye make it.*

(Exodus 25:1,2; 8,9)

When Moses spoke to the children of Israel concerning the materials required for the building of the tabernacle, they began to bring offerings to those skilled workmen who were to fashion the tabernacle. The givers responded with such enthusiasm that they had to finally be restrained, for the "stuff" they brought was more than enough.

> *And they spake unto Moses, saying, The people bring much more than enough for the service of the work, which the LORD commanded to make.*
>
> *And Moses gave commandment, and they caused it to be proclaimed throughout the camp, saying, Let neither man nor woman make any more work for the offering of the sanctuary. So the people were restrained from bringing.*
>
> *For the stuff they had was sufficient for all the work to make it, and too much.* (Exodus 36:5-7)

Obviously this is a reminder that if the Gospel of Grace is preached to believers, without the condemnation of the law, which is meant for unbelievers only, then willing hearts are stirred and there is no lack of material or Spiritual substance with which to promote the Lord's Gospel. This is also representative as to how much God treasures the willing heart which He gracefully places within all believers. For it is of the substance of our willing hearts, and with the Spirit of Christ that is within the heart of each believer, of which the Tabernacle in Heaven is built.

> *And when he was demanded of the Pharisees, when the kingdom of God should come, he*

answered them and said, The kingdom of God
cometh not with observation:
Neither shall they say, Lo here! or, lo there! for,
behold, the kingdom of God is within you.
(Luke 17:20,21)

And again:

Know ye not that ye are the temple of God, and
that the Spirit of God dwelleth in you?
If any man defile the temple of God, him shall
God destroy; for the temple of God is holy, <u>which</u>
<u>temple ye are</u>...
Do ye not know that they which minister about
holy things live of the things of the temple? <u>and</u>
<u>they which wait at the altar are partakers with</u>
<u>the altar?</u>
Even so hath the Lord ordained that they which
preach the gospel should live of the gospel.
(1 Corinthians 3:16,17; 9:13,14)

God appointed Bezalel, a man whose name means "in the shadow of God" to be the general superintendent of the tabernacle's construction. His job was to design and teach others, in the many skilful arts required for it's construction. Be assured that the Spirit of God will also teach and strengthen all those who diligently seek and respond to His will, the fine art of building a Tabernacle of Praise to God, within the heart of the believer. A Tabernacle fit for Him to dwell in.

The Ark of the Covenant

And let them make me a sanctuary; that I may
dwell among them.
According to all that I shew thee, after the
pattern of the tabernacle, and the pattern of all
the instruments thereof, even so shall ye make it.
And they shall make an ark of shittim wood: two

cubits and a half shall be the length thereof, and a cubit and a half the breadth thereof, and a cubit and a half the height thereof.

And thou shalt overlay it with pure gold, within and without shalt thou overlay it, and shalt make upon it a crown of gold round about.

(Exodus 25:8-11)

The Ark of the Covenant, which God instructed Moses to include in the tabernacle, was to be placed within the inner sanctuary of the tabernacle. This was to be the dwelling place of God's glorious presence on earth, within the closed second veil. Only the High Priests were allowed to go beyond the second veil annually, and then only to sprinkle blood on the Mercy Seat, in order that the Covenant of Promise God made to the children of Israel through Abraham, might be renewed for another year.

Although the term "Ark of the Covenant" does not appear in the Book of the Exodus, this term appears eighty five times in other Books of the Old Testament, beginning in Numbers 10:33. The "Ark of the Covenant" refers to the same Ark which the Lord instructed Moses to build, and is referred to as the "Ark of the Testimony" in the Book of Exodus, eighty two times. The term "Ark of the Covenant" appears only one time in the New Testament, in the fourth verse of chapter nine of the Book of Hebrews.

If the Ark which the Lord instructed Moses to have built, was referred to as the Ark of the Covenant, then we should determine which Covenant the Ark represented. As mentioned previously the word "Covenant" in the Old Testament is a translation of the Hebrew word, "beriyth", and refers to the Covenant confirmed by God to Abram, by the passing between two pieces of divided flesh. God's imposing of the ten commandments upon the unbelieving children of Israel, who subsequently were to die in the Sinai desert, makes no mention of the "passing between two pieces of flesh". It is obvious that the passing between two pieces of flesh refers to the Covenant God Graciously gave to all believers through Father Abraham.

> *And it came to pass, that, when the sun went down, and it was dark, behold a smoking furnace, and a burning lamp that passed between those pieces.*
>
> *In the same day the LORD made a Covenant with Abram, saying, Unto thy seed have I given this land, from the river of Egypt unto the great river, the river Euphrates:* (Genesis 15:17,18)

King David knew of the secret place of the Lord's Covenant, the Covenant given by God when He passed between two pieces of divided flesh. David knew the Father as being a God of Covenanted mercy and truth, a God who pardoned all sin and iniquity that he might enter boldly, even to abide, into the secret place of the Most High.

> *All the paths of the LORD are mercy and truth unto such as keep his Covenant and his testimonies.*
>
> *For thy name's sake, O LORD, pardon mine iniquity; for it is great.*
>
> *What man is he that feareth the LORD? him shall he teach in the way that he shall choose.*
>
> *His soul shall dwell at ease; and his seed shall inherit the earth.*
>
> *The secret of the LORD is with them that fear him; and he will shew them his Covenant.* (Psalms 25:10-14)

And again:

> *He that dwelleth in the secret place of the most High shall abide under the shadow of the Almighty. I will say of the LORD, He is my refuge and my fortress: my God; in him will I trust.* (Psalms 91:1,2)

God instructed Moses to have the Ark constructed of acacia

wood, another name for shittim wood, and then to incase it in pure gold. The spiritual message here of acacia wood covered with gold is beautiful, and speaks of the abundance of God's Grace and merciful intent toward the blood redeemed. Acacia wood is one of the most knotted and twisted types of wood that exists, which in the making of the Ark of the Covenant, speaks of the knotted twisted heart of unredeemed natural man, the old man of the flesh with which all humans, since the fall of Adam and Eve, were born. The covering of gold of the entire Ark, speaks of the covering of the righteous judgements of the Lord which covers all who have received the blessing of the promise, the promise which God made to all believers through Abraham.

The fear of the LORD is clean, enduring for ever: the judgments of the LORD are true and righteous altogether.

More to be desired are they than gold, yea, than much fine gold: sweeter also than honey and the honeycomb.

Moreover by them is thy servant warned: and in keeping of them there is great reward.

(Psalms 19:9-11)

The promise made to Abraham was that of the blessing of the Spirit of Christ to come, which was conferred upon all believers, ever since the time Melchizedek blessed him with bread and wine, 430 years before the ten commandments. The blessing of Abraham, the secret of the Covenant of Grace God made to all believers through him, comes only to those believers who accept that Melchizedek was a pre-incarnate appearing of the Lord Jesus Christ. Christ went to the Cross for this reason, to redeem believers from the curse of the law, that we might be blessed with faithful Abraham.

Christ hath redeemed us from the curse of the law, being made a curse for us: for it is written, Cursed is every one that hangeth on a tree:

That the blessing of Abraham might come on the Gentiles through Jesus Christ; that we might receive the promise of the Spirit through faith.

Brethren, I speak after the manner of men; Though it be but a man's Covenant, yet if it be confirmed, no man disannulleth, or addeth thereto.

Now to Abraham and his seed were the promises made. He saith not, And to seeds, as of many; but as of one, And to thy seed, which is Christ.

And this I say, that the Covenant, that was confirmed before of God in Christ, the law, which was four hundred and thirty years after, cannot disannul, that it should make the promise of none effect. (Galatians 3:13-17)

God's merciful righteous judgements imputes that power which, through faith in the blood of Christ, covers believers with God's very nature, pure gold. The Lord only sees His righteousness children as covered with His gold, and does not consider nor condemn believers for their old twisted and gnarled nature.

Job knew of the righteous judgements of the Lord which comes from the Mercy Seat. This perfect man was renewed in the Spirit, through trials and the judgements of righteousness which purges the dross of unbelief, and in the end, brought him forth as refined pure gold.

Oh that I knew where I might find him! that I might come even to his seat!

I would order my cause before him, and fill my mouth with arguments.

I would know the words which he would answer me, and understand what he would say unto me.

Will he plead against me with his great power? No; but he would put strength in me.

There the righteous might dispute with him; so should I be delivered for ever from my judge.

Behold, I go forward, but he is not there; and backward, but I cannot perceive him:

On the left hand, where he doth work, but I cannot behold him: he hideth himself on the right hand, that I cannot see him:

But he knoweth the way that I take: <u>when he hath tried me, I shall come forth as gold.</u>

(Job 23:3-10)

The four golden rings on the corners of the Ark were designed to hold two gold covered staves which were never to be removed.

And thou shalt cast four rings of gold for it, and put them in the four corners thereof; and two rings shall be in the one side of it, and two rings in the other side of it.

And thou shalt make staves of shittim wood, and overlay them with gold.

And thou shalt put the staves into the rings by the sides of the ark, that the ark may be borne with them.

The staves shall be in the rings of the ark: they shall not be taken from it. (Exodus 25:12-15)

There are probably many reasons why these gold covered staves were never to be taken out of their rings. The one most evident is that the golden Ark of the Covenant was not to be moved except upon the shoulders of the Kohathites. The message of God's Covenanted blessing and Grace, is to be conveyed only by those who shoulder the responsibility to present the Gospel to believers as the pure righteous judgements of gold, not of condemnation or the curse of the law.

The Contents of the Ark

> *And thou shalt put into the ark the testimony which I shall give thee.* (Exodus 25:16)

And:

> *And after the second veil, the tabernacle which is called the Holiest of all;*
> *Which had the golden censer, and the ark of the Covenant overlaid round about with gold, wherein was the golden pot that had manna, and Aaron's rod that budded, and the tables of the Covenant;*
> *And over it the cherubims of glory shadowing the mercyseat; of which we cannot now speak particularly.* (Hebrews 9:3,4)

As we see in the verse above, Moses is instructed to put the tables of stone into the Ark, under the Mercy Seat, as a Testimony to future generations, that all memory of the curse of the law is covered by God's mercy. In spite of this revelation of God's Sovereign Grace and mercy the children of Israel chose not to believe, as a consequence they perished in the wilderness, because of the hardness of their hearts.

> *But with whom was he grieved forty years? was it not with them that had sinned, whose carcases fell in the wilderness?*
> *And to whom sware he that they should not enter into his rest, but to them that believed not?*
> *So we see that they could not enter in because of unbelief.* (Hebrews 3:17-19)

The second item to be sealed under the Mercy Seat was Aaron's rod that budded, it was to be kept in the Ark of the Covenant as a token against the rebellious children of Israel. They failed to recognize that Aaron, their High Priest, although a temporary High Priest because he was only a mortal human and subject to death, represented the High Priestly ministry of Jesus Christ, a High Priest forever in the order of Mechizedek.

And Moses spoke unto the children of Israel, and every one of their princes gave him a rod apiece, for each prince one, according to their fathers' houses, even twelve rods: and the rod of Aaron was among their rods.

And Moses laid up the rods before the LORD in the tabernacle of witness.

And it came to pass, that on the morrow Moses went into the tabernacle of witness; and, behold, the rod of Aaron for the house of Levi was budded, and brought forth buds, and bloomed blossoms, and yielded almonds.

And Moses brought out all the rods from before the LORD unto all the children of Israel: and they looked, and took every man his rod.

And the LORD said unto Moses, Bring Aaron's rod again before the testimony, to be kept for a token against the rebels; and thou shalt quite take away their murmurings from me, that they die not.

And Moses did so: as the LORD commanded him, so did he. (Numbers 17:6-11)

Aaron's rod typified the rod of God's Divine power given to the fallible Aaronic priesthood of the flesh, which was only a human symbol of the promise of the perfect priesthood of the Christ to come. God made an oath and promised, witnessed by the appearing of Melchisedec to Abraham, that Jesus the Christ alone was ordained to be the eternal perfect High Priest. All fallible earthly priests were ordained of men, and their position was not confirmed of God through an oath.

And inasmuch as not without an oath he was made priest:

(For those priests were made without an oath;
but this with an oath by him that said unto him,
The Lord sware and will not repent, Thou art a
priest for ever after the order of Melchisedec:)
By so much was Jesus made a surety of a better
testament.

And they truly were many priests, because they
were not suffered to continue by reason of death:
But this man, because he continueth ever, hath
an unchangeable priesthood.

Wherefore he is able also to save them to the
uttermost that come unto God by him, seeing he
ever liveth to make intercession for them.

(Hebrews 7:20-25)

So the inclusion of Aaron's rod that budded within the Ark, was a Testimony of the promise of an eternal High Priest to come, not born of sinful man, but made like unto the Son of God. This promise was fulfilled, when entrance into the Holy of Holies was made available to God's Covenanted people, through faith in the blood and body of Jesus the Christ. With the perfect sacrifice of the eternal High Priest, at Christ's death and resurrection, the veil of the temple was rent from top to bottom, that believers from then on, might enter boldly into the Holiest of all.

The third Testimony which is covered by the Mercy Seat, is the golden pot that contained a sample of manna, the bread of the life of the flesh, which God supplied to the children in the wilderness for forty years.

And the house of Israel called the name thereof
Manna: and it was like coriander seed, white;
and the taste of it was like wafers made with
honey.

And Moses said, This is the thing which the
LORD commandeth, Fill an omer of it to be kept
for your generations; that they may see the bread

*wherewith I have fed you in the wilderness, when
I brought you forth from the land of Egypt.*
*And Moses said unto Aaron, Take a pot, and put
an omer full of manna therein, and lay it up
before the LORD, to be kept for your
generations.*
*As the LORD commanded Moses, so Aaron laid
it up before the Testimony, to be kept.*
(Exodus 16:31-34)

The manna in the wilderness was a physical representation of a Spiritual truth; that man must feast on the Word of God in order to survive Spiritually.

*And he humbled thee, and suffered thee to
hunger, and fed thee with manna, which thou
knewest not, neither did thy fathers know; that he
might make thee know that man doth not live by
bread only, but by every word that proceedeth
out of the mouth of the LORD doth man live.*
(Deuteronomy 8:3)

The provision of daily manna ceased when the children entered the promised land, they then fed on the provisions of the promised land. The need for a physical reminder of the promise of the Word of God to come, was nullified and made void when Jesus Christ, the living Word, appeared to mankind in the flesh.

*Our fathers did eat manna in the desert; as it is
written, He gave them bread from heaven to eat.*
*Then Jesus said unto them, Verily, verily, I say
unto you, Moses gave you not that bread from
heaven; but my Father giveth you the true bread
from heaven.*
*For the bread of God is he which cometh down
from heaven, and giveth life unto the world.*
*Then said they unto him, Lord, evermore give us
this bread.*

And Jesus said unto them, I am the bread of life:
he that cometh to me shall never hunger; and he
that believeth on me shall never thirst.
But I said unto you, That ye also have seen me,
and believe not. (John 6:31-36)

Faith in the sprinkled blood of the cross of Christ upon the Mercy Seat in Heaven, gives believers access to the source of the bread of life, the bread of life which is continually rained upon us from heaven. At the time of Moses, even as today, there are those who have not become aware that the Mercy Seat is the source of the Word, and it is there that it is impressed upon our hearts by the Holy Spirit. Sadly, there are still those believers who consider the word of the ten commandments as the source of their daily bread, the letter of the law to guide them in their Christian walk. Unfortunately, there are many who believe that the source of Spiritual life comes from trying to keep the cruel letter of the law of the ten commandments. The ten commandments were imposed upon unbelievers, and are meant to condemn the guilty.

This I say then, Walk in the Spirit, and ye shall
not fulfil the lust of the flesh.
For the flesh lusteth against the Spirit, and the
Spirit against the flesh: and these are contrary
the one to the other: so that ye cannot do the
things that ye would.
But if ye be led of the Spirit, ye are not under the
law. (Galatians 5:16-18)

And again:

Now the end of the commandment is charity out
of a pure heart, and of a good conscience, and of
faith unfeigned:
From which some having swerved have turned
aside unto vain jangling;
Desiring to be teachers of the law;
understanding neither what they say, nor

whereof they affirm.

But we know that the law is good, if a man use it lawfully;

<u>*Knowing this, that the law is not made for a righteous man, but for the lawless*</u> *and disobedient, for the ungodly and for sinners, for unholy and profane, for murderers of fathers and murderers of mothers, for manslayers,*

(1 Timothy 1:5-9)

It is interesting to note that there were no doors on the Ark of the Covenant, nor any other means of access. The three articles which God instructed Moses to put under the Mercy Seat, were not meant to be viewed or removed. The Mercy Seat permanently covered the three symbols of the provisions of the flesh. The Mercy Seat speaks of the gift of God's righteous judgements upon all believers, it separates and mercifully puts under it the memory and guilt of the flesh. However the law of the flesh still remains as a curse to those who do not understand that God has put away all memory of the sins of the flesh, through the provisions of His Grace and mercy. This was as true in the Old Testament as it is in the New.

Now this I say, brethren, that flesh and blood cannot inherit the kingdom of God; neither doth corruption inherit incorruption.

Behold, I shew you a mystery; We shall not all sleep, but we shall all be changed,

In a moment, in the twinkling of an eye, at the last trump: for the trumpet shall sound, and the dead shall be raised incorruptible, and we shall be changed.

For this corruptible must put on incorruption, and this mortal must put on immortality.

So when this corruptible shall have put on incorruption, and this mortal shall have put on immortality, then shall be brought to pass the saying that is written, Death is swallowed up in victory.

O death, where is thy sting? O grave, where is thy victory?

The sting of death is sin; and the strength of sin is the law. (1 Corinthians 15:50-56)

The Mercy Seat

And thou shalt make a mercy seat of pure gold: two cubits and a half shall be the length thereof, and a cubit and a half the breadth thereof. (Exodus 25:17)

The High Priest in the Old Testament, entered into the Holy of Holies, behind the closed veil, once a year on the day of atonement. He sprinkled the blood of the slain animal seven times on the Mercy Seat, this made atonement for, but only covered the sins of the children of Israel for another year.

And he shall take of the blood of the bullock, and sprinkle it with his finger upon the mercy seat eastward; and before the mercy seat shall he sprinkle of the blood with his finger seven times. (Leviticus 16:14)

For today's believer, the sprinkling of the blood of our High Priest, Jesus Christ, upon the present Seat of Mercy and Grace in the Heavenly Throne Room, completely, once and for all, has done away with all memory of sin and iniquity. The Throne of Grace is only accessible to those who count the blood of the Covenant, which God made to all believers through Abraham, which Jesus ratified by His own blood, efficacious enough to present them to the Father in His very own Holiness, righteousness and perfection. Therefore, it is crucial that believers see the importance of remembering, that the blood of the Covenant speaks of the Spirit of Grace, not guilt.

> *He that despised Moses' law died without mercy under two or three witnesses:*
>
> *Of how much sorer punishment, suppose ye, shall he be thought worthy, who hath trodden under foot the Son of God, and hath counted the blood of the Covenant, wherewith he was sanctified, an unholy thing, and hath done despite unto the Spirit of grace?*
>
> (Hebrews 10:28,29)

At the pure golden Mercy Seat in the Heavens, within the secret place of the Most High, is given every New Covenant believer the assurance of God's righteous judgement of mercy and grace. Here, at the Mercy Seat within the Holy of Holies, the believer is made conscious of and given the assurance of eternal peace and rest. Here, under the shadow of His wings, is given the confirmation of the fulfilment of God's perfect will through faith in the sprinkled blood of the Christ, our continual High Priest in the order of Melchisedec. Here is the beginning and end of our salvation made manifest. Here the believer awakens to the reality of the fulfilment of God's purpose for redeemed man. Here believers have become conformed, and are being conformed, into God's holiness and perfection. Here believers have been moulded into God's very nature. Here carnal life is not given consideration, nor is the memory of foolish works of the flesh of any consequence.

> *For by one offering he hath perfected for ever them that are sanctified.*
>
> *Whereof the Holy Ghost also is a witness to us: for after that he had said before,*
>
> *This is the Covenant that I will make with them after those days, saith the Lord, I will put my laws into their hearts, and in their minds will I*

write them;
And their sins and iniquities will I remember no
more.
Now where remission of these is, there is no
more offering for sin.
Having therefore, brethren, boldness to enter
into the holiest by the blood of Jesus,
By a new and living way, which he hath
consecrated for us, through the veil, that is to
say, his flesh;
And having an high priest over the house of
God;
Let us draw near with a true heart in full
assurance of faith, having our hearts sprinkled
from an evil conscience, and our bodies washed
with pure water. (Hebrews 10:15-22)

The Meeting Place

And thou shalt make two cherubims of gold, of
beaten work shalt thou make them, in the two
ends of the mercy seat.
And make one cherub on the one end, and the
other cherub on the other end: even of the mercy
seat shall ye make the cherubims on the two ends
thereof.
And the cherubims shall stretch forth their wings
on high, covering the mercy seat with their
wings, and their faces shall look one to another;
toward the mercy seat shall the faces of the
cherubims be.
And thou shalt put the mercy seat above upon the
ark; and in the ark thou shalt put the testimony
that I shall give thee. (Exodus 25:18-21)

The cherubs of Glory majestically cast the shadow of their wings upon the Mercy Seat, here believers are invited to dwell in the continual knowledge of the presence of the Holy Spirit. The awareness of dwelling in the presence of His glory is that joy which is unspeakable.

> *He that dwelleth in the secret place of the most High shall abide under the shadow of the Almighty.*
>
> *I will say of the LORD, He is my refuge and my fortress: my God; in him will I trust.*
>
> *Surely he shall deliver thee from the snare of the fowler, and from the noisome pestilence.*
>
> *He shall cover thee with his feathers, and under his wings shalt thou trust: his truth shall be thy shield and buckler.*
>
> *Thou shalt not be afraid for the terror by night; nor for the arrow that flieth by day;*
> (Psalms 91:1-5)

This is the present dwelling place of the Spirit filled believer, not for those who have any regard for the law of the flesh, but for those only who have full appreciation that the blood of Christ has given us the righteousness of God.

Here at the Mercy Seat, within the Holy of Holies, the believer is able to view God with another perspective, in the new light of His Glory. Seeing the blood of the cross of Christ sprinkled on the Mercy Seat, we remember the blood of the New Covenant in a new light. When we drink of the blood of the New Covenant we remember what the blood of Jesus has done for us, not as a reminder of our own forgotten sin and guilt nature.

> *And there I will meet with thee, and I will commune with thee from above the mercy seat, from between the two cherubims which are upon the ark of the testimony, of all things which I will give thee in commandment unto the children of Israel.* (Exodus 25:22)

The Altar of Incense

God spoke to Moses regarding the Altar of Incense.

> *And thou shalt make an altar to burn incense upon: of shittim wood shalt thou make it.*
>
> *A cubit shall be the length thereof, and a cubit the breadth thereof; foursquare shall it be: and two cubits shall be the height thereof: the horns thereof shall be of the same.*
>
> *And thou shalt overlay it with pure gold, the top thereof, and the sides thereof round about, and the horns thereof; and thou shalt make unto it a crown of gold round about.*
>
> *And two golden rings shalt thou make to it under the crown of it, by the two corners thereof, upon the two sides of it shalt thou make it; and they shall be for places for the staves to bear it withal.*
>
> *And thou shalt make the staves of shittim wood, and overlay them with gold.*
>
> <u>*And thou shalt put it before the vail that is by the ark of the testimony, before the mercy seat that is over the testimony, where I will meet with thee.*</u>
>
> (Exodus 30:1-6)

In the tabernacle of Moses in the wilderness, the Altar of Incense was to be placed before the second veil, that is outside the closed veil which enclosed the Holy of Holies, the secret dwelling place of the Glory of God. It's purpose was unique in that it's function was to offer up a perpetual sweet smelling incense before the Lord. Aaron, the High Priest, was instructed to offer up incense before the Lord twice a day, morning and evening. The morning and evening offerings were to insure that there was a continual sweet odour of incense before the Lord at all times.

And Aaron shall burn thereon sweet incense every morning: when he dresseth the lamps, he shall burn incense upon it.

And when Aaron lighteth the lamps at even, he shall burn incense upon it, a <u>perpetual</u> incense before the LORD throughout your generations.

(Exodus 30:7,8)

The Altar of Incense served an entirely different purpose than did the Brazen Altar. The Brazen or Brass Altar was situated outside the entrance of the tabernacle of the congregation, outside of the first veil. The Brazen Altar was the Altar upon which the sacrificial animals were slain, they typified the offering of the body of Christ. The blood of these sacrifices was the means whereby the Levites daily cleansed and serviced the tabernacle between the first and second veils, they served in the tabernacle of the congregation inside the first veil but not within the second veil.

Now when these things were thus ordained, the priests went always into the first tabernacle, accomplishing the service of God.

But into the second went the high priest alone once every year, not without blood, which he offered for himself, and for the errors of the people:

The Holy Ghost this signifying, that the way into the holiest of all was not yet made manifest, while as the first tabernacle was yet standing.

(Hebrews 9:6-8)

Prior to God sending His only begotten Son, the second veil which covered the Holy of Holies remained intact. Only after the perfect sacrifice of Jesus Christ on the cross was the second veil of the tabernacle rent from top to bottom. This was true of both the earthly tabernacle as well as the Heavenly Tabernacle. The Altar of Incense, in both cases, speaks of the continual intercession to God, of the High Priest(s), on behalf of believers.

But now, the second inner veil of the Heavenly Tabernacle being rent, Jesus Christ continually and joyfully bids believers to enter into the Holy of Holies to dwell with Him, through faith in what His blood has accomplished for us. Jesus Christ has become the believers Altar of Incense, the believers mediator, in the Heavenly Tabernacle.

It is still absolutely necessary for unbelievers to first accept that Christ died on the cross for the sin of mankind, but then, having once believed He suffered on the cross, and now recognize that He is risen, and appearing for believers at the right hand of the Father, Jesus Christ ever since has become our Altar of Incense. Through faith in the blood of Jesus Christ, believers may now continually offer up a sweet smelling incense to the Lord, the sacrifice of praise, having been glorified in Him within the second veil.

> *We have an altar, whereof they have no right to eat which serve the tabernacle.*
> *For the bodies of those beasts, whose blood is brought into the sanctuary by the high priest for sin, are burned without the camp.*
> *Wherefore Jesus also, that he might sanctify the people with his own blood, suffered without the gate.*
> *Let us go forth therefore unto him without the camp, bearing his reproach.*
> *For here have we no continuing city, but we seek one to come.*
> *By him therefore let us offer the sacrifice of praise to God continually, that is, the fruit of our lips giving thanks to his name.*
> (Hebrews 13:10-15)

There are infinitely many more aspects and truths of the Gospel of Grace, and the power of the blood of Christ, which the

Holy Spirit would reveal to us, through the knowledge of the mystery of the Gospel spoken of in the tabernacle of Moses. We have only looked into a very small fraction of the truths of the Gospel of Grace and rest, which the tabernacle spoke to the children of Israel, as recorded below.

> *Let us therefore fear, lest, a promise being left us*
> *of entering into his rest, any of you should seem*
> *to come short of it.*
> *For unto us was the gospel preached, as well as*
> *unto them: but the word preached did not profit*
> *them, not being mixed with faith in them that*
> *heard it.* (Hebrews 4:1,2)

Here we have only scratched the surface of the revelation of truth that is spoken of by the knowledge of the purpose of the Ark of the Covenant and of the Altar of Incense within the tabernacle of God's Covenant of Grace in the Old Testament.

The theme of the Book of Exodus, as with the other four Books of the Pentateuch, brings us to focus on what God's continual purpose is for mankind, which is to simply accept all His love for us through faith in the blood Covenant of the promised Christ. The word translated "law" in the Old Testament is generally of the Hebrew word "Torah", and does not generally refer to the ten commandments. To consider the heart of the Pentateuch as the "law" and an extension of the ten commandments is to ignore the Spirit of God's Grace and mercy. Every animal sacrifice ever offered was meant to reflect the promise of the blood of the perfect sacrifice to come, that of the blood of Christ. As we saw in the Book of the Exodus, most of the subject matter speaks of the Gospel of Grace as depicted in the building of the Tabernacle of Witness in the wilderness. To consider the ten commandments imposed upon the children of Israel, at their request, on Mount Sinai, as being the primary Covenant of the Old Testament is to ignore the Covenant given Abraham 430 years earlier. The first generation of the children of

Israel died in the wilderness through lack of faith in God's
Covenant He made to all believers through Abraham, they did not
die in the wilderness because they could not keep an impossible
law given on Mount Sinai. To consider Christianity as having it's
roots and tenancy in the ten commandments is to ignore the fact
that all believers are the seed of Abraham and not the seed of
Moses.

> *Christ hath redeemed us from the curse of the*
> *law, being made a curse for us: for it is written,*
> *Cursed is every one that hangeth on a tree:*
> *That the blessing of Abraham might come on the*
> *Gentiles through Jesus Christ; that we might*
> *receive the promise of the Spirit through faith...*
> *And if ye be Christ's, then are ye Abraham's*
> *seed, and heirs according to the promise.*
> (Galatians 3:13,14;29)

Redemption does not come from Mount Sinai through the
children of bondage born to Hagar, but through the seed of
Abraham and Mount Zion and from Jerusalem, which is the
mother of all believers.

> *For ye are not come unto the mount that might*
> *be touched, and that burned with fire, nor unto*
> *blackness, and darkness, and tempest,*
> *And the sound of a trumpet, and the voice of*
> *words; which voice they that heard intreated that*
> *the word should not be spoken to them any more:*
> *(For they could not endure that which was*
> *commanded, And if so much as a beast touch the*
> *mountain, it shall be stoned, or thrust through*
> *with a dart:*
> *And so terrible was the sight, that Moses said, I*
> *exceedingly fear and quake:)*
> *But ye are come unto mount Sion, and unto the*
> *city of the living God, the heavenly Jerusalem,*
> *and to an innumerable company of angels,*

To the general assembly and church of the firstborn, which are written in heaven, and to God the Judge of all, and to the spirits of just men made perfect,

And to Jesus the mediator of the new Covenant, and to the blood of sprinkling, that speaketh better things than that of Abel.

(Hebrews 12:18-24)

8

PALESTINIAN COVENANT
Conditional Inheritance

The Palestinian Covenant is the second of two conditional Covenants, effectually a reaffirmation of the ten commandments, imposed by God, again through Moses, to unbelieving Israel. Moses told the second generation of the children of Israel of the conditions of this Covenant prior to their being allowed to cross the river Jordan, and enter into the promised land of Canaan.

The first generation had died in the wilderness, because they had not demonstrated faith in the Covenant God had made to them and all believers, through Abraham. The Covenant of Promise that God Sovereignly made to all believers through Abraham is also the Covenant of Grace through which children of Israel were brought out of the furnace of Egypt. God reminded them of this at the time He was imposing the ten commandments upon them.

> *And God spoke all these words, saying,*
> *I am the LORD thy God, which have brought*
> *thee out of the land of Egypt, out of the house of*
> *bondage.* (Exodus 20:1,2)

God underlined their own inability to attain righteousness by imposing the ten commandments upon them, at their request, at

Mount Sinai. The ten commandments were added because they failed to see that they had transgressed the law of God's unconditional love, the Covenant of the Promise of Christ to come, through the Abrahamic Covenant. Because they had not turned to seek the Lord's gift of righteousness through faith in the Covenant God had made to them and all believers through Abraham, 430 years earlier, God swore that the first generation who were led out of Egypt, would not enter into the promised land and His rest, but would die in the wilderness.

Harden not your hearts, as in the provocation, in the day of temptation in the wilderness:

When your fathers tempted me, proved me, and saw my works forty years.

Wherefore I was grieved with that generation, and said, They do alway err in their heart; and they have not known my ways.

So I sware in my wrath, They shall not enter into my rest.)

Take heed, brethren, lest there be in any of you an evil heart of unbelief, in departing from the living God.

But exhort one another daily, while it is called To day; lest any of you be hardened through the deceitfulness of sin.

For we are made partakers of Christ, if we hold the beginning of our confidence stedfast unto the end;

While it is said, To day if ye will hear his voice, harden not your hearts, as in the provocation.

For some, when they had heard, did provoke: howbeit not all that came out of Egypt by Moses. But with whom was he grieved forty years? was it not with them that had sinned, whose carcases fell in the wilderness?

> *And to whom sware he that they should not enter*
> *into his rest, but to them that believed not?*
> *So we see that they could not enter in because of*
> *unbelief.* (Hebrews 3:8-19)

The impossible condition that they keep the Covenant of Sinai, which the previous generation could not keep, were the same restrictive conditions by which the second generation were allowed to enter the land of Canaan.

> *These are the words of the Covenant, which the*
> *LORD commanded Moses to make with the*
> *children of Israel in the land of Moab, beside the*
> *Covenant which he made with them in Horeb.*
>
> *And Moses called unto all Israel, and said unto*
> *them, Ye have seen all that the LORD did before*
> *your eyes in the land of Egypt unto Pharaoh, and*
> *unto all his servants, and unto all his land;*
>
> *The great temptations which thine eyes have*
> *seen, the signs, and those great miracles:*
>
> *Yet the LORD hath not given you an heart to*
> *perceive, and eyes to see, and ears to hear, unto*
> *this day.*
>
> *And I have led you forty years in the wilderness:*
> *your clothes are not waxen old upon you, and thy*
> *shoe is not waxen old upon thy foot.*
>
> *Ye have not eaten bread, neither have ye drunk*
> *wine or strong drink: that ye might know that I*
> *am the LORD your God.* (Deuteronomy 29:1-6)

Here in Moab, while preparing to entering the promised land, the second generation were being given another opportunity to awaken to the gift of righteousness, which may only be realized through faith in the unconditional Covenant of Promise which God gave to all believers through Abraham. Once again God was promising the children of Israel, through Moses, that their continued inheritance in the promised land was conditional upon their awakening to His Covenant which He had made with their fathers, Abraham, Isaac and Jacob. The entire chapter of Psalms 106 is another testimony as to the Lord's goodness toward Israel, but a sad commentary as well, as to the hardness of their unbelieving hearts.

> *Many times did he deliver them; but they provoked him with their counsel, and were brought low for their iniquity.*
> *Nevertheless he regarded their affliction, when he heard their cry:*
> *And he remembered for them his Covenant, and repented according to the multitude of his mercies.*
> *He made them also to be pitied of all those that carried them captives.*
> *Save us, O LORD our God, and gather us from among the heathen, to give thanks unto thy holy name, and to triumph in thy praise.*
> *Blessed be the Lord God of Israel from everlasting to everlasting: and let all the people say, Amen. Praise ye the LORD.*
> (Psalms 106:43-48)

Wherefore they were given a choice as to which Covenant they would respond to, even as are believers today.

> *See, I have set before thee this day life and good, and death and evil;*
> *In that I command thee this day to love the LORD thy God, to walk in his ways, and to keep his commandments and his statutes and his judgments, that thou mayest live and multiply: and the LORD thy God shall bless thee in the land whither thou goest to possess it.*
> *But if thine heart turn away, so that thou wilt not hear, but shalt be drawn away, and worship*

other gods, and serve them;
I denounce unto you this day, that ye shall surely
perish, and that ye shall not prolong your days
upon the land, whither thou passest over Jordan
to go to possess it.
I call heaven and earth to record this day against
you, that I have set before you life and death,
blessing and cursing: therefore choose life, that
both thou and thy seed may live:
That thou mayest love the LORD thy God, and
that thou mayest obey his voice, and that thou
mayest cleave unto him: for he is thy life, and the
length of thy days: <u>that thou mayest dwell in the</u>
<u>land which the LORD sware unto thy fathers, to</u>
<u>Abraham, to Isaac, and to Jacob, to give them.</u>
(Deuteronomy 30:15-20)

Israel as a nation, as of this day, still have not learned that righteousness is a gift of grace, they still give more credence to the ten commandments imposed upon them at Sinai, than they do to the Covenant God gave to all believers through Abraham.

Who is a God like unto thee, that pardoneth
iniquity, and passeth by the transgression of the
remnant of his heritage? he retaineth not his
anger for ever, because he delighteth in mercy.
He will turn again, he will have compassion
upon us; he will subdue our iniquities; and thou
wilt cast all their sins into the depths of the sea.
<u>Thou wilt perform the truth to Jacob, and the</u>
<u>mercy to Abraham, which thou hast sworn unto</u>
<u>our fathers from the days of old.</u>
(Micah 7:18-20)

As promised by God, Israel as a nation, the sons of Jacob through Abraham, will find no righteousness or peace until they come to understand that the conditional Mosaic law is an offence and sets aside the Covenant He gave to all believers through Abraham. It is only a softened heart, a new heart of the Spirit, through which the believers eyes are opened to perceive the difference between the conditional Covenant of Mount Sinai and the unconditional Covenant God made to all His seed through Abraham. May the author remind the reader:

> *And Moses called unto all Israel, and said unto*
> *them, Ye have seen all that the LORD did before*
> *your eyes in the land of Egypt unto Pharaoh, and*
> *unto all his servants, and unto all his land;*
> *The great temptations which thine eyes have*
> *seen, the signs, and those great miracles:*
> *Yet the LORD hath not given you an heart to*
> *perceive, and eyes to see, and ears to hear, unto*
> *this day.* (Deuteronomy 29:2-4)

God's gracious giving of the conditional Palestinian Covenant to the children of Israel was yet another opportunity for all succeeding generations to awaken to the unconditional Covenant and oath God made to them through the Father of faith, the patriarch Abraham.

Here, prior to the crossing of the river Jordan, in warning an unbelieving generation before they entered the promised land, God once again demonstrates His mercy and unconditional love toward an unworthy people, as He did throughout their wilderness journey. Moses warned them that failing to recognize God's goodness would result in the loss of God's blessing, and eventually bring about God's wrath, and consequently their dispersion from the land of promise.

> *Keep therefore the words of this Covenant, and*
> *do them, that ye may prosper in all that ye do....*
> *Even all nations shall say, Wherefore hath the*
> *LORD done thus unto this land? what [meaneth]*
> *the heat of this great anger?*
> *Then men shall say, Because they have forsaken*

> *the Covenant of the LORD God of their fathers,*
> *which he made with them when he brought them*
> *forth out of the land of Egypt:*
> *For they went and served other gods, and*
> *worshipped them, god whom they knew not, and*
> *[whom] he had not given unto them:*
> *And the anger of the LORD was kindled against*
> *this land, to bring upon it all the curses that are*
> *written in this book:*
> *And the LORD rooted them out of their land in*
> *anger, and in wrath, and in great indignation,*
> *and cast them into another land, as [it is] this*
> *day.* (Deuteronomy 29:9,24-28)

The Scriptures above show how the Lord desired to show mercy and grace to the children of Israel, if only they would believe and receive the unconditional Covenant He made to all believers through Abraham, and come to understand that His love and imputed righteousness, were then, as they are now, all sufficient and complete. Verse 28 foretells of the banishment into Babylon of the children of Israel. Because of their hardened hearts they attempted to keep the conditions of the Palestinian Covenant, rather than accept the Covenant of Grace made available to them through the Covenant God made to them through Abraham. This is still the problem with the nation Israel today, they continue to look to Moses as their leader, rather than accept the fact that they are not only the physical seed of Abraham, but the Spiritual seed of Abraham as well.

If we relate this crossing of the River Jordan to the tabernacle which God instructed Moses to build as a pattern of the Heavenly Tabernacle, the River Jordan represents the second veil which inclosed the Holy of Holies. The children of Israel were given perfect positional inheritance of the promised land, but did not enter in and experience this promised perfection because of unbelief. Instead they were only allowed to enter through the first veil of the tabernacle, and tried to fulfill the law of Moses and the Palestinian Covenant through their own will power.

Believers today have the same choice to make as did the Israelites. We have a choice as to which Covenant governs our lives, the conditional Covenant of the letter of the law imposed upon unbelievers at Mount Sinai, and here again at the Jordan, or the unconditional Covenant of Grace given to all believers through Abraham. We have a choice as to which veil or which body of water we travel beyond, the first veil of the Red Sea or the second veil of the River Jordan. Do we chose to stay beyond the Red Sea in the wilderness of the law, or do we chose to enter the promised land beyond the river Jordan, through faith in the blood of Christ and the promise given us through Abraham?

It was the Lord's desire that the children would awaken and soften their hearts to simply receive the gift of His righteousness, their birthright, the blessing of the seed of Abraham. Had they put their faith in the blood of the promised Christ, God would have blessed them and would have allowed them to stay in the Holy Land, and Mount Zion. However their hardened hearts did not allow them to move beyond their desert experience at Mount Sinai, and consequently they were cursed as promised, and dispersed from the promised land.

Again, believers today have this same choice to make; at which Mount shall we worship, Mount Sinai and the law, or Mount Zion the City of Grace. Essau's "fornication" was the fact that he sold his birthright to Jacob, as the seed of Abraham he sold the blessing of Abraham which was his rightful inheritance, and so put himself back under the law of Sinai.

> *Looking diligently lest any man fail of the grace*
> *of God; lest any root of bitterness springing up*
> *trouble you, and thereby many be defiled;*
> *Lest there be any fornicator, or profane person,*
> *as Esau, who for one morsel of meat sold his*
> *birthright.*

For ye know how that afterward, when he would have inherited the blessing, he was rejected: for he found no place of repentance, though he sought it carefully with tears.

For ye are not come unto the mount that might be touched, and that burned with fire, nor unto blackness, and darkness, and tempest,

And the sound of a trumpet, and the voice of words; which voice they that heard intreated that the word should not be spoken to them any more:

(For they could not endure that which was commanded, And if so much as a beast touch the mountain, it shall be stoned, or thrust through with a dart:

And so terrible was the sight, that Moses said, I exceedingly fear and quake:)

But ye are come unto mount Sion, and unto the city of the living God, the heavenly Jerusalem, and to an innumerable company of angels,

To the general assembly and church of the firstborn, which are written in heaven, and to God the Judge of all, and to the spirits of just men made perfect,

And to Jesus the mediator of the new Covenant, and to the blood of sprinkling, that speaketh better things than that of Abel.

See that ye refuse not him that speaketh. For if they escaped not who refused him that spake on earth, much more shall not we escape, if we turn away from him that speaketh from heaven:
(Hebrews 12:15-25)

As God promised, because they did not relent, and went about trying to establish their own righteousness through the impossible conditions of the Palestinian Covenant, which confirmed the cruel letter of the law, some of them were exiled into Assyria beginning in 734 B. C., others into Babylon beginning in 608 B. C., their temple in Jerusalem finally being destroyed in 586 B. C. The remnant, the poorest of the poor whom God always preserves for Himself, were not exiled and were allowed to remain at Jerusalem, the City of the living God. The exiles, or captivities of the children of Israel are another study and recorded in many Old Testament Scriptures.

The prophet Jeremiah warned of the desolation and exile that would come to Jerusalem and Israel as a consequence of God's chosen people not accepting the Covenant of the God of Abraham, Isaac and Jacob. May this author remind the reader, that in the Scriptures below, the word "Covenant" in each case, is a translation of the Hebrew word "beriyth", which means "cutting" or "walking between two pieces of divided flesh". The first 45 chapters of the Book of Jeremiah are an example of the unheeded warning of God's wrath to come upon Judah and Jerusalem because of the unbelief of that Covenant, for example:

> *The word that came to Jeremiah from the LORD, saying, Hear ye the words of this <u>Covenant, and speak unto the men of Judah, and to the inhabitants of Jerusalem; And say thou unto them, Thus saith the LORD God of Israel; Cursed [be] the man that obeyeth not the words of this Covenant,*
> *Which I commanded your fathers in the day [that] I brought them forth out of the land of Egypt, from the iron furnace, saying, Obey*
> *my voice, and do them, according to all which I command you: so shall ye be my people, and I will be your God:*
> *That I may perform the oath which I have sworn unto your fathers, to give them a land flowing with milk and honey, as [it is] this day. Then</u>*

answered I, and said, So be it, O LORD.

Then the LORD said unto me, Proclaim all these words in the cities of Judah, and in the streets of Jerusalem, saying, Hear ye the words of this Covenant, and do them.

For I earnestly protested unto your fathers in the day [that] I brought them up out of the land of Egypt, [even] unto this day, rising early and protesting, saying, Obey my voice.

Yet they obeyed not, nor inclined their ear, but walked every one in the imagination of their evil heart: therefore I will bring upon them all the words of this Covenant, which I commanded [them] to do; but they did [them] not.

And the LORD said unto me, A conspiracy is found among the men of Judah, and among the inhabitants of Jerusalem.

They are turned back to the iniquities of their forefathers, which refused to hear my words; and they went after other gods to serve them: the house of Israel and the house of Judah have broken my Covenant which I made with their fathers.

Therefore thus saith the LORD, Behold, I will bring evil upon them, which they shall not be able to escape; and though they shall cry unto me, I will not hearken unto them.

Then shall the cities of Judah and inhabitants of Jerusalem go, and cry unto the gods unto whom they offer incense: but they shall not save them at all in the time of their trouble.

(Jeremiah 11:1-12)

However the same weeping prophet had made it very clear to the Children of Israel that God had not abandoned them altogether, He sent them into exile for seventy years to humble them in the hope that they might once again remember Him as a God of unconditional love. God once again, showing mercy and giving His chosen nation another chance to accept the land of milk and honey, as a gift of the Covenant He had made to them earlier through Abraham. As it was then, so it is now, the biggest stumbling block of Christianity is our inability, through lack of faith in the blood of Christ, to accept the goodness of God.

For example:

> *For I know the thoughts that I think toward you, saith the LORD, thoughts of peace, and not of evil, to give you an expected end.*
> *Then shall ye call upon me, and ye shall go and pray unto me, and I will hearken unto you.*
> *And ye shall seek me, and find [me], when ye shall search for me with all your heart.*
> *And I will be found of you, saith the LORD: and I will turn away your captivity, and I will gather you from all the nations, and from all the places whither I have driven you, saith the LORD; and I will bring you again into the place whence I caused you to be carried away captive.*

(Jeremiah 29:11-14)

After having been taken into captivity by Nebuchadnezzar, the king of Babylon, and having been allowed to return to the land of Palestine, the children of Israel still had not awakened to the gift of their righteousness through the Abrahamic Covenant. As a result, they were once again destined to be driven from the land of their inheritance, 70 years after Jesus' ministry on earth. Again Jeremiah prophesied of their second dispersion. He also prophesied of the Lord once again regathering His chosen nation to the promised land, and of the promise of the ushering in of the Davidic Covenant, which will be realized at the time the Lord, once again, returns to earth as King of Jerusalem, to administer righteousness to his people, the seed of Abraham through (Israel) Jacob.

> *Woe be unto the pastors that destroy and scatter the sheep of my pasture! saith the LORD.*
>
> *Therefore thus saith the LORD God of Israel against the pastors that feed my people; Ye have scattered my flock, and driven them away, and have not visited them: behold, I will visit upon you the evil of your doings, saith the LORD.*
>
> *And I will gather the remnant of my flock out of all countries whither I have driven them, and will bring them again to their folds; and they shall be fruitful and increase.*
>
> *And I will set up shepherds over them which shall feed them: and they shall fear no more, nor be dismayed, neither shall they be lacking, saith the LORD.*
>
> *Behold, the days come, saith the LORD, that I will raise unto David a righteous Branch, and a King shall reign and prosper, and shall execute judgment and justice in the earth.*
>
> *In his days Judah shall be saved, and Israel shall dwell safely: and this [is] his name whereby he shall be called, THE LORD OUR RIGHTEOUSNESS.*
>
> *Therefore, behold, the days come, saith the LORD, that they shall no more say, The LORD liveth, which brought up the children of Israel out of the land of Egypt;*
>
> *But, The LORD liveth, which brought up and which led the seed of the house of Israel out of the north country, and from all countries whither I had driven them; and they shall dwell in their own land.* (Jeremiah 23:1-8)

Chapter 30 of Deuteronomy also foretells of the day when Israel will finally possess the promised land, under the unconditional Covenant which He made to all believers through Abraham.

> *That then the LORD thy God will turn thy captivity, and have compassion upon thee, and will return and gather thee from all the nations, whither the LORD thy God hath scattered thee.*
>
> *If [any] of thine be driven out unto the outmost [parts] of heaven, from thence will the LORD thy God gather thee, and from thence will he fetch thee:*
>
> *And the LORD thy God will bring thee into the land which thy fathers possessed, and thou shalt possess it; and he will do thee good, and multiply thee above thy fathers.*
>
> *And the LORD thy God will circumcise thine heart, and the heart of thy seed, to love the LORD thy God with all thine heart, and with all thy soul, that thou mayest live.*

(Deuteronomy 30:3-6)

The Israelites were allowed to rebuild their temple and return to Jerusalem, in various stages, prior to the dedication of the temple in 516 B. C. After that time, they were once again given yet another chance to awaken to righteousness, and were allowed to return to the promised land until 70 years after the Lord appeared to them, at His first Advent, as Jesus the Christ.

Because, as a nation they did not believe the earthly ministry of God's only begotten Son, their temple was destroyed by the Romans in 70 A. D. They were once again driven from the land of their inheritance. This time they were dispersed into all the nations of the earth.

Yet not without hope were they driven from the land and scattered among the nations, for the Lord has promised that at the end time He will restore Israel to its previous glory, and He will circumcise their hearts, that they may dwell in the land which He swore unto their fathers, to Abraham, to Isaac, and to Jacob, to give them.

> *And it shall come to pass, when all these things are come upon thee, the blessing and the curse, which I have set before thee, and thou shalt call [them] to mind among all the nations, whither the LORD thy God hath driven thee,*
>
> *And shalt return unto the LORD thy God, and shalt obey his voice according to all that I command thee this day, thou and thy children, with all thine heart, and with all thy soul;*
>
> *That then the LORD thy God will turn thy captivity, and have compassion upon thee, and will return and gather thee from all the nations, whither the LORD thy God hath scattered thee.*
>
> *If [any] of thine be driven out unto the outmost [parts] of heaven, from thence will the LORD thy God gather thee, and from thence will he fetch thee: And the LORD thy God will bring thee into the land which thy fathers possessed, and thou shalt possess it; and he will do thee good, and multiply thee above thy fathers.*
>
> *And the LORD thy God will circumcise thine heart, and the heart of thy seed, to love the LORD thy God with all thine heart, and with all thy soul, that thou mayest live.*
>
> (Deuteronomy 30:1-6)

Also:

> *I call heaven and earth to record this day against you, [that] I have set before you life and death, blessing and cursing: therefore choose life, that both thou and thy seed may live:*
>
> *That thou mayest love the LORD thy God, [and]*

that thou mayest obey his voice, and that thou
mayest cleave unto him: for he [is] thy life, and
the length of thy days: that thou mayest dwell in
the land which the LORD sware unto thy fathers,
to <u>Abraham, to Isaac, and to Jacob, to give them.</u>
(Deuteronomy 30:19,20)

The desolation of the land of Palestine prior to 1948, and the conflict in the middle east surrounding Jerusalem and Israel since, are sadly, proof of the consequences of the ineptitude of man to respond to God's will through dependancy upon his own strength. Surely if mankind might learn anything from history, it is that man cannot govern himself.

The children of Israel as a nation, since 1948, when the state of Israel was first formed, have begun to be regathered into their own land by the Lord, just as He has promised. However, as of this date, the nation of Israel as a whole, still remain under the conditional Palestinian Covenant. Because their eyes have not been opened, they live before the closed veil of unbelief, still not having accepted the unconditional Abrahamic Covenant. Israel as a nation, until this day, have not awakened to the unconditional gift of God's righteousness and perfection which is theirs through belief in the Covenant God made to them through Abraham. They may recognize Abraham as their father after the flesh, and as a result they still attempt to adhere to the cruel laws of the many commandments, and as a consequence are blinded to the impossibility of attaining righteousness through the law. Neither have their eyes been opened to the unconditional God given gift of righteousness, their inheritance, through the Covenant God made to them through Abraham. The law of the commandments, is only abolished to those who accept the blessing of the Covenant God made to all believers through Abraham, only then is the second veil opened.

Seeing then that we have such hope, we use great
plainness of speech:

*And not as Moses, which put a vail over his face,
that the children of Israel could not stedfastly
look to the end of that which is abolished:*

*But their minds were blinded: for until this day
remaineth the same vail untaken away in the
reading of the old testament; which vail is done
away in Christ.*

*But even unto this day, when Moses is read, the
vail is upon their heart.*

*Nevertheless when it shall turn to the Lord, the
vail shall be taken away.* (2 Corinthians 3:12-16)

This is as true today as it was in the time of Jesus. During His time on earth the Pharisees were in a constant conflict with Jesus because they did not comprehend the freedom and truth to be found in the Abrahamic Covenant. As He told the Pharisees in John 8, where Jesus equates the seed of Abraham with all the children of God, not just the Jew.

*And ye shall know the truth, and the truth shall
make you free.*

*They answered him, We be Abraham's seed, and
were never in bondage to any man: how sayest
thou, Ye shall be made free?*

*Jesus answered them, Verily, verily, I say unto you,
Whosoever committeth sin is the servant of sin.*

*And the servant abideth not in the house for
ever: [but] the Son abideth ever.*

*If the Son therefore shall make you free, ye shall
be free indeed.*

*I know that ye are Abraham's seed; but ye seek to
kill me, because my word hath no place in you.*

*I speak that which I have seen with my Father:
and ye do that which ye have seen with your
father.*

They answered and said unto him, Abraham is

our father. Jesus saith unto them, If ye were
Abraham's children, ye would do the works of
Abraham.
But now ye seek to kill me, a man that hath told
you the truth, which I have heard of God: this did
not Abraham.
Ye do the deeds of your father. Then said they to
him, We be not born of fornication; we have one
Father, [even] God.
Jesus said unto them, If God were your Father,
ye would love me: for I proceeded forth and
came from God; neither came I of myself, but he
sent me. (John 8:32-42)

The provisions of the Palestinian Covenant, through legalistic conviction, once again demonstrate God's love, Sovereign Grace and mercy. He appeals once again to the children of Israel, and all succeeding generations, up to and including our present generation, to simply receive the righteousness of God, through faith in the blood of His Covenant.

We see demonstrated, in the history of the people of Israel, the confusion that results, when a people or a nation, forget and depart from God's first Covenant of the Promise, the Abrahamic Covenant.

The present day denominational Christian church, being an unbelieving heir of Abraham's promise, has also placed herself under the curse of the conditional Covenants, and the curse of the sin of the law. They too wait without the Holy place with a veil upon their hearts.

In a moment, in the twinkling of an eye, at the
last trump: for the trumpet shall sound, and the
dead shall be raised incorruptible, and we shall
be changed.
For this corruptible must put on incorruption,
and this mortal must put on immortality.

So when this corruptible shall have put on incorruption, and this mortal shall have put on immortality, then shall be brought to pass the saying that is written, Death is swallowed up in victory.

death, where is thy sting? O grave, where is thy victory?

<u>*The sting of death is sin; and the strength of sin is the law.*</u>

But thanks be to God, which giveth us the victory through our Lord Jesus Christ.

(1 Corinthians 15:52-57)

The present day visible church has become blindly dependant upon self motivation and moral platitudes in vain attempts to obtain self righteousness through the law of Moses.

The present day visible denominational church does not realize that the veil, and the curse of the law of the ten commandments given through Moses, is only done away with through the recognition of the Covenant given all believers through Abraham, the Covenant through which believers are given the promise of the Spirit of the Lord.

For as many as are of the works of the law are under the curse: for it is written, Cursed is every one that continueth not in all things which are written in the book of the law to do them.

But that no man is justified by the law in the sight of God, it is evident: for, The just shall live by faith.

And the law is not of faith: but, The man that doeth them shall live in them.

<u>*Christ hath redeemed us from the curse of the law,*</u> *being made a curse for us: for it is written, Cursed is every one that hangeth on a tree:*

<u>*That the blessing of Abraham might come on the*</u>

Gentiles through Jesus Christ; that we might receive the promise of the Spirit through faith.
(Galatians 3:10-14)

It is through the body of Jesus Christ, and faith in His blood of the New Covenant, which rent open the veil, giving believers entrance into the Heavenly Throne of Grace, which fulfilled the Covenant of Promise made to Abraham and his seed. Abraham's faith in the promise of the redeeming blood of Christ to come, has been referred to throughout Scriptures, in both the Old and New Testaments.

By faith Abraham, when he was tried, offered up Isaac: and he that had received the promises offered up his only begotten son,
Of whom it was said, That in Isaac shall thy seed be called:
Accounting that God was able to raise him up, even from the dead; from whence also he received him in a figure.
(Hebrews 11:17-19)

God confirmed to Abram the promise of the redeeming blood of Christ to come, when Mechizedek met him and ministered to him with bread and wine, the promise of the body and blood of Christ.

And Melchizedek king of Salem brought forth bread and wine: and he was the priest of the most high God.
And he blessed him, and said, Blessed be Abram of the most high God, possessor of heaven and earth:
And blessed be the most high God, which hath delivered thine enemies into thy hand. And he gave him tithes of all. (Genesis 14:18-20)

The promise to the seed of Abraham, that of the redeeming blood of Christ to come, was confirmed to Abraham by God, in

Christ, 430 years before the curse of the law was imposed upon the children of Israel.

> *Now to Abraham and his seed were the promises made. He saith not, And to seeds, as of many; but as of one, And to thy seed, which is Christ.*
>
> *And this I say, that the Covenant, that was confirmed before of God in Christ, the law, which was four hundred and thirty years after, cannot disannul, that it should make the promise of none effect.*
>
> *For if the inheritance be of the law, it is no more of promise: but God gave it to Abraham by promise.* (Galatians 3:16-18)

Faith in the redeeming blood of Jesus Christ, our mediator of the New Covenant, our High Priest in the order of Melchizedek, at the right hand of the Father, fully meets all the demands of the law. The law of the ten commandments was never meant to justify, or provide for further ongoing salvation to believers, but the ten commandments were imposed to convict the unrighteous of their impossible, lost condition.

> *Now the end of the commandment is charity out of a pure heart, and of a good conscience, and of faith unfeigned:*
>
> *From which some having swerved have turned aside unto vain jangling;*
>
> *Desiring to be teachers of the law; understanding neither what they say, nor whereof they affirm.*
>
> *But we know that the law is good, if a man use it lawfully;*
>
> *Knowing this, that the law is not made for a righteous man, but for the lawless and disobedient, for the ungodly and for sinners, for*

unholy and profane, for murderers of fathers and
murderers of mothers, for manslayers,
(1 Timothy 1:5-9)

The choice is still for the individual; Choose you this day whom you will serve, the blessing of the seed of Father Abraham, or the cursing of the law.

And it shall come to pass, when all these things
are come upon thee, the blessing and the curse,
which I have set before thee, and thou shalt call
them to mind among all the nations, whither the
LORD thy God hath driven thee,

And shalt return unto the LORD thy God, and
shalt obey his voice according to all that I
command thee this day, thou and thy children,
with all thine heart, and with all thy soul;

That then the LORD thy God will turn thy
captivity, and have compassion upon thee, and
will return and gather thee from all the nations,
whither the LORD thy God hath scattered thee.

If any of thine be driven out unto the outmost
parts of heaven, from thence will the LORD thy
God gather thee, and from thence will he fetch
thee:

And the LORD thy God will bring thee into the
land which thy fathers possessed, and thou shalt
possess it; and he will do thee good, and multiply
thee above thy fathers.

And the LORD thy God will circumcise thine
heart, and the heart of thy seed, to love the
LORD thy God with all thine heart, and with all
thy soul, that thou mayest live.

And the LORD thy God will put all these curses
upon thine enemies, and on them that hate thee,
which persecuted thee.

And thou shalt return and obey the voice of the LORD, and do all his commandments which I command thee this day.

And the LORD thy God will make thee plenteous in every work of thine hand, in the fruit of thy body, and in the fruit of thy cattle, and in the fruit of thy land, for good: for the LORD will again rejoice over thee for good, as he rejoiced over thy fathers:

If thou shalt hearken unto the voice of the LORD thy God, to keep his commandments and his statutes which are written in this book of the law, and if thou turn unto the LORD thy God with all thine heart, and with all thy soul.

For this commandment which I command thee this day, it is not hidden from thee, neither is it far off.

It is not in heaven, that thou shouldest say, Who shall go up for us to heaven, and bring it unto us, that we may hear it, and do it?

Neither is it beyond the sea, that thou shouldest say, Who shall go over the sea for us, and bring it unto us, that we may hear it, and do it?

But the word is very nigh unto thee, in thy mouth, and in thy heart, that thou mayest do it.

See, I have set before thee this day life and good, and death and evil;In that I command thee this day to love the LORD thy God, to walk in his ways, and to keep his commandments and his statutes and his judgments, that thou mayest live and multiply: and the LORD thy God shall bless thee in the land whither thou goest to possess it.

But if thine heart turn away, so that thou wilt not hear, but shalt be drawn away,

and worship other gods, and serve them;

I denounce unto you this day, that ye shall surely perish, and that ye shall not prolong your days upon the land, whither thou passest over Jordan to go to possess it.

I call heaven and earth to record this day against you, that I have set before you life and death, blessing and cursing: therefore choose life, that both thou and thy seed may live:

That thou mayest love the LORD thy God, and that thou mayest obey his voice, and that thou mayest cleave unto him: for he is thy life, and the length of thy days: <u>that thou mayest dwell in the land which the LORD sware unto thy fathers, to Abraham, to Isaac, and to Jacob, to give them.</u>

(Deuteronomy 30:1-20)

9

DAVIDIC COVENANT
Testimony

The Davidic Covenant is the unconditional promise God made to the nation Israel that they would one day, once again, when the Messiah's returns as the King of Kings and Lord of Lords, be ruled by David's seed, Jesus Christ at His second coming.

> *And the ten horns which thou sawest are ten kings, which have received no kingdom as yet; but receive power as kings one hour with the beast.*
>
> *These have one mind, and shall give their power and strength unto the beast.*
>
> *These shall make war with the Lamb, and the Lamb shall overcome them: for he is Lord of lords, and King of kings: and they that are with him are called, and chosen, and faithful.*
> (Revelation 17:12-14)

The intent of God's heart for His chosen people, in giving the Davidic Covenant to the nation Israel, as with all previous unconditional Covenants, was to awaken mankind to the righteousness that a loving God has made available to all who would simply believe and receive His word. As with all previous Covenants this righteousness is only imputed to the believing individual, through faith in the atoning blood of Jesus Christ. As the prophet Zechariah prophesied, "they will look on me whom they have pierced".

> *And it shall come to pass in that day, that I will seek to destroy all the nations that come against Jerusalem.*
> *And I will pour upon the house of David, and upon the inhabitants of Jerusalem, the spirit of grace and of supplications: and they shall look upon me whom they have pierced, and they shall mourn for him, as one mourneth for his only son, and shall be in bitterness for him, as one that is in bitterness for his firstborn.*
> (Zechariah 12:9,10)

All references made to the word "Covenant" in referring to the Davidic Covenant, is again the interpretation of the Hebrew word "beriyth", which means: "walking between two pieces of divided flesh," as in the first Covenant of Promise which God made to Abraham.

The Davidic Covenant will usher in the one thousand year millennium Kingdom Age.

> *In that day will I raise up the tabernacle of David that is fallen, and close up the breaches thereof; and I will raise up his ruins, and I will build it as in the days of old:*
> *That they may possess the remnant of Edom, and of all the heathen, which are called by my name, saith the LORD that doeth this.*
> *Behold, the days come, saith the LORD, that the plowman shall overtake the reaper, and the treader of grapes him that soweth seed; and the mountains shall drop sweet wine, and all the hills shall melt.*

> *And I will bring again the captivity of my people*
> *of Israel, and they shall build the waste cities,*
> *and inhabit them; and they shall plant vineyards,*
> *and drink the wine thereof; they shall also make*
> *gardens, and eat the fruit of them.*
> *And I will plant them upon their land, and they*
> *shall no more be pulled up out of their land*
> *which I have given them, saith the LORD thy*
> *God.* (Amos 9:11-15)

Second Samuel chapter 7 is another section of Scripture that is often referred to as the revelation of the Davidic Covenant. It is confirmed again in Psalms 89, as we shall see below.

> *For the LORD is our defence; and the Holy One*
> *of Israel is our king.*
> *Then thou spakest in vision to thy holy one, and*
> *saidst, I have laid help upon one that is mighty;*
> *I have exalted one chosen out of the people.*
> *I have found David my servant; with my holy oil*
> *have I anointed him:*
> *With whom my hand shall be established: mine*
> *arm also shall strengthen him.*
> *The enemy shall not exact upon him; nor the son*
> *of wickedness afflict him.*
> *And I will beat down his foes before his face, and*
> *plague them that hate him.*
> *But my faithfulness and my mercy shall be with*
> *him: and in my name shall his horn be exalted.*
> *I will set his hand also in the sea, and his right*
> *hand in the rivers.*
> *He shall cry unto me, Thou art my father, my*
> *God, and the rock of my salvation.*
> *Also I will make him my firstborn, higher than*
> *the kings of the earth.*
> *My mercy will I keep for him for evermore, and*

my Covenant shall stand fast with him.

His seed also will I make to endure for ever, and his throne as the days of heaven.

If his children forsake my law, and walk not in my judgments;

If they break my statutes, and keep not my commandments;

Then will I visit their transgression with the rod, and their iniquity with stripes.

Nevertheless my lovingkindness will I not utterly take from him, nor suffer my faithfulness to fail.

My Covenant will I not break, nor alter the thing that is gone out of my lips.

Once have I sworn by my holiness that I will not lie unto David.

His seed shall endure forever, and his throne as the sun before me.

It shall be established for ever as the moon, and as a faithful witness in heaven. Selah

(Psalms 89:18-37)

Like all unconditional Covenants of Promise, the Davidic Covenant was first offered by God to his chosen nation, Israel, the only stipulation being that they must believe and receive them. In verses 30-32 of the above portion of Scripture, we see a warning, that unbelief of the promise will be visited with reproof from the Lord. Never the less, says the Lord, He will be faithful as He promised, and will never remove this Davidic Covenant from His chosen people.

For thus saith the LORD; David shall never want a man to sit upon the throne of the house of Israel;

Neither shall the priests the Levites want a man before me to offer burnt offerings, and to kindle meat offerings, and to do sacrifice continually.

And the word of the LORD came unto Jeremiah, saying,

Thus saith the LORD; If ye can break my Covenant of the day, and my Covenant of the night, and that there should not be day and night in their season;

Then may also my Covenant be broken with David my servant, that he should not have a son to reign upon his throne; and with the Levites the priests, my ministers.

As the host of heaven cannot be numbered, neither the sand of the sea measured: so will I multiply the seed of David my servant, and the Levites that minister unto me.

(Jeremiah 33:17-22)

At Jesus Christ's incarnation He came as a Suffering Servant, as the Lamb of God who took away the sin of the world, who suffered the cruel cross that His blood might become the propitiation whereby regenerated man might be reconciled to God. The blood of Christ also made manifest and confirmed to believers the immutability of the Davidic Covenant.

The Apostle James makes mention of the Davidic Covenant as recorded in the Book of Acts, while debating God's intention as to whom were to be the prime recipients of the Gospel at the time of the incarnate appearing of Jesus Christ, the Jewish or Gentile nations.

And after they had held their peace, James answered, saying, Men and brethren, hearken unto me:

Simeon hath declared how God at the first did visit the Gentiles, to take out of them a people for his name.

And to this agree the words of the prophets; as it is written,

After this I will return, and will build again the tabernacle of David, which is fallen down; and I will build again the ruins thereof, and I will set it up:

That the residue of men might seek after the Lord, and all the Gentiles, upon whom my name is called, saith the Lord, who doeth all these things.

Known unto God are all his works from the beginning of the world.

Wherefore my sentence is, that we trouble not them, which from among the Gentiles are turned to God: (Acts 15:13-19)

The above Scriptures confirming that the Gentiles were to be the first beneficiaries of the Gospel, as the prophets of old had testified. *After this I will return*, that is after the days of the Gentile nations, the Jewish nation would again become the prime recipient of God's Grace, through the Davidic Covenant. It is when Jesus Christ returns again in might and power, that *He will* rebuild the Tabernacle of David, a Tabernacle not built by the hands of man. The Tabernacle of the Covenant of David, or the key of David, is to be rebuilt by God, referring to the rebuilding and restoring of a Theocratic Kingdom by His Spirit to the nation Israel, not a visible building of things which do appear.

Our fathers had the tabernacle of witness in the wilderness, as he had appointed, speaking unto Moses, that he should make it according to the fashion that he had seen.

Which also our fathers that came after brought in with Jesus into the possession of the Gentiles, whom God drave out before the face of our fathers, unto the days of David;

Who found favour before God, and desired to find a tabernacle for the God of Jacob...

> *Ye stiffnecked and uncircumcised in heart and*
> *ears, ye do always resist the Holy Ghost: as your*
> *fathers did, so do ye.*
> *Which of the prophets have not your fathers*
> *persecuted? and they have slain them which*
> *shewed before of the coming of the Just One; of*
> *whom ye have been now the betrayers and*
> *murderers:* (Acts 7:44-46; 51,52)

From the above Scriptures it is evident, that the Jewish nation and the Christian "nations" are under two distinct and separate Covenants. Christians are presently under the Gospel of Grace through faith in the blood of Christ, as *God promised to Abraham and his seed.* The children of Israel as a nation, as of this day, still remain under the cruel letter of the law of the ten commandments given through Moses, and dependant upon physical circumcision of the flesh. This will change when The Messiah returns and the Promised Covenant is *fulfilled to the seed of David*. For, at that time, Israel as a nation, will once again be awakened and realize that they are the chosen people of God, the seed of Abraham and David, but not Moses. Until that time, Jew and Gentile are of two separated seeds, two separated Covenants, yet all believers become the same seed in Jesus Christ.

> *The book of the generation of Jesus Christ, the*
> *son of David, the son of Abraham.*
> (Matthew 1:1)

Also:

> *That the blessing of Abraham might come on the*
> *Gentiles through Jesus Christ; that we might*
> *receive the promise of the Spirit through faith.*
> *Brethren, I speak after the manner of men;*
> *Though it be but a man's Covenant, yet if it be*
> *confirmed, no man disannulleth, or addeth*
> *thereto.*
> *Now to Abraham and his seed were the promises*
> *made. He saith not, And to seeds, as of many; but*

as of one, And to thy seed, which is Christ.
(Galatians 3:14-16)

Reference to the Davidic Covenant may be found in many Scriptures in the Bible, and though not directly mentioned, is alluded to in many others. The theme of the Book of Amos is to exhort the Jewish nation "to return unto Me" an appeal to recognize that God will, through the promise of the Davidic Covenant, graft Israel into the Olive Branch, Jesus Christ, once again. In the Scriptures below the Lord reaffirms His Promise that Israel will once again be grafted into the Olive Tree, Jesus Christ.

For if God spared not the natural branches, take heed lest he also spare not thee.

Behold therefore the goodness and severity of God: on them which fell, severity; but toward thee, goodness, if thou continue in his goodness: otherwise thou also shalt be cut off.

And they also, if they abide not still in unbelief, shall be graffed in: for God is able to graff them in again.

For if thou wert cut out of the olive tree which is wild by nature, and wert graffed contrary to nature into a good olive tree: how much more shall these, which be the natural branches, be graffed into their own olive tree?

For I would not, brethren, that ye should be ignorant of this mystery, lest ye should be wise in your own conceits; that blindness in part is happened to Israel, until the fulness of the Gentiles be come in.

And so all Israel shall be saved: as it is written, There shall come out of Sion the Deliverer, and shall turn away ungodliness from Jacob:

For this is my Covenant unto them, when I shall take away their sins.

(Romans 11:21-27)

The heart of the Zionist is quickened by the hope of the promise of the Messiah's return, as revealed in the Davidic Covenant. Israel will once again become heirs and the prime recipients of the Covenants of Grace when Christ sets his feet upon the Mount of Olives. Christ will then reign in Jerusalem, the City of David, as David did when he reigned as king of Jerusalem, as a type of Christ. Jerusalem, the earthly city of David, will then be revealed to all of mankind as the City of righteousness and peace. It is only upon the Messiah's return that true peace, and the Spirit of Grace, will come to the nation Israel. Finally, once again Israel will be ruled by a Theocratic government under the Kingship of the Messiah.

And his feet shall stand in that day upon the mount of Olives, which [is] before Jerusalem on the east, and the mount of Olives shall cleave in the midst thereof toward the east and toward the west, [and there shall be] a very great valley; and half of the mountain shall remove toward the north, and half of it toward the south.

(Zechariah 14:4)

And again:

And I will pour upon the house of David, and upon the inhabitants of Jerusalem, the spirit of grace and of supplications: <u>and they shall look upon me whom they have pierced</u>, and they shall mourn for him, as one mourneth for [his] only [son], and shall be in bitterness for him, as one that is in bitterness for [his] firstborn.

(Zechariah 12:10)

We see the Davidic Covenant as being the dividing wall which separates Israel as a nation and all present day Christian believers. For teachers to teach that present day Israel and Christians are under the same Covenant is to ignore the differences between the Davidic and Abrahamic Covenants. On one side of the division is the Jewish nation, still under the curse of the law, but looking forward to the coming of the promised Messiah, on the other is the body of believers who have recognized that the promise of the Holy Spirit has come through the blessing of Abraham, and the God/person of Jesus Christ.

> *So then they which be of faith are blessed with faithful Abraham.*
>
> *For as many as are of the works of the law are under the curse: for it is written, Cursed is every one that continueth not in all things which are written in the book of the law to do them.*
>
> *But that no man is justified by the law in the sight of God, it is evident: for,*
>
> *The just shall live by faith.*
>
> *And the law is not of faith: but, The man that doeth them shall live in them.*
>
> *Christ hath redeemed us from the curse of the law, being made a curse for us: for it is written, Cursed is every one that hangeth on a tree:*
>
> *That the blessing of Abraham might come on the Gentiles through Jesus Christ; that we might receive the promise of the Spirit through faith.*
>
> (Galatians 3:9-14)

At the return of Jesus Christ, Israel will once again become the prime beneficiaries of God's Grace through the Davidic Covenant. However, all those who have faith in the sprinkled blood of Christ, whether Jew or Gentile, enjoy the benefits of His Kingship and Lordship NOW.

The people of Israel as a nation, are presently blinded because of their inherited faith in their own ability to understand and keep the law of Moses, and consequently are presently separated from the Covenant of Grace which was given to believers through our Father Abraham. At our Lord's return, Israel will once again be grafted into the Olive Tree from which they were broken off, and once again become the recipients of the efficacious grace of the Abrahamic and other unconditional Covenants of Promise.

> *And they also, if they abide not still in unbelief, shall be graffed in: for God is able to graff them in again.* (Romans 11:23)

Also:

> *Yet the number of the children of Israel shall be as the sand of the sea, which cannot be measured nor numbered; and it shall come to pass, [that] in the place where it was said unto them, Ye [are] not my people, [there] it shall be said unto them, [Ye are] the sons of the living God.* (Hosea 1:10)

All Covenants given to man by God were given initially to Israel. All nations are presently blessed through the promises first given to the Jewish nation through the Abrahamic Covenant. Because Israel as a nation have not believed, they have not inherited these blessings.

> *Then the LORD said unto Moses, Now shalt thou see what I will do to Pharaoh: for with a strong hand shall he let them go, and with a strong hand shall he drive them out of his land.*
>
> *And God spake unto Moses, and said unto him, I am the LORD:*
>
> *And I appeared unto Abraham, unto Isaac, and unto Jacob, by the name of God Almighty, but by my name JEHOVAH was I not known to them.*
>
> *And I have also established my Covenant with them, to give them the land of Canaan, the land of their pilgrimage, wherein they were strangers.*
>
> *And I have also heard the groaning of the children of Israel, whom the Egyptians keep in*

bondage; and I have remembered my Covenant.
Wherefore say unto the children of Israel, I am
the LORD, and I will bring you out from under
the burdens of the Egyptians, and I will rid you
out of their bondage, and I will redeem you with
a stretched out arm, and with great judgments:
And I will take you to me for a people, and I will
be to you a God: and ye shall know that I am the
LORD your God, which bringeth you out from
under the burdens of the Egyptians.
And I will bring you in unto the land, concerning
the which I did swear to give it to Abraham, to
Isaac, and to Jacob; and I will give it you for an
heritage: I am the LORD.
And Moses spake so unto the children of Israel:
but they hearkened not unto Moses for anguish
of spirit, and for cruel bondage.
(Exodus 6:1-9)

The above Scriptures confirm, once again, that the children
of Israel were delivered and received redemption through the
provisions of the Abrahamic Covenant. There is no redemption
without faith in the blood of Jesus Christ, therefore it is necessary
that God's children, at that time even as it is today, be ever
mindful that the Abrahamic Covenant was ratified and ministered
to Abraham by Mechizedek, through God's oath and promise of
redeeming blood of Jesus Christ to come. Had the children of
Israel not had faith in the redeeming blood of Jesus Christ, and
kept the first Passover by sprinkling blood upon each of their
door posts, their first born would have perished when the death
angel (Satan) passed through the land of Egypt, on the night
before they were delivered from the bondage of the world
system.

By faith Moses, when he was come to years,
refused to be called the son of Pharaoh's

daughter; Choosing rather to suffer affliction with the people of God, than to enjoy the pleasures of sin for a season;
<u>*Esteeming the reproach of Christ greater riches than the treasures in Egypt:*</u> *for he had respect unto the recompence of the reward.*
By faith he forsook Egypt, not fearing the wrath of the king: for he endured, as seeing him who is invisible.
Through faith he kept the passover, and the sprinkling of blood, lest he that destroyed the firstborn should touch them. (Hebrews 11:24-28)

We also see from the previous Scriptures, (Exodus 6:1-9), that although the children of Israel recognized God as God Almighty (Elohim), they did not recognize Him as being JEHOVAH (their saviour and deliverer). The above Scriptures clearly state, that had they had faith in what the Lord had spoken to them through Moses and the Tabernacle of Witness, the children of Israel would have inherited all of the promised land, and Spiritual blessings which were offered them under the Covenant of Grace, the everlasting Covenant made to all believers through Abraham. Over and over the Word says "I will", that is unconditionally, the Lord desired to give the children of Israel all things pertaining to life and Godliness, but they did not listen to Moses because of "anguish of spirit, and for cruel bondage." This is still true of the nation Israel and all unbelievers in the Covenant of Abraham, TODAY.

Because the children of Israel did not believe and simply accept the freedom given them through the Covenant God made to them through their Father Abraham, by default these Covenants were given to the Gentile nations, in order to stir the jealousy of the Israeli nation. As it is today.

Of the Rock [that] begat thee thou art unmindful, and hast forgotten God that formed thee.

> And when the LORD saw [it], he abhorred
> [them], because of the provoking of his sons, and
> of his daughters.
> And he said, I will hide my face from them, I will
> see what their end [shall be]: for they [are] a
> very froward generation, children in whom [is]
> no faith.
> They have moved me to jealousy with [that
> which is] not God; they have provoked me to
> anger with their vanities: and I will move them
> to jealousy with [those which are] not a people;
> I will provoke them to anger with a foolish
> nation. (Deuteronomy 32:18-21)

Also:

> But I say, Did not Israel know? First Moses
> saith, I will provoke you to jealousy by [them
> that are] no people, [and] by a foolish
> nation I will anger you. (Romans 10:19)

The Covenants of Promises will once again primarily pertain to Israel after the time of the Gentiles is fulfilled, at the time when Jesus Christ returns to this earth.

> Who are Israelites; to whom [pertaineth] the
> adoption, and the glory, and the Covenants, and
> the giving of the law, and the service [of God],
> and the promises; (Romans 9:4)

And again:

> O ye seed of Israel his servant, ye children of
> Jacob, his chosen ones.
> He [is] the LORD our God; his judgments [are]
> in all the earth.
> Be ye mindful always of his Covenant; the word
> [which] he commanded to a thousand
> generations;
> [Even of the Covenant] which he made with

Abraham, and of his oath unto Isaac;
And hath confirmed the same to Jacob for a law,
[and] to Israel [for] an everlasting Covenant,
Saying, Unto thee will I give the land of Canaan,
the lot of your inheritance;
(1 Chronicles 16:13-18)

The above Scriptures are recorded as a Song of Praise, offered to God by David, after he and the children of Israel had brought the Ark of the Covenant from the house of Abinadab to Jerusalem. David here testifying of the significance of the Ark of the Covenant, which was a figure of the Ark in the Heavenly Tabernacle (Hebrews 9:9). The Ark of the Covenant that was in the house of Abinadab was a symbol of God's oath and unconditional Covenant made to Abraham and his seed, through Jacob. When the Messiah returns as King over the nation of Israel, He will make manifest the Covenant of Promise He made to them as the seed of Jacob, through the Davidic Covenant.

A very graphic account of the children of Israel's deliverance and journey, from the land of Egypt, testifying of their unbelief and hardness of heart, is recorded in Psalms 105 and 106. Notice again, as you read these Scriptures. Although Israel had initially been given the Covenants of Promise, it was because of their unbelief, that the Lord temporarily has excluded Israel from the blessings of the Covenants, and has given them to other nations.

And he gave them into the hand of the heathen;
and they that hated them ruled over them.
(Psalms 106:41)

And again:

Ho, every one that thirsteth, come ye to the
waters, and he that hath no money; come ye, buy,
and eat; yea, come, buy wine and milk without
money and without price.
Wherefore do ye spend money for [that which is]
not bread? and your labour for [that which]
satisfieth not? hearken diligently unto me, and

eat ye [that which is] good, and let your soul delight itself in fatness.

Incline your ear, and come unto me: <u>hear, and your soul shall live; and I will make an everlasting Covenant with you, [even] the sure mercies of David.</u>

Behold, I have given him [for] a witness to the people, a leader and commander to the people.

Behold, thou shalt call a nation [that] thou knowest not, and nations [that] knew not thee shall run unto thee because of the LORD thy God, and for the Holy One of Israel; for he hath glorified thee. (Isaiah 55:1-5)

All who believe, whether Jew or Gentile, are invited to come and drink freely of the goodness of God and the sure mercies of His Kingdom, NOW! and need not wait for the Davidic Covenant to be made manifest. As Jesus said to the Pharisees who looked for further evidence of the Kingdom of God.

And when he was demanded of the Pharisees, when the kingdom of God should come, he answered them and said, The kingdom of God cometh not with observation:

<u>Neither shall they say, Lo here! or, lo there! for, behold, the kingdom of God is within you.</u>

(Luke 17:20,21)

We see from the Scripture quotation above that the Kingdom of God, for which all men longingly look, dwells in the heart of each believer, NOW! Regardless of attempts to prove otherwise, the theological community cannot deny that the Greek word interpreted "within" here, means exactly what is stated, that is, the Kingdom of God literally dwells in the heart of each believer, each individual believer is the Lords dwelling place, His Tabernacle.

What? know ye not that your body is the temple of the Holy Ghost which is in you, which ye have

of God, and ye are not your own?
(1 Corinthians 1:19)

Throughout the New Testament Jesus Christ is known as The Son of David, showing that His appearing was full evidence that the Davidic Kingdom and the Kingdom of God were now coincidently revealed and are synonymies.

> *While the Pharisees were gathered together, Jesus asked them,*
>
> *Saying, What think ye of Christ? whose son is he? They say unto him, [The son] of David.*
>
> *He saith unto them, How then doth David in spirit call him Lord, saying,*
>
> *The Lord said unto my Lord, Sit thou on my right hand, till I make thine enemies thy footstool?*
>
> *If David then call him Lord, how is he his son?*
>
> *And no man was able to answer him a word, neither durst any [man] from that day forth ask him any more [questions].*
>
> (Matthew 22:41-46)

At His first Advent, under the provisions of the Abrahamic Covenant, Jesus came as a suffering servant, lowly and riding on an ass.

> *Rejoice greatly, O daughter of Zion; shout, O daughter of Jerusalem: behold, thy King cometh unto thee: he is just, and having salvation; lowly, and riding upon an ass, and upon a colt the foal of an ass.* (Zechariah 9:9)

At the time Bethlehem was referred to as the city of David, when He came as a babe wrapped in swaddling clothes.

> *And Joseph also went up from Galilee, out of the city of Nazareth, into Judaea, <u>unto the city of David, which is called Beth-lehem;</u>*
>
> *(because he was of the house and lineage of David:)*

To be taxed with Mary his espoused wife, being great with child.

And so it was, that, while they were there, the days were accomplished that she should be delivered.

And she brought forth her firstborn son, and wrapped him in swaddling clothes, and laid him in a manger; because there was no room for them in the inn.

And there were in the same country shepherds abiding in the field, keeping watch over their flock by night.

And, lo, the angel of the Lord came upon them, and the glory of the Lord shone round about them: and they were sore afraid.

And the angel said unto them, Fear not: for, behold, I bring you good tidings of great joy, which shall be to all people.

For unto you is born this day in the city of David a Saviour, which is Christ the Lord.

(Luke 2:4-11)

Because they did not understand the two different Advents and the two different Covenants, there was confusion, even as there is today.

Many of the people therefore, when they heard this saying, said,

Of a truth this is the Prophet.

Others said, This is the Christ. But some said, Shall Christ come out of Galilee?

Hath not the scripture said, That Christ cometh of the seed of David, and out of the town of Beth-lehem, where David was?

So there was a division among the people because of him. (John 7:40-43)

Bethlehem was prophesied as the city of David in the Old Testament as well, the birthplace of Jesus Christ's appearing at His first Advent.

And Samuel did that which the LORD spake, and came to Beth-lehem.

And the elders of the town trembled at his coming, and said, Comest thou peaceably?...

And Samuel said unto Jesse, Are here all [thy] children? And he said, There remaineth yet the youngest, and, behold, he keepeth the sheep.

And Samuel said unto Jesse, Send and fetch him: for we will not sit down till he come hither.

And he sent, and brought him in. Now he [was] ruddy, [and] withal of a beautiful countenance, and goodly to look to. And the LORD said, Arise, anoint him: for this [is] he.

Then Samuel took the horn of oil, and anointed him in the midst of his brethren: and the spirit of the LORD came upon David from that day forward. So Samuel rose up, and went to Ramah....

Then answered one of the servants, and said, Behold, I have seen a son of Jesse the Beth-lehemite, [that is] cunning in playing, and a mighty valiant man, and a man of war, and prudent in matters, and a comely person, and the LORD [is] with him....

And Saul said to him, Whose son [art] thou, [thou] young man? And David answered, I [am] the son of thy servant Jesse the Beth-lehemite.

(1 Samuel 16:4;11-13;18;17:58)

Also:

But thou, Beth-lehem Ephratah, [though] thou be little among the thousands of Judah, [yet] out

*of thee shall he come forth unto me [that is] to be
ruler in Israel; whose goings forth [have been]
from of old, from everlasting.* (Micah 5:2)

At Christ's second Advent, Jerusalem will be reaffirmed as
the City of David, the City of the great King.

*But I say unto you, Swear not at all; neither by
heaven; for it is God's throne:*
*Nor by the earth; for it is his footstool: neither
by Jerusalem; for it is the city of the great King.*
(Matthew 5:34,35)

Again:

*Great is the LORD, and greatly to be praised in
the city of our God, in the mountain of his
holiness.*
*Beautiful for situation, the joy of the whole
earth, is mount Zion, on the sides of the north,
the city of the great King.*
(Psalms 48:1,2)

Even today, Christ the believers Heavenly High Priest and
mediator, dwells in the Heavenly Jerusalem, on Mount Zion. At
the right hand of the Father, Christ is no longer a suffering
servant but the King of Jerusalem, the City of King David.

*But ye are come unto mount Sion, and unto the
city of the living God, the heavenly Jerusalem,
and to an innumerable company of angels,*
*To the general assembly and church of the
firstborn, which are written in heaven, and to
God the Judge of all, and to the spirits of just
men made perfect,*
*And to Jesus the mediator of the new Covenant,
and to the blood of sprinkling, that speaketh
better things than that of Abel.*
(Hebrews 12:22-24)

This division of the first and second Advent, need not be the source of any friction between Jew and Gentile, for this was God's perfect will in delivering all believers, whether Jew or Gentile, through the same Abrahamic Covenant of Grace, confirmed by the two Advents of our Lord and Saviour, Jesus the Christ. Whether lowly and riding on a donkey as Saviour for the Gentile nations, or as the King of Jerusalem at His Second Coming, Jesus Christ is the same, yesterday, today and forever.

> *For I would not, brethren, that ye should be ignorant of this mystery, lest ye should be wise in your own conceits; that blindness in part is happened to Israel, until the fulness of the Gentiles be come in.*
>
> *And so all Israel shall be saved: as it is written, There shall come out of Sion the Deliverer, and shall turn away ungodliness from Jacob:*
>
> *For this [is] my Covenant unto them, when I shall take away their sins.* (Romans 11:25-27)

In that day, righteous judgements through faith in Christ's blood will purge the hearts of believing Israel, and the glorious benefits of the Davidic Covenant will be made manifest by the Messiah.

> *And David reigned over all Israel; and David executed judgment and justice unto all his people.* (2 Samuel 8:15)

Until that day the Lord God reigns in the heart of ALL believers, whether they be Jew or Gentile, through the righteous judgements of Jesus Christ our High Priest. Jesus Christ, called of God a High Priest forever in the order of Melchisedec. Melchisedec, who blessed Abraham, and confirmed the Covenant of Grace to all his seed through bread and wine, the body and blood of Christ.

> *O ye seed of Israel his servant, ye children of Jacob, his chosen ones.*

*He [is] the LORD our God; his judgments [are]
in all the earth.*

*Be ye mindful always of his Covenant; the word
[which] he commanded to a thousand
generations; [Even of the Covenant] which he
made with Abraham, and of his oath unto Isaac;
And hath confirmed the same to Jacob for a law,
[and] to Israel [for] an everlasting Covenant,
(1 Chronicles 16:13-17)*

The message of the Davidic Covenant is then that; in that day, when the Lord sets His feet upon the Mount of Olives, the Jews, as a nation, will be awakened to the gift of God's righteousness, through faith in the blood of the Christ whom they had pierced, which is their inheritance as the seed of Abraham. At this time Israel will be grafted again into the Olive Tree, and once again, become the blessed of The BRANCH. At the same time, the time of the Gentile nations will have been fulfilled.

Both Jew and Gentile have been made heirs of the everlasting, unconditional New Covenant of Promise as the seed of Abraham, through faith in the blood of Christ, but under two distinctly separate dispensations. These two dispensations of God's Grace have been separated by the two appearances of our Lord Jesus Christ. At His first appearing He was the Suffering Servant, lowly and riding on a donkey, at the second appearing He will be revealed as the King of Kings and Lord of Lords.

Jews and Gentiles will then, both having been born again by grace through faith in the blood of Christ, and both having been made recipients of the blessing of righteousness and perfection as the seed of Abraham, become one in the mystical body of Christ. But until "that day" Jew and Gentile are distinct and separated by the two different dispensations of the same unconditional Covenant.

This author then would ask the theological community, why is the present "church age" taught that believing Jews and

Gentiles are united as Judeo/Christians? Obviously we are separated by two separate dispensations. Why is this confusion propagated to believers who earnestly search for a pure distinct Gospel? Why are believers, who are honestly seeking first and foremost for the righteousness of the Kingdom of God, being misled by teachers who dispense the cruel letter of the law to believers, a law which is meant for unbelievers, rather than the Spirit of Grace, which is only dispensed from the Throne of Grace?

Believers cannot be under both, the law of the ten commandments, as is the Jewish nation presently, and the Law of Grace, as are all believers who have faith in the sprinkling of the blood of Jesus Christ on the Mercy Seat. Law and Grace cannot co-exist. The law is from Mount Sinai, Grace is dispensed from Mount Zion, the City of the living God. Therefore, once again this author reminds you of the Scriptural quotation:

> *For ye are not come unto the mount that might be touched, and that burned with fire, nor unto blackness, and darkness, and tempest,*
> *And the sound of a trumpet, and the voice of words; which voice they that heard intreated that the word should not be spoken to them any more:*
> *(For they could not endure that which was commanded, And if so much as a beast touch the mountain, it shall be stoned, or thrust through with a dart:*
> *And so terrible was the sight, that Moses said, I exceedingly fear and quake:)*
> *But ye are come unto mount Sion, and unto the city of the living God, the heavenly Jerusalem, and to an innumerable company of angels,*
> *To the general assembly and church of the firstborn, which are written in heaven, and to God the Judge of all, and to the spirits of just*

men made perfect,
And to Jesus the mediator of the new Covenant,
and to the blood of sprinkling, that speaketh
better things than that of Abel.
(Hebrews 12:18-24)

10

NEW COVENANT
Fulfilment

The theme of this chapter is unity and perfection through Christ's New Covenant mediation.

The New Covenant is one of the least taught and consequently least understood doctrines in Christianity today. The New Covenant has been made manifest by the blood of Jesus Christ and pertains, in all it fulness and benefits, to the Gentile nations, TODAY! As a result it would seem, that the present day denominational church has forsaken the benefits and first principles of the oracles of God. Denominational church's have departed from God's primary Covenant of Promise made to Abraham and his seed, as did the children of Israel, and its fulfilment to the Gentiles through the blood of Christ in the New Covenant.

The New Covenant is very succinctly outlined in the entire eighth chapter of the Book of Hebrews. In order that the exact articulation of the New Covenant, or that Covenant which was ratified when Christ ascended into Heaven with His own atoning blood as a propitiation, not go unread, it is reprinted here.

The New Covenant:

> *Now of the things which we have spoken [this is]*

*the sum: We have such an high priest, who is set
on the right hand of the throne of the Majesty
in the heavens;*

*A minister of the sanctuary, and of the true
tabernacle, which the Lord pitched, and not
man.*

*For every high priest is ordained to offer gifts
and sacrifices:*

*wherefore [it is] of necessity that this man have
somewhat also to offer.*

*For if he were on earth, he should not be a
priest, seeing that there are priests that offer
gifts according to the law:*

*Who serve unto the example and shadow of
heavenly things, as Moses was admonished of
God when he was about to make the tabernacle:
for, See, saith he, [that] thou make all things
according to the pattern shewed to thee in the
mount.*

*But now hath he obtained a more excellent
ministry, by how much also he is the mediator of
a better Covenant, which was established
upon better promises.*

*For if that first [Covenant] had been faultless,
then should no place have been sought for the
second.*

*For finding fault with them, he saith, Behold, the
days come, saith the Lord, when I will make a
new Covenant with the house of Israel
and with the house of Judah:*

*Not according to the Covenant that I made with
their fathers in the day when I took them by the
hand to lead them out of the land of Egypt;
because they continued not in my Covenant, and*

I regarded them not, saith the Lord.

For this [is] the Covenant that I will make with the house of Israel after those days, saith the Lord; I will put my laws into their mind, and write them in their hearts: and I will be to them a God, and they shall be to me a people:

And they shall not teach every man his neighbour, and every man his brother, saying, Know the Lord: for all shall know me, from the least to the greatest.

For I will be merciful to their unrighteousness, and their sins and their iniquities will I remember no more.

In that he saith, A new [Covenant], he hath made the first old. Now that which decayeth and waxeth old [is] ready to vanish away.

(Hebrews 8:1-13)

The above Scriptures are the heart of the Gospel of Sovereign Grace, they describe the New Covenant which is built upon better promises than the Old Covenant of Promise which God made with all believers through Abraham. Better because the Mosaic tabernacle in the wilderness was only a figure of the true. Better because the promise of a better sacrifice was accomplished when God sent His only Son, Jesus Christ, to fulfill that promise. Better because the veil to the Holy of Holies has now been rent from top to bottom exposing and making accessible the secret place of the Most High to New Covenant believers. Better because we NOW have a High Priest with a more excellent ministry. We now have an High Priest whom God has set forth to be a propitiation, through faith in His perfect blood sacrifice, rather than the imperfect sacrifice of the blood of bulls and goats.

Tragically, there are doctrines of major importance in the Bible that the vast majority of clergy and theologians will not or cannot deal with, at the very least they are not giving these doctrines the emphasis they deserve. Unfortunately, this seems to be true of the clarification of the New Covenant as it pertains, first to the Gentile, and secondarily in the end times to the nation of Israel.

All of the Bible, in both the Old and New Testaments, which are unerringly the revelation of God's justification and salvation plan for mankind, is summed up in the New Covenant, the Covenant of the Blood of Christ. Many of us are quite familiar with the so called law of Moses or the ten commandments, which are a part of a conditional Covenant, and readily recall that they are found in Exodus 20. However the Scriptural location of the articulation of the New Covenant, is not as well known, as a matter of fact it seems to be one of the best kept secrets in Christianity today. Both the unconditional Covenant of Grace and the conditional letter of the law of Moses run parallel to each other throughout the Bible, however their relationship, and separation from each other, are seldom explained by expositors. The Scriptures alone give the best clarification of their relative purposes.

Because Israel, as a nation, have not recognized the intent of God's heart in the giving of the Covenant of Grace to them through His Covenant to Abraham as his seed, they have been temporarily cut from the benefits of the New Covenant until the time of the Gentiles has been fulfilled. Individual Jews have been given the same opportunity to receive Jesus Christ as their Lord and Saviour as have all believers, but as a nation, Israel has been blinded to the truth of Jesus Christ's first Advent. However when, Jesus Christ the Messiah returns, at His second Advent, Israel as a nation will once again be grafted into the Olive Tree, under the provisions of the Davidic Covenant, and once again become The BRANCH. At that time all believers of the nation of Israel will receive the full benefits of the New Covenant of Grace.

Please note that in the Scriptures above, the Lord takes upon Himself all the responsibility to motivate hearts and deliver believers from sin and iniquities. Never once does He mention "Thou Shalt", as did the letter of the law of Moses. The New Covenant is unconditional, in it the Lord states very clearly, several times that, "HE WILL" build up the heart of believers and separate the sin and guilt of our iniquitous nature from His memory and condemnation. The New Covenant only asks that we recognize God's Sovereign Grace and goodness. This freedom from the law of condemnation was also true of God's Promise to Abraham, which He made with the nation Israel at the time He gave the promise.

> And *I will* make thee exceeding fruitful, and *I will* make nations of thee, and kings shall come out of thee.
>
> And *I will* establish my Covenant between me and thee and thy seed after thee in their generations for an everlasting Covenant, to be a God unto thee, and to thy seed after thee.
>
> And *I will* give unto thee, and to thy seed after thee, the land wherein thou art a stranger, all the land of Canaan, for an everlasting possession; and *I will* be their God. (Genesis 17:6-8)

Two of the kings which came out of the loins of Abraham as promised in Genesis 35:11, is Jesus Christ the King of Righteousness and Peace, and King David whose Covenant will be fulfilled at the Second Advent of Jesus Christ.

Other than to simply believe through faith in the blood of the better sacrifice, there are no conditions to God's gift of the land of promise. All believers, whether Jew or Gentile, presently have been given the positional blessings to live in Spiritual Mount Zion, through faith, and are eligible to receive through our Lord Jesus Christ, all Spiritual blessings in heavenly places. Once again I quote:

> But ye are come unto mount Sion, and unto the city of the living God, the heavenly Jerusalem,

and to an innumerable company of angels,
To the general assembly and church of the
firstborn, which are written in heaven, and to
God the Judge of all, and to the spirits
of just men made perfect, and to Jesus the
mediator of the new Covenant, and to the blood
of sprinkling, that speaketh better things than
[that of] Abel. (Hebrews 12:22-24)

Of very special note is Hebrews 8:12, where the word says, "your sins and iniquities I will remember no more." Can we suppose this really means what it says? Can this really be true, that God does not remember the believers sins and iniquities? What is the catch? Where is the but...? This promise of the absolution of sin, through Christ's High Priestly ministry, is the most startling revelation of the New Covenant. This is the New Covenant to which we drink of His blood at every communion service, as we partake of the Lord's table. The promises given here are ratified by the Lord's blood.

And he took the cup, and gave thanks, and gave
[it] to them, saying, Drink ye all of it;
For this is my blood of the new testament, which
is shed for many for the remission of sins.
(Matthew 26:27,28)

I wonder how many believers accept and realize that this provision of God's mercy toward our unrighteousness applies not only when we first give our hearts and lives to the Lord for His direction, but that He does not hold the guilt of our sins and iniquities in remembrance for the rest of our lives, even unto the day we stand before the judgement seat of Christ. At the judgement seat of Christ believers will be rewarded for the works done in the Spirit of Grace while in the body, our sin nature and worthless deeds will be burned as stubble.

For we must all appear before the judgment seat
of Christ; that every one may receive the things
[done] in [his] body, according to that he hath

done, whether [it be] good or bad.
(2 Corinthians 5:10)

And again:

Now if any man build upon this foundation gold,
silver, precious stones, wood, hay, stubble;
Every man's work shall be made manifest: for
the day shall declare it, because it shall be
revealed by fire; and the fire shall try every
man's work of what sort it is.
If any man's work abide which he hath built
thereupon, he shall receive a reward.
If any man's work shall be burned, he shall suffer
loss: but he himself shall be saved; yet so as by
fire. (1 Corinthians 3:12-15)

Both these Covenants, the New Covenant and the Covenant given to all believers through Abraham, were fulfilled for believers through the faithfulness of the revealed blood of Christ at His incarnation, typified when Melchizedek appeared to Abraham as the priest of the Most High God, in the Old Testament. There are many, many more provisions of God's Grace made available to believers through these two Covenants, but the promise that He will remember the sins and iniquities of believers no more, is by far the best news that one could hope for. It indeed is the basis of the hope we have in being made one with the Father, through the recognition of the reconciling blood of Jesus shed on the cross, and sprinkled on the Mercy Seat in Heaven. It is in the realization that through faith in the blood of Christ, and upon the purging of an otherwise guilty conscience, we need not be conscious of any condemnation because of the guilt of sin. If we recognize, and take advantage of the provisions of Christ's present High Priestly ministry at the right hand of the Father, we become totally confident of His righteousness within our hearts. Only the Spirit of His indwelling righteousness, and the provisions of God's mercy, allow believers to come boldly before the Throne of Grace.

*For the word of God [is] quick, and powerful,
and sharper than any twoedged sword, piercing
even to the dividing asunder of soul and spirit,
and of the joints and marrow, and [is] a
discerner of the thoughts and intents of the heart.
Neither is there any creature that is not manifest
in his sight:
but all things [are] naked and opened unto the
eyes of him with whom we have to do.
Seeing then that we have a great high priest, that
is passed into the heavens, Jesus the Son of God,
let us hold fast [our] profession.
For we have not an high priest which cannot be
touched with the feeling of our infirmities; but
was in all points tempted like as [we are, yet]
without sin.
Let us therefore come boldly unto the throne of
grace, that we may obtain mercy, and find grace
to help in time of need.* (Hebrews 4:12-16)

It is only through the acknowledgement of what the Holy
Spirit says through the provisions of the New Covenant, and the
perfection that is our new nature in Christ, through which
believers are given the boldness to enter the Holy of Holies.

*But this man, after he had offered one sacrifice
for sins for ever, sat down on the right hand of
God; From henceforth expecting till his enemies
be made his footstool.
For by one offering he hath perfected for ever
them that are sanctified.
[Whereof] the Holy Ghost also is a witness to us:
for after that he had said before,
This [is] the Covenant that I will make with them
after those days, saith the Lord, I will put my
laws into their hearts, and in their minds will I*

write them; And their sins and iniquities will I remember no more.

Now where remission of these [is, there is] no more offering for sin.

Having therefore, brethren, boldness to enter into the holiest by the blood of Jesus,

By a new and living way, which he hath consecrated for us, through the veil, that is to say, his flesh; And [having] an high priest over the house of God; Let us draw near with a true heart in full assurance of faith,

having our hearts sprinkled from an evil conscience, and our bodies washed with pure water.

Let us hold fast the profession of [our] faith without wavering; (for he [is] faithful that promised; (Hebrews 10:12-23)

The word boldly, in the above two Scriptures, is translated from the Greek word PARRHESIA, which is interpreted in most Bible dictionaries as: "the absence of fear in speaking boldly; hence, confidence, cheerful courage, boldness, without any connection necessarily with speech."

The state of "Parrhesia" or the boldness to dwell in the very presence of God, was the same boldness with which Adam and Eve walked naked and open in the Garden of Eden, prior to the fall. So then faith in the atoning blood of Jesus Christ which believers are asked to drink of, when celebrating Communion, gives us this "parrhesia" boldness to come and dwell with Him in His very presence at the Mercy Seat. The atoning blood of Christ, sprinkled on the Mercy Seat, has redeemed and separated believers from the wrath and curse of our sinful flesh nature, so that we might enter boldly through the second veil into the very Holy of Holies.

May we conclude that faith in the efficacy of the continual

blood of sprinkling, by our High Priest, is necessary to receive the promises of positional perfection through the Covenants of Grace? Is it not evident that a believer only experiences more of his positional perfection, as he grows in the Spirit through faith in the perfecting power of the sprinkling of the blood of Christ, His mediator and High Priest?

> *He that dwelleth in the secret place of the most High shall abide under the shadow of the Almighty.*
>
> *I will say of the LORD, He is my refuge and my fortress: my God; in him will I trust.*
>
> *Surely he shall deliver thee from the snare of the fowler, and from the noisome pestilence.*
>
> *He shall cover thee with his feathers, and under his wings shalt thou trust: his truth shall be thy shield and buckler.*
>
> *Thou shalt not be afraid for the terror by night; nor for the arrow that flieth by day;*
>
> *Nor for the pestilence that walketh in darkness; nor for the destruction that wasteth at noonday.*
>
> *A thousand shall fall at thy side, and ten thousand at thy right hand; but it shall not come nigh thee.*
>
> *Only with thine eyes shalt thou behold and see the reward of the wicked.*
>
> *Because thou hast made the LORD, which is my refuge, even the most High, thy habitation;*
>
> *There shall no evil befall thee, neither shall any plague come nigh thy dwelling* (Psalms 91:1-10)

Certainly there is no provision for our flesh to enter the Holy Place, and come boldly before the Throne of Grace in our natural state. We cannot come in the boldness of flesh, but we are exhorted to come boldly in the Spirit of His righteousness which dwells within the heart of each born again believer. If we have faith in the power of His Word, we will have considered our flesh nature as having been separated from our Spirit nature, by the sword of the Word, through the Covenant of Grace. We will have considered ourselves to be dead indeed unto sin but alive unto Christ.

> *Knowing that Christ being raised from the dead dieth no more; death hath no more dominion over him. For in that he died, he died unto sin once: but in that he liveth, he liveth unto God.*
> *Likewise reckon ye also yourselves to be dead indeed unto sin, but alive unto God through Jesus Christ our Lord.* (Romans 6:9-11)

The Spiritually <u>perfected</u> are invited to come in total abandonment of our fleshly nature, because we have a High Priest who suffered as we, and knows all about our infirmities.

> *For we have not an high priest which cannot be touched with the feeling of our infirmities; but was in all points tempted like as [we are, yet] without sin.*
> *Let us therefore come <u>boldly</u> unto the throne of grace, that we may obtain mercy, and find grace to help in time of need.* (Hebrews 4:15,16)

If we allow the Holy Spirit to reveal this doctrine to our hearts, we will come to understand that it is here, at the Throne of Grace, and here only, that we receive mercy, freedom from guilt, and obtain further salvation, through faith in the blood of Christ, our High Priest in the order of Melchisedec. As in the Old Testament, it is God's intent that His people meet and abide with Him before the Throne of Grace, within the second veil. It is He who is more anxious than we, to meet with us here, continually, even to dwell here, as we saw in Psalms 91 above.

We cannot have knowledge in that of which we are unaware, therefore, if we do not know of the Scriptures that tell us of our <u>position</u> in Christ, we cannot <u>experience</u> the benefits of that position, because of unbelief. We of ourselves have no faith, but we are given faith to the extent we are able to believe in God's faithfulness. We cannot count Him faithful if we do not know "The Word" that describes His nature and faithfulness. If we are not aware that we can come boldly to the Throne of Grace, without guilt, then we suffer without the second veil in our unbelief, and effectually ignore His Glory, nor do we experience complete freedom from the thoughts of guilt of our past sin and iniquity. This freedom from the quilt of sin and iniquity is the theme and blessing of the New Covenant.

> *My people are destroyed for lack of knowledge:*
> *because thou hast rejected knowledge, I will also*
> *reject thee, that thou shalt be no priest to me:*
> *seeing thou hast forgotten the law of thy God, I*
> *will also forget thy children.*
> *As they were increased, so they sinned against*
> *me: [therefore] will I change their glory into*
> *shame.*
> *They eat up the sin of my people, and they set*
> *their heart on their iniquity.*
> *And there shall be, like people, like priest: and I*
> *will punish them for their ways, and reward them*
> *their doings.* (Hosea 4:6,7)

If we do not know, that under the New Covenant, He no longer remembers the believers sins and iniquities, then we suffer according to the flesh, under the law. If we, through our own will, set our hearts on trying to rid ourselves of the thoughts of our iniquitous nature, we do not, nor cannot walk in the boldness of His Holy Spirit to the extent God would have us. It is an offence to the provisions of His Grace, if we continue to focus our attention on, and pamper, a sin nature which Jesus Christ paid so dearly to have buried with Him in our baptism. If we, through ignorance of the Word, dwell upon our sin nature and try to correct the old man of the flesh, we cannot walk in the Spirit of

Divine Grace. What foolish pride to think for one minute that I could add to the sufficiency of His perfect sacrifice through attempting to correct my flesh nature.

At the communion table, believers are exhorted to remember what faith in the blood of the body of Christ has done, and is presently doing for us within the second veil, on the Mercy Seat in the Heavenly Jerusalem. We are exhorted to examine ourselves, to ask ourselves if we have total confidence in the perfect sinless righteousness with which He presents us to the Father.

I'm sure many pastors and theologians will cringe at the thought of preaching this doctrine, the liberty of the New Covenant, doctrine which provides for the guilt of sin and iniquities having been removed from God's memory. However not to accept this doctrine is to do despite to the Spirit of Grace and allow the opinions of man to devour us.

> *Thou art of purer eyes than to behold evil, and*
> *canst not look on iniquity:* wherefore lookest
> *thou upon them that deal treacherously, and*
> *holdest thy tongue when the wicked devoureth*
> *the man that is more righteous than he.*
> (Habakukk 1:13)

Those believers who began in the Spirit and have now become so foolish as to think that further perfection comes through the moral law, have again closed the veil which Jesus Christ paid so dearly to have rent, by the perfect sacrifice of His body and the sprinkling of His atoning blood on the Mercy Seat in Heaven. If believers ignore or are ignorant of the great salvation that is available to them within the Holy place, and again resort to the moral law in order to lay again the foundation of repentance from the dead works of the flesh, they are asking Jesus Christ to be crucified over and over again.

> *Therefore leaving the principles of the doctrine*
> *of Christ, let us go on unto perfection; not laying*

again the foundation of repentance from dead
works, and of faith toward God,
Of the doctrine of baptisms, and of laying on of
hands, and of resurrection of the dead, and of
eternal judgment.
And this will we do, if God permit.
For it is impossible for those who were once
enlightened, and have tasted of the heavenly gift,
and were made partakers of the Holy Ghost,
And have tasted the good word of God, and the
powers of the world to come,
If they shall fall away, to renew them again unto
repentance; seeing they crucify to themselves the
Son of God afresh, and put him to an open
shame. (Hebrews 6:1-6)

Believers who, after having once been saved at the Cross, but now attempt to adhere to the law of the ten commandments have no concept of what it means to be led of the Holy Spirit. Believers who walk in the provisions of the New Covenant are given the liberty to do as they please, those who remain under a moral code cannot understand, nor appreciate that those who dwell in the secret place of the Most High have no desire to walk in the flesh, nor have they any desire to abuse the liberty whereby they have been set free.

Forasmuch as ye are manifestly declared to be
the epistle of Christ ministered by us, written not
with ink, but with the Spirit of the living God; not
in tables of stone, but in fleshy tables of the
heart.
And such trust have we through Christ to
God-ward:
Not that we are sufficient of ourselves to think
any thing as of ourselves; but our sufficiency is
of God;

Who also hath made us able ministers of the new testament; not of the letter, but of the spirit: for the letter killeth, but the spirit giveth life.

But if the ministration of death, written and engraven in stones, was glorious, so that the children of Israel could not stedfastly behold the face of Moses for the glory of his countenance; which glory was to be done away:

How shall not the ministration of the spirit be rather glorious?

For if the ministration of condemnation be glory, much more doth the ministration of righteousness exceed in glory.

For even that which was made glorious had no glory in this respect, by reason of the glory that excelleth.

For if that which is done away was glorious, much more that which remaineth is glorious.

Seeing then that we have such hope, we use great plainness of speech:

And not as Moses, which put a vail over his face, that the children of Israel could not stedfastly look to the end of that which is abolished:

But their minds were blinded: for until this day remaineth the same vail untaken away in the reading of the old testament; which vail is done away in Christ.

But even unto this day, when Moses is read, the vail is upon their heart.

Nevertheless when it shall turn to the Lord, the vail shall be taken away.

Now the Lord is that Spirit: and where the Spirit of the Lord is, there is liberty.

(2 Corinthians 3:3-17)

Certainly the writer of Psalms 91 was not without faults of

the flesh, yet David writes of his experience of dwelling within the secret place, the Holy of Holies, where no flesh is to be found. Although David's imperfections are well recorded in Scripture, he was judged of God as one having a perfect heart, and being a man after God's own heart. Indeed, Paul informs us that Jesus Himself was made of the seed of David.

> *Concerning his Son Jesus Christ our Lord,*
> *which was made of the seed of David according*
> *to the flesh;* (Romans 1:3)

God's desire for believers, is that we simply accept His provision for our perfection through faith in His High Priestly ministry at the right hand of the Father.

All believers recognize that it was God's Sovereign love toward us which gave us the provision of redemption through faith in the blood of Jesus' death and resurrection. Why then would we doubt that His declaration of His perfect love toward us, would not desire to continue, or perfect us in His charitable love? The author will remind readers later on that the Greek word "Teleios" speaks of his declaration of perfect love for us and is our perfect position in him. The Greek word, "Teleioo" speaks of His provision for us to continue to grow, or become more mature in experiencing that perfect love. It is our acceptance of His perfect love that matures us in that love, and it is His continuing love that casts out fear.

> *For this is the Covenant that I will make with the*
> *house of Israel after those days, saith the Lord; I*
> *will put my laws into their mind, and write them*
> *in their hearts: and I will be to them a God, and*
> *they shall be to me a people:* (Hebrews 8:10)

Also:

> *There is no fear in love; but perfect love casteth*
> *out fear: because fear hath torment. He that*
> *feareth is not made perfect in love.*
> *We love him, because he first loved us.*
> (1 John 4:18,19)

As we are led to understand from the Scriptures above, His love casts out fear. These same Scriptures confirm that God works from the inside out, not first through the flesh and then into the heart. It is by imputing His laws into our heart that flesh is circumcised. To attempt to change our reactions to circumstances without first allowing God to change our heart, is to live by a law of self determination. Abraham received God's declaration of righteousness before he was circumcised; first righteousness and then circumcision, first the heart and then further ongoing salvation.

> *Cometh this blessedness then upon the circumcision only, or upon the uncircumcision also? for we say that faith was reckoned to Abraham for righteousness.*
>
> *How was it then reckoned? when he was in circumcision, or in uncircumcision? Not in circumcision, but in uncircumcision.*
>
> *And he received the sign of circumcision, a seal of the righteousness of the faith which he had yet being uncircumcised: that he might be the father of all them that believe, though they be not circumcised; that righteousness might be imputed unto them also:*
>
> *And the father of circumcision to them who are not of the circumcision only, but who also walk in the steps of that faith of our father Abraham, which he had being yet uncircumcised.*
>
> (Romans 4:9-12)

For Abram, circumcision of the flesh was a sign of having accepted God's declaration of his perfection. Positional perfection of the Spirit is a token of the Covenant God made to all believers through Abraham. Ongoing cutting off of the flesh of the natural man, and salvation to the uttermost is experienced through faith in the atoning blood of our High Priest, Jesus

Christ. Abraham experienced salvation to the uttermost through faith in the promise of the coming High Priest as revealed to him in Melchisedec, through bread and wine.

> *And when Abram was ninety years old and nine,*
> *the LORD appeared to Abram, and said unto*
> *him, I am the Almighty God; walk before me, and*
> *be thou perfect.*
> *And I will make my Covenant between me and*
> *thee, and will multiply thee exceedingly...*
> *This is my Covenant, which ye shall keep,*
> *between me and you and thy seed after thee;*
> *Every man child among you shall be*
> *circumcised.*
> *And ye shall circumcise the flesh of your*
> *foreskin; and it shall be a token of the Covenant*
> *betwixt me and you.* (Genesis 17:1,2; 10,11)

Many, many times I have heard Bible teachers and preachers proclaim "that no one is perfect", the implication being that we must recognize our desperate sinful nature and accept the fact that even as believers, we could never live up to God's expectations. This teaching is very disturbing and is Scripturally incorrect, indeed this view is one of the major reasons the denominational church is in such a weakened state today.

It is this same negative response to God's Sovereign Grace, in the Covenant God made to them through Abraham, which caused the Israelites to be exiled into bondage. This state of the believers imperfection is true of the natural man and our fleshly nature, indeed we are evil in the natural, and cannot keep the law.

> *The heart [is] deceitful above all [things], and*
> *desperately wicked: who can know it?*
> (Jeremiah 17:9)

And again:

> *For I know that in me (that is, in my flesh,)*
> *dwelleth no good thing: for to will is present with*

*me; but [how] to perform that which is good I
find not.* (Romans 7:18)

However; If we walk in the Spirit nature we are not under the
law and confines of the flesh nature, which has been and is being
removed from the believer, through faith in the atoning blood of
Christ's present, continual High Priestly ministry.

*[This] I say then, Walk in the Spirit, and ye shall
not fulfil the lust of the flesh.*

*For the flesh lusteth against the Spirit, and the
Spirit against the flesh: and these are contrary
the one to the other: so that ye cannot do the
things that ye would.*

*But if ye be led of the Spirit, ye are not under the
law.* (Galatians 5:16-18)

The benefits and provisions of Christ's High Priestly
intercessory ministry at the right hand of the Father, is not
generally understood or preached by the present day institutional,
or man controlled church, and because of this would-be believers
are missing one of the main purposes of His death and
resurrection, that is to present believers in Christ's sinless
perfection to the Father. For it is Jesus Christ, through the perfect
sacrifice of his atoning blood who has paid the price of perfect
redemption. He alone is worthy. Unless believers have the very
righteousness of God we cannot enter the Kingdom of Heaven,
there is only one advocate that is able and worthy to accomplish
this for us. This is why Jesus, in the Sermon on the Mount said:

*{Be ye therefore perfect, even as your Father
which is in heaven is perfect.}* (Matthew 5:48)

And again, in the same sermon:

*{For I say unto you, That except your
righteousness shall exceed [the righteousness]
of the scribes and Pharisees, ye shall in no case
enter into the kingdom of heaven.}*
(Matthew 5:20)

A true understanding of the doctrine of the High Priestly Ministry of Christ, as mediator of the New Covenant, is a doctrine that would clarify much of the confusion and dogmatic divisions in Christianity today. Through faith in the blood of Christ, all Christian denominations truly have been given the opportunity to set aside doctrinal principles and differences, and be yielded to the unifying glory which the Father instills in the heart of every believer. If believers were to accept the significance of the glory bestowed upon them, through the ever present High Priestly ministry of Christ, then dogmatic differences would disappear.

> *Sanctify them through thy truth: thy word is truth.*
>
> *As thou hast sent me into the world, even so have I also sent them into the world.*
>
> *And for their sakes I sanctify myself, that they also might be sanctified through the truth.*
>
> *Neither pray I for these alone, but for them also which shall believe on me through their word;*
>
> *That they all may be one; as thou, Father, art in me, and I in thee, that they also may be one in us: that the world may believe that thou hast sent me.*
>
> *And the glory which thou gavest me I have given them; that they may be one, even as we are one:* <u>*I in them, and thou in me, that they may be made perfect in one; and that the world may know that thou hast sent me, and hast loved them, as thou hast loved me.*</u> (John 17:17-23)

The above quotation is from the section of Scripture which is known as "Christ's High Priestly intercessory prayer". His concern and continual prayer for His bride, the church, has not changed, for He is the same today as He was yesterday. He has not ceased to pray for the glory, unity and perfection of believers, as we see recorded in the Scriptures above, prior to his crucifixion, when he prayed for all believers that they would share in the glory with which He and the Father are united. The glory which He would share with believers is diminished by denominational divisions, shameful divisions that put a veil over the provisions of grace. Christ is not divided, but, because we as individuals look to church leaders and denominational principles instead of Spirit revealed doctrines for day-to-day guidance, we miss what the Holy Spirit would say to each of us individually, and put denominational loyalties before individual responses to the Gospel.

> *For ye are yet carnal: for whereas there is among you envying, and strife, and divisions, are ye not carnal, and walk as men?*
>
> *For while one saith, I am of Paul; and another, I am of Apollos; are ye not carnal?*
>
> *Who then is Paul, and who is Apollos, but ministers by whom ye believed, even as the Lord gave to every man?*
>
> *I have planted, Apollos watered; but God gave the increase.*
>
> *So then neither is he that planteth any thing, neither he that watereth; but God that giveth the increase.*
>
> *Now he that planteth and he that watereth are one: and every man shall receive his own reward according to his own labour.*
>
> (1 Corinthians 3:3-8)

In the Scriptures above, as in many other Scriptures, believers are given to understand that each person individually is exhorted to respond to the leading of the Holy Spirit, each through his own Spirit revealed knowledge of the Gospel. If believers would come to understand the provisions of Christ's present High Priestly ministry, which is administered to our hearts through faith in the power of the blood of the New

Covenant, perhaps we would come to speak the same thing.

> *Now I beseech you, brethren, by the name of our Lord Jesus Christ, that ye all speak the same thing, and that there be no divisions among you; but that ye be perfectly joined together in the same mind and in the same judgment.*
>
> *For it hath been declared unto me of you, my brethren, by them which are of the house of Chloe, that there are contentions among you.*
>
> *Now this I say, that every one of you saith, I am of Paul; and I of Apollos; and I of Cephas; and I of Christ.*
>
> *Is Christ divided? was Paul crucified for you? or were ye baptized in the name of Paul?*

(1 Corinthians 1:10-13)

This unity of Spirit and speech will only come about as the bride of Christ is awakened to the gift of her perfect righteousness, only to be experienced through faith in the blood of Christ's present High Priestly ministry at the right hand of the Father.

Present church teaching does not accentuate this provision of Christ's present High Priestly ministry at the right hand of the Father, through which all believers are separated from the guilt of their past sin nature. I have seen many statements of faith of various denominational churches and the vast majority readily confess that Christ is ascended into heaven and is seated at the right hand of God, and that He will return. However, these so called statements of faith do not emphasize in any way that He is available to perfectly cleanse and make whole, believers from all unrighteousness, NOW! at this very moment, through His present High Priestly ministry at the Mercy Seat in Heaven. This omission, of His intercession at the right hand of the Father, in the statements of faith, began as far back as the introduction of the Apostles creed in the 2nd century A. D. As in most statements of faith published by the denominational man controlled church's of today, the shorter form of that creed stated: "That they believe in God the Father Almighty, and in Jesus Christ His Only Son our Lord etc..and that He ascended into heaven and is seated at the right hand of the Father, and from thence He shall come to judge the quick and the dead...etc." The desire of God's heart is that believers, through the leading of the Holy Spirit, enter and dwell with Him in the secret place of the Most High, is nowhere mentioned in these creeds.

Although some of the statements of faith mention His intercessory ministry, the full recognition of the exciting provision of further blood cleansing and perfection at the Mercy Seat, is little emphasized. The mention of the perfecting power of the sprinkling of His blood on the Mercy Seat, which power is able to purge the conscience of the believer, is given scant attention if acknowledged at all. Every believer is the beneficiary of the following verse, hopefully the doctrine below will be written upon each heart by the witness of the Divine Spirit.

For by one offering he hath perfected for ever
them that are sanctified. (Hebrews 10:14)

Sanctification and Christ's perfect indwelling Spirit are one and the same. They both speak of being completely separated and free to accept the leading of the Holy Spirit, to live out the will of God, separated from the will of the flesh. To be sanctified, is to give God the glory for His having separated the believers perfect Holy Spirit nature, from his flesh nature. This sanctification is extended to all the seed of Abraham, this is the outworking of the cutting of the Covenant, the "beriyth" with which God passed between the animals when He Sovereignly sealed His Covenant to Abraham.

It is beneficial to look up the word "sanctification" in a Bible dictionary, that it might be confirmed to the heart of the believer, it's full meaning.

If individual believers in the body of Christ understood, as a first priority, the provisions of His sanctifying blood which is theirs through His High Priestly ministry at the right hand of the Father, then the present priorities of denominationalism and dogmatic platitudes would come to be understood for what they really are, vanity.

Denominational divisions are the result of man's interpretation of the Scriptures without placing full dependency upon the witness of the Holy Spirit. Man, restricted by his human nature, cannot relay the truth to another mans heart. The Holy Spirit alone is able to reveal to the believers heart the true meaning of Scriptures, which further forms and anoints in us the mind of Christ. Should we then not come to the conclusion that believers need not look to other men, no matter how well respected they are, to interpret Scriptures for them? Should we not come to the conclusion that the Holy Spirit alone is able to teach our hearts the unity which is of the truth?

> *Let that therefore abide in you, which ye have*
> *heard from the beginning. If that which ye have*
> *heard from the beginning shall remain in you, ye*
> *also shall continue in the Son, and in the Father.*
> *And this is the promise that he hath promised us,*
> *even eternal life.*
> *These things have I written unto you concerning*
> *them that seduce you.*
> *But the anointing which ye have received of him*
> *abideth in you, and ye need not that any man*
> *teach you: but as the same anointing teacheth*
> *you of all things, and is truth, and is no lie, and*
> *even as it hath taught you, ye shall abide in him.*
> *And now, little children, abide in him; that, when*
> *he shall appear, we may have confidence, and*
> *not be ashamed before him at his coming.*
> (1 John 2:24-28)

Because they looked to the man Moses, instead of having

faith in the Covenant of Promise God made to them through Abraham, the children of Israel, as a nation, have been temporarily cut off from Christ the Vine. They have forgotten the Covenant of Promise through which they might be sanctified.

> *Even all nations shall say, Wherefore hath the LORD done thus unto this land? what meaneth the heat of this great anger?*
>
> *Then men shall say, Because they have forsaken the Covenant of the LORD God of their fathers, which he made with them when he brought them forth out of the land of Egypt:*
>
> *For they went and served other gods, and worshipped them, gods whom they knew not, and whom he had not given unto them:*
>
> *And the anger of the LORD was kindled against this land, to bring upon it all the curses that are written in this book:*
>
> *And the LORD rooted them out of their land in anger, and in wrath, and in great indignation, and cast them into another land, as it is this day.*
>
> *The secret things belong unto the LORD our God: but those things which are revealed belong unto us and to our children for ever, that we may do all the words of this law.*
>
> (Deuteronomy 29:24-29)

The children of Israel had forgotten that their entrance into Canaan would be blessed only if they remembered God's Covenant which He swore to Abraham and his seed.

> *In that I command thee this day to love the LORD thy God, to walk in his ways, and to keep his commandments and his statutes and his judgments, that thou mayest live and multiply: and the LORD thy God shall bless thee in the land whither thou goest to possess it.*

*But if thine heart turn away, so that thou wilt not
hear, but shalt be drawn away, and worship
other gods, and serve them;*

*I denounce unto you this day, that ye shall surely
perish, and that ye shall not prolong your days
upon the land, whither thou passest over Jordan
to go to possess it.*

*I call heaven and earth to record this day against
you, that I have set before you life and death,
blessing and cursing: therefore choose life, that
both thou and thy seed may live:*

*That thou mayest love the LORD thy God, and
that thou mayest obey his voice, and that thou
mayest cleave unto him: for he is thy life, and the
length of thy days: that thou mayest dwell in the
land which the LORD sware unto thy fathers, <u>to
Abraham, to Isaac, and to Jacob, to give them.</u>*

(Deuteronomy 30:16-20)

The New Covenant, as recorded in Hebrews chapter eight,
being the revealed glory of the promise God made to His people
through Abraham, has also to a large degree, been forgotten by
the present day virtual church. The children of Israel perished in
the wilderness because they looked upon the man Moses as their
deliverer and ignored the Covenant of Promise God made to
them through Abraham and confirmed in Moses' writings, the
Pentateuch. Jesus warned the Pharisees of their continued
ignorance of the promise God made to all believers through
Abraham, those who put their trust in the man Moses instead of
what was revealed of God through Moses' writings.

*I am come in my Father's name, and ye receive
me not: if another shall come in his own name,
him ye will receive.*

*How can ye believe, which receive honour one of
another, and seek not the honour that cometh*

from God only?
Do not think that I will accuse you to the Father:
there is one that accuseth you, even Moses, in
whom ye trust.
For had ye believed Moses, ye would have
believed me: for he wrote of me. (John 5:43-46)

Likewise, New Covenant believers, because they too have ignored the Covenant God made to us through Abraham, have reverted once again to depend upon church leaders to act as their prime mediators between themselves and God. Christian unity will only become manifest when believers allow the Holy Spirit to mediate and interpret the truth to our hearts, through belief in the first principles of the oracles of God, His Holy Covenants, separate from the influence of denominational church dogma. It is the Lord who promises unity of believers in the Spirit and that through Him alone. If believers would listen to what He would say to the church through the Holy Spirit, man's divisive dogmatic professions of conceived truth would become of little significance. Through Christ's present High Priestly ministry, a Priest forever in the order of Melchisedek, He alone becomes the individual believers mediator of the New Covenant.

For there is one God, and one mediator between
God and men, the man Christ Jesus;
Who gave himself a ransom for all, to be testified
in due time. (1 Timothy 2:5,6)

This truth of Christ's present intercession at the right hand of the Father, which affords us ongoing daily salvation, is a little recognized provision of God's love given to all believers through His Sovereign Grace. Until we believers come to know and accept the glorious provisions and benefits that are ours through the New Covenant, and the present High Priestly ministry of Christ at the right hand of the Father, we are ignoring the efficacy of Christ's blood to purge and purify our consciences from the guilt and sin of our original Adamic nature. Christ's present joy at the right hand of the Father not only includes presenting His glorious pure bride, the mystical church, to the Father in His spotless perfection, but to continually offer to every individual believer further ongoing salvation to the uttermost. As we have read in his High Priestly prayer in John 17 previously, the Lord continually further purifies His church through righteous judgements from the Throne of Grace. God's desire to meet with His Holy people at the Mercy Seat was also expressed in the Old Testament, in the Tabernacle of Witness.

> And there *I will* meet with thee, and *I will* commune with thee from above the mercy seat, from between the two cherubims which [are] upon the ark of the testimony, of all [things] which *I will* give thee in commandment unto the children of Israel. (Exodus 25:22)

Christ NOW continually sanctifies believers who have faith in the blood perfecting and cleansing provisions of His High Priestly Ministry. God still desires that believers continually dwell in His presence at the Mercy Seat.

> For by one offering he hath perfected for ever them that are sanctified.
> Whereof the Holy Ghost also is a witness to us: for after that he had said before,
> This is the Covenant that I will make with them after those days, saith the Lord, I will put my laws into their hearts, and in their minds will I write them; And their sins and iniquities will I remember no more.
> Now where remission of these is, there is no more offering for sin.
> Having therefore, brethren, boldness to enter into the holiest by the blood of Jesus,
> By a new and living way, which he hath consecrated for us, through the veil, that is to

say, his flesh;
And having an high priest over the house of
God;
Let us draw near with a true heart in full
assurance of faith, having our hearts sprinkled
from an evil conscience, and our bodies washed
with pure water. (Hebrews 10:14-22)

It is here within the Holy of Holies, where God desires to meet with His people whom He has justified and declared righteous through faith in what the blood of Christ has done, and is continually doing for us NOW. It is His will that we should meet with Him there, therefore, we need not consider such a thought of entering into the Holy of Holies with trepidation and false guilt. Not only is it His will for us to come into His very presence but to ignore this provision is to do despite to the Spirit of Grace, and in so doing we limit the glory with which He would clothe every believer.

God's invitation for those believers who walk in the Spirit and not in the flesh, to enter and dwell with Him, is for the continual present NOW. Dwelling in His presence is only for those believers who have accepted the provisions of the New Covenant as quoted above where the Lord has promised that He will no longer remember our sins and iniquities. Believers who have faith in the blood of Christ to have completely separated and circumcised their flesh from the Spirit of Christ which indwells us, are encouraged to come boldly to the very Throne Room of God, NOW. If believers cannot accept the glorious provisions of the New Covenant which totally separates flesh and Spirit then the thoughts of coming into the Lord's very presence is viewed with trepidation and fear. It is only through faith in the blood of Christ to perfectly cleanse and present believers to the Father in His righteousness, that believers are invited to enter in the very presence of His very Holiness, because in Him there is no unholiness. It is only when believers, through faith in the sprinkled blood of Christ, have been clothed in the pure white robes of God's righteousness, that we are enabled to enter boldly to the Throne of Grace. None are worthy of their own righteousness to come before His Holy presence, but the Lamb who was slain before the foundation of the world is worthy, and He continually presents believers in His perfection through our faith in His sprinkled blood on the Mercy Seat.

Believers need not attempt to reach some "super Christian" status through our own efforts, before being eligible to come boldly before God's presence at the Mercy Seat. The indwelling Holy Spirit of the righteousness of God, which has been imputed to all believers, is our entrance to the very Throne Room of Grace and meant to be experienced NOW. Although He is passed into the heavens, and we remain on this earth in the flesh, we are invited, through the Spirit of Christ, to come boldly into His very presence.

> *But ye are come unto mount Sion, and unto the city of the living God, the heavenly Jerusalem, and to an innumerable company of angels,*
>
> *To the general assembly and church of the firstborn, which are written in heaven, and to God the Judge of all, and to the spirits of just men made perfect,*
>
> *And to Jesus the mediator of the new Covenant, and to the blood of sprinkling, that speaketh better things than that of Abel.*
>
> (Hebrews 12:22-24)

Indeed, not to understand through the Scriptures that it is the will of the Father for believers to enter His Holy presence, within the second veil, is to ignore the provisions of grace and the power of the blood of the New Covenant.

> *He that despised Moses' law died without mercy under two or three witnesses:*
>
> *Of how much sorer punishment, suppose ye,*

shall he be thought worthy, who hath trodden under foot the Son of God, and hath counted the blood of the Covenant, wherewith he was sanctified, an unholy thing, and hath done despite unto the Spirit of grace?
(Hebrews 10:28,29)

When Christ's flesh was broken on the cross, the veil in the temple was rent from top to bottom, both in the earthly tabernacle which God gave to the children of Israel through Moses on Mount Sinai, which was a figure of the true, but the veil in the true Heavenly Tabernacle was also rent. Therefore, through Christ's blood and His body we have access into the very presence of God's glory.

And almost all things are by the law purged with blood; and without shedding of blood is no remission.

It was therefore necessary that the patterns of things in the heavens should be purified with these; but the heavenly things themselves with better sacrifices than these.

For Christ is not entered into the holy places made with hands, which are the figures of the true; but into heaven itself, now to appear in the presence of God for us:

Nor yet that he should offer himself often, as the high priest entereth into the holy place every year with blood of others;

For then must he often have suffered since the foundation of the world: but now once in the end of the world hath he appeared to put away sin by the sacrifice of himself. (Hebrews 9:22-26)

Free access into the Holiest is the heart of the Sovereign Grace of the New Covenant, this is the provision of the blood of Christ, drink freely of it and thereby glorify Him.

For I have received of the Lord that which also I

delivered unto you, That the Lord Jesus the same
night in which he was betrayed took bread:
And when he had given thanks, he brake it, and
said, Take, eat: this is my body, which is broken
for you: this do in remembrance of me.
After the same manner also he took the cup,
when he had supped, saying, This cup is the new
testament in my blood: this do ye, as oft as ye
drink it, in remembrance of me.
For as often as ye eat this bread, and drink this
cup, ye do shew the Lord's death till he come.
Wherefore whosoever shall eat this bread, and
drink this cup of the Lord, unworthily, shall be
guilty of the body and blood of the Lord.
(1 Corinthians 11:23-27)

As we see quoted in the Scriptures above the Lord asks believers, when they drink and eat of the emblems of the New Covenant to do so in remembrance of Him. We are exhorted to remember what the sacrifice of His blood and body has accomplished for us. As we saw in the quotation of Hebrews 10:19,20 above, believers are exhorted to remember that it is the offering of Christ's body and blood which has given believers the boldness to enter into the Holiest, the Throne of Grace, that we might obtain mercy and find grace to help in the time of need.

I know of nowhere in Scripture where believers, prior to partaking of the emblems of the blood and body of Christ, are required of the Lord to review their sins and iniquities, as we are so often reminded of by present day teachers. To review the sinful nature of our flesh is to count the blood of the Lamb slain from the foundation of the world, as not having made believers worthy to approach the Throne of Grace with boldness.

Surely we are to examine ourselves, but the Scriptures say we are to examine ourselves in regards to the degree we have accepted, and are walking in the Spirit of faith. Believers are exhorted to contemplate the degree to which we have accepted God's Grace and mercy as having separated and sanctified us unto Himself. To look back again upon the guilt of our sin nature is to deny the separating power of the atoning blood of Christ, to have completely cleansed believers from all unrighteousness. How would the blood which Jesus Christ shed on the cross as our atonement and sanctification, which also at the same time set aside the believers sin nature, speak of our need to once again look upon and convict us of the guilt of that sin nature? For God has divided and removed our old sin nature, separated from The Spirit of Christ which lives within the believer, as far as the east is from the west.

Believers are exhorted through the Scriptures to judge themselves, to show themselves approved unto God through the study and belief in His Word. Faith in the circumcising power of the sharp sword of the Word determines the degree to which the flesh has been separated from The Spirit of Christ within the heart of the believer. It is for our redemption the Father gave His only begotten Son and sent Him into the world, not for condemnation, but to give believers a sentence of "not guilty". Therefore may we again conclude that to contemplate the old man of our circumcised sin nature, as not having been crucified with Christ, is to ask Him to be crucified again? Could it be that to consider the robes of righteousness, with which God has clothed believers, as having been spotted by the remembrance of sin, is to drink of this cup of His blood and to eat of the bread of His body, unworthily? May we conclude that to "do this in remembrance of me" is to recognize that the blood of the New Covenant speaks of our High Priest as being anointed to continually present believers in His very own perfection to the Father?

We may thus also conclude that the true unity of all New Covenant believers, will only become our experience when we recognize that we are perfectly united in God's Glory, at the

Throne of Grace. The unity of the mystery of the pure spotless bride of Christ, will only become a reality, when we accept that we are anointed to dwell in God's very presence, through faith in the sprinkled blood of our Saviour, Jesus Christ, our High Priest forever in the order of Melchisedec.

> *But ye, beloved, building up yourselves on your most holy faith, praying in the Holy Ghost,*
> *Keep yourselves in the love of God, looking for the mercy of our Lord Jesus Christ unto eternal life.*
> *And of some have compassion, making a difference:*
> *And others save with fear, pulling them out of the fire; hating even the garment spotted by the flesh.*
> <u>*Now unto him that is able to keep you from falling, and to present you faultless before the presence of his glory with exceeding joy,*</u>
> *To the only wise God our Saviour, be glory and majesty, dominion and power, both now and ever. Amen.* (Jude 20-25)

Also:

> *Now the God of peace, that brought again from the dead our Lord Jesus, that great shepherd of the sheep, through the blood of the everlasting Covenant,*
> <u>*Make you perfect in every good work to do his will,*</u> *working in you that which is wellpleasing in his sight, through Jesus Christ; to whom be glory for ever and ever. Amen.* (Hebrews 13:20,21)

11

PERFECTION
Teleioo, Teleios

Maturing through experiencing the Spirit of God's perfection, and having been declared positionally perfect, are in most instances in the New Testament, interpretations of two Greek words, Teleioo and Teleios.

Teleios is the Greek word interpreted as "perfect" and is an expression of God's declaration of His perfection in our <u>Spirit</u> nature only, it does not suggest that in our flesh dwells any good thing. Teleios perfection is the believers foundational position in Him. God's declaration of the believers justified nature, through faith in the blood of Christ, that is, God's declaration of the believer's <u>positional</u> righteousness perfection, is described by the word Teleios.

> *Who shall lay any thing to the charge of God's*
> *elect? It is God that justifieth.* (Romans 8:33)

An example of Teleios perfection is included in the Scripture below, where both words interpreted as perfect, are the Greek word Teleios.

> *Be ye therefore perfect, even as your Father*
> *which is in heaven is perfect.* (Matthew 5:48)

Teleioo is a Greek word also interpreted as "perfect" and refers to our imperfect responses, through our imperfect works of unbelief, to His perfect Spirit within. Teleioo perfecting is experiencing or growing, or conforming, or being made into the likeness of His perfect Spirit which indwells the heart of every believer. Teleioo speaks of <u>experiencing</u> ongoing daily salvation, through the present High Priestly ministry of Christ, at the Throne of Grace.

> *Wherefore he is able also to save them to the*
> *uttermost that come unto God by him, seeing he*
> *ever liveth to make intercession for them.*
> *For such an high priest became us, who is holy,*
> *harmless, undefiled, separate from sinners, and*
> *made higher than the heavens;*
> (Hebrews 7:25,26)

Spiritual growth has nothing to do with the flesh nature, for the old man of the flesh cannot be improved upon, for the old nature is dead and was buried in baptism.

Any good expository dictionary will confirm that the meaning of the word "Teleioo" is as follows: "bring to an end by completing or perfecting, the perfecting of faith by works, as Christ assured completion of His earthly course in the accomplishment of the Father's will." So we see that it is this word which denotes a growing or maturing process. A Scriptural example of the use of this word is:

> *I in them, and thou in me, that they may <u>be made</u>*
> <u>*perfect in one*</u>*; and that the world may know that*
> *thou hast sent me, and hast loved them, as thou*
> *hast loved me.* (John 17:23)

In chapter three of the book of Philippians we see an example of these two Greek words Teleios and Teleioo used and interpreted as the English word "perfect".

> *Not as though I had already attained, either were*
> *already perfect: but I follow after, if that I may*
> *apprehend that for which also I am apprehended*
> *of Christ Jesus.* (Philippians 3:12)

In the Scripture above "Teleioo" is used to denote Paul's admission of his incompleteness and his immaturity in Christ's gift of His perfection. However Paul recognizes that he may follow after the perfection which he is apprehended of Christ, and continues to follow after the leading of the perfect Spirit of Christ within. We see the word "Teleios" used in contradistinction in the Scripture below.

> Let us therefore, <u>as many as be perfect</u>, be thus minded: and if in any thing ye be otherwise minded, God shall reveal even this unto you. (Philippians 3:15)

Above Paul is saying that as many as <u>be perfect</u>, or declared righteous by the Father, and those who have fully accepted their God given positional perfection in Christ, be mindful of the unity of the brotherhood, which is made manifest in the knowledge of the power of Christ's resurrection. The consciousness of neither positional nor experiential perfection is possible without the believer first having recognized that his flesh nature has been circumcised completely from his God given Holy Spirit nature, even as God performed this separation of flesh and Spirit to Abraham and all his seed. This process is called sanctification.

> For both he that sanctifieth and they who are sanctified [are] all of one: for which cause he is not ashamed to call them brethren, (Hebrews 2:11)

A third Greek word which is, in other instances interpreted as "perfect", is the word "Katartizo", which also refers to the unity of believers upon confession of their perfection through God's provisions, is quoted below.

> Finally, brethren, farewell. Be perfect, be of good comfort, be of one mind, live in peace; and the God of love and peace shall be with you. (2 Corinthians 13:11)

Generally speaking, perfection of Saints is interpreted as growing into Christian maturity. It is true that many Scriptures testify of the maturing process afforded believers, through the Holy Spirit's leading as in the verses below, where perfection is the interpretation of the Greek word "katartizo".

> *And he gave some, apostles; and some, prophets; and some, evangelists; and some, pastors and teachers;*
> *For the perfecting of the saints, for the work of the ministry, for the edifying of the body of Christ:* (Ephesians 4:11,12)

The same word is translated as being perfectly joined together in agreement, in the Testimony of Jesus Christ through the confirmation of the Holy Spirit, as in the Scripture below.

> *Now I beseech you, brethren, by the name of our Lord Jesus Christ, that ye all speak the same thing, and [that] there be no divisions among you; but [that] ye be perfectly joined together in the same mind and in the same judgment.*
> (1 Corinthians 1:10)

Also, Jesus Himself has been depicted as growing into perfection, or being made perfect, into the perfection his Father had given him from the beginning.

> *And being made perfect, he became the author of eternal salvation unto all them that obey him;*
> (Hebrews 5:9)

So this Word speaks of the perfecting or growing in the unity of the Glory of the Gospel, of the growing <u>experience</u> in the God given <u>position</u> which is the believers portion through faith in the blood of the New Covenant.

As long as believers continue to deny Christ's perfection in their Spirit nature and look at their own imperfection in the flesh, we will never be able to recognize Christ's perfection in other believers. Until believers accept the fact that it is no longer the flesh which governs our responses to God's righteousness, but it is The Spirit of Christ's perfection who dwells within that guides us, we will never be united in the Glory of His perfection. There will never be any unity of believers in the flesh, believers are only united as one through His Spirit.

In the Old Testament, the Hebrew word most commonly translated into English as the word "perfect" is the word "Tamiym". "Tamiym" compares most favourably with the Greek word "Teleios" as described above, it denotes entirety, integrity, truth, without blemish, complete, full, perfect, undefiled, without spot, upright or whole. In context, this verse was given to the children of Israel in order to encourage them to sanctify or separate themselves from the pollution of other nations.

> *Thou shalt be perfect with the LORD thy God.*

(Deuteronomy 18:13)

Also the Hebrew word "Tamiym" is translated as the word denoting <u>positional</u> perfection when God declared Abraham and his seed to be perfect and righteous before Him.

> *And when Abram was ninety years old and nine,*
> *the LORD appeared to Abram, and said unto*
> *him, <u>I am the Almighty God; walk before me, and</u>*
> *<u>be thou perfect.</u>*
> *And I will make my Covenant between me and*
> *thee, and will multiply thee exceedingly.*
> *And Abram fell on his face: and God talked with*
> *him, saying,*
> *As for me, behold, my Covenant is with thee,*
> *and thou shalt be a father of many nations.*
> *Neither shall thy name any more be called*
> *Abram, but thy name shall be Abraham; for a*
> *father of many nations have I made thee.*

(Genesis 17:1-5)

In the verses above it is evident that Abraham did not experience perfection before he was given positional perfection. Abraham never did experience perfection in the flesh, nor did God rescind his positional perfection when his faith wavered. God declared Abraham's perfection and righteousness to be that of a Spiritual nature, separate from the flesh.

The Hebrew word "shalem" in the Old Testament favourably corresponds to the Greek word "teleioo", which we have seen from the Scriptures above, refers to <u>experiencing</u>, maturing or growing in the <u>positional perfection</u> which God has given every believer, through faith in the blood of Christ. This Hebrew word denotes a response to the gift of God, a building process, as in the Scripture below where Solomon's temple was being built until it was perfected.

> *Now all the work of Solomon was prepared unto*
> *the day of the foundation of the house of the*
> *LORD, and until it was finished.*
> *[So] the house of the LORD was perfected.*
> (2 Chronicles 8:16)

Below we see an example of the response of a heart being matured by the acknowledgement of the Lord's provisions through his statutes and commandments.

> *Let your heart therefore be perfect with the*
> *LORD our God, to walk in his statutes, and to*
> *keep his commandments, as at this day.*
> (1 Kings 8:61)

In conclusion, believers will never be unified in the body of Christ, until we recognize that we have been given a new perfect nature in Christ, sanctified and separated from our old sin nature of the flesh and the first Adam.

12

WHY MUST BELIEVERS BE PERFECT?

All believers in the atoning blood of Jesus Christ, who would enter the Kingdom of Heaven, have been judged and declared righteous and perfect, because it is God who justifies. God the Father has made provision for all believers to become partakers of His Divine perfect nature, through faith in the blood of the perfect sacrifice, Jesus Christ.

> *Be ye therefore perfect, even as your Father*
> *which is in heaven is perfect.* (Matthew 5:48)

Even before the flood, perfection was imputed to those whom God chose. By Grace He separated and delivered the righteous believers from the condemned unbelievers.

> *But Noah found grace in the eyes of the LORD.*
> *These are the generations of Noah: Noah was a*
> *just man and perfect in his generations, and*
> *Noah walked with God.* (Genesis 6:8,9)

Even as God commanded Father Abraham, through whom all believers receive the blessing of God's righteousness and perfection, in Jesus Christ.

And when Abram was ninety years old and nine, the LORD appeared to Abram, and said unto him, I am the Almighty God; walk before me, and be thou perfect.

And I will make my Covenant between me and thee, and will multiply thee exceedingly.

And Abram fell on his face: and God talked with him, saying,

As for me, behold, my Covenant is with thee, and thou shalt be a father of many nations.

Neither shall thy name any more be called Abram, but thy name shall be Abraham; for a father of many nations have I made thee.

(Genesis 17:1-5)

Even as the children of Israel were admonished of the Lord to keep themselves Holy and perfect before Him through His provisions.

For all that do these things are an abomination unto the LORD: and because of these abominations the LORD thy God doth drive them out from before thee.

Thou shalt be perfect with the LORD thy God.

(Deuteronomy 18:12,13)

Even as King David glorified God for the gift of His perfection, the perfection which David acknowledged as the source of his strength and power, through the Word.

As for God, his way is perfect; the word of the LORD is tried: he is a buckler to all them that trust in him.

For who is God, save the LORD? and who is a rock, save our God?

God is my strength and power: and he maketh my way perfect.

(2 Samuel 22:31-33; Psalms 18:30-32)

The peace of the Lord rests upon the righteous, those who accept His perfection.

Mark the perfect man, and behold the upright: for the end of that man is peace.

But the transgressors shall be destroyed together: the end of the wicked shall be cut off.

But the salvation of the righteous is of the LORD: he is their strength in the time of trouble.

(Psalms 37:37-39)

Also:

Finally, brethren, farewell. Be perfect, be of good comfort, be of one mind, live in peace; and the God of love and peace shall be with you.

(2 Corinthians 13:11)

Job, a man whom God tested severely in order that He might bless Job with even more abundance than that which he had previously, was perfect in all his ways even before his testings.

There was a man in the land of Uz, whose name was Job; and that man was perfect and upright, and one that feared God, and eschewed evil.

(Job 1:1)

Also:

And the LORD said unto Satan, Hast thou considered my servant Job, that there is none like him in the earth, a perfect and an upright man, one that feareth God, and escheweth evil?

(Job 1:8)

In the book of the Proverbs, we read that it is through the acknowledgement of righteous perfection that the upright are directed in His way.

The righteousness of the perfect shall direct his way: but the wicked shall fall by his own wickedness. (Proverbs 11:5)

How good must we be in order to enter the Kingdom of Heaven? In Matthew 19:16-22 we read of the rich young ruler who was admonished of the Lord, that if he would enter into heaven he must have perfectly kept the ten commandments, which he claimed to have done. Had he done so, Jesus would have considered him to be perfect, having been declared righteous and positionally of full age, "Teleios". Although he claimed to have kept the ten commandments from his youth up, it was obvious from Jesus' further comment, that even had he done so, he was still not righteous enough to enter the Kingdom of Heaven nor to be His Disciple. It is obvious from Scripture that all men were born with a sinful nature, and had the rich young ruler, who was born of the same sinful Adamic nature as are all men, through his own will kept all the commandments from his youth up, he still would not have attained the righteousness required of God, to enter His Kingdom. The truth remains that natural man may not enter the Kingdom of God, until he is reborn of the Spirit as he has not been declared righteous and perfect, justified. In order that the rich man might prove his sincerity, Jesus told him he must sell his earthly possessions and give to the poor, thereby demonstrating that he valued the righteous judgements of Christ and the treasures of heaven, more than his earthly riches. This he did not do.

> *Jesus said unto him, {If thou wilt be perfect, go [and] sell that thou hast, and give to the poor, and thou shalt have treasure in heaven: and come [and] follow me.}*
>
> *But when the young man heard that saying, he went away sorrowful: for he had great possessions." (Matthew 19:21,22)*

From the verse above we understand that the rich young ruler valued his own earthly riches more than the treasure of eternal riches in Christ's perfection. He had not, nor could he have as he claimed, kept the ten commandments, for he obviously loved his riches more than the Lord God or he would have sold them in order to seek the righteousness of the Kingdom of God. Nor did he love his neighbour as himself, or he would have been willing to share his wealth.

Again in Matthew chapter five, in the Sermon on the Mount, Jesus tells us:

> *{For I say unto you, That except your righteousness shall exceed [the righteousness] of the scribes and Pharisees, ye shall in no case enter into the kingdom of heaven.}*
>
> (Matthew 5:20)

Few of us have attempted, through our flesh nature, to keep the letter of the law of Moses as scrupulously as did the scribes and Pharisees, for they tried to adhere to over 600 rules. Obviously then, as Jesus stated in this, His Sermon on the Mount, the Pharisees were not made righteous through their attempts to obtain the status of righteousness through the law of the commandments. If then believer's righteousness must exceed the righteousness of the Pharisees, how then are believers to receive this righteousness? Jesus answers this question for us in the last verse of His Sermon on the Mount

> *{Be ye therefore perfect, even as your Father which is in heaven is perfect.}*
>
> (Matthew 5:48)

The blood of Christ was, and still remains a perfecting sacrifice, because Father God declared and accepted it as perfect, otherwise there would be need for more than one sacrifice to make sinners whole and complete in Him.

> *For by one offering he hath <u>perfected</u> for ever them that are sanctified.*
>
> (Hebrews 10:14)

Also:

> *If therefore <u>perfection</u> were by the Levitical priesthood, (for under it the people received the law,) what further need [was there] that another priest should rise after the order of Melchisedec,*

and not be called after the order of Aaron?
(Hebrews 7:11)

Above we see that it was necessary that Christ should become the perfect sacrifice and also our perfect High Priest, in order that believers need not attempt to achieve perfection through the commandments of the law, as did the Pharisees.

In the Scriptures below, we are once more reminded that the perfect church, the mysterious body of Christ, the Spirit of just men made perfect, is only unified through faith in the blood of the perfect sacrifice, Jesus Christ, our High Priest forever, in the order of Melchisedec.

> *But ye are come unto mount Sion, and unto the city of the living God, the heavenly Jerusalem, and to an innumerable company of angels,*
> *To the general assembly and church of the firstborn, which are written in heaven, and to God the Judge of all, and to the spirits of just men made perfect,*
> *And to Jesus the mediator of the new Covenant, and to the blood of sprinkling, that speaketh better things than that of Abel.*
> (Hebrews 12:22-24)

Prior to Jesus' crucifixion, He prayed to our Father in Heaven as our High Priest, as an example of His present High Priestly ministry at the right hand of the Father. An example of the Spirit in which He prays for all believers, NOW!

> *Neither pray I for these alone, but for them also which shall believe on me through their word;*
> *That they all may be one; as thou, Father, art in me, and I in thee, that they also may be one in us: that the world may believe that thou hast sent me.*
> *And the glory which thou gavest me I have given them; that they may be one, even as we are one:*
> *I in them, and thou in me, that they may be made*

*perfect in one; and that the world may know that
thou hast sent me, and hast loved them, as thou
hast loved me.* (John 17:20-23)

There is no provision for imperfection, uncleanliness or unrighteousness in the Kingdom of God. His mystical church is the pure holy spotless bride of Christ, NOW!

*Husbands, love your wives, even as Christ also
loved the church, and gave himself for it;*

*That he might sanctify and cleanse it with the
washing of water by the word,*

*That he might present it to himself a glorious
church, not having spot, or wrinkle, or any such
thing; but that it should be holy and without
blemish.*

*So ought men to love their wives as their own
bodies. He that loveth his wife loveth himself.*

*For no man ever yet hated his own flesh; but
nourisheth and cherisheth it, even as the Lord
the church:*

*For we are members of his body, of his flesh, and
of his bones.*

*For this cause shall a man leave his father and
mother, and shall be joined unto his wife, and
they two shall be one flesh.*

*This is a great mystery: but I speak concerning
Christ and the church.* (Ephesians 5:25-32)

Certainly the believers perfection in Christ is a mystery even as the body of Christ, the true unified church, is a mystery. Present day ministers who are ordained to preach the Word of God, are admonished to edify the mysterious church, the body of Christ, with the message of perfection and consequential unity in Christ.

*And he gave some, apostles; and some, prophets;
and some, evangelists; and some, pastors and*

teachers;

For the perfecting of the saints, for the work of
the ministry, for the edifying of the body of
Christ:

Till we all come in the unity of the faith, and of
the knowledge of the Son of God, unto a perfect
man, unto the measure of the stature of the
fulness of Christ: (Ephesians 4:11-13)

Have we, as believers, through present day preaching, been given to understand that the work of the ministry of pastors and teachers is to make known the unity and perfection of the faithful in Christ's perfection? This unity and perfection of the mysterious body of Christ will only come about, when we awaken to the knowledge that the blood of Christ, through His present High Priestly ministry at the right hand of the Father, continually presents believers to God in His very own perfection.

If God declares believers to be perfect and righteous before Him, through faith in the sprinkling of the blood of Christ on the Mercy Seat, then how perfect and righteous are those whom God has declared to be perfect and righteous?

13

ACCEPTING OUR POSITION IN HIM

The biggest challenge facing individual Christians, as we seek first the Kingdom of God and His righteousness, is in child like faith to continually and unconditionally keep our hearts open to the leading of the Holy Spirit, to simply believe and accept the goodness of God. Only through faith in the power of the blood of Christ are we able to accept the manifold gifts He has given us through God's will, and His Covenants to mankind. The history of His mystical church is founded upon His Covenants, not upon man's recorded observations and denominational responses of His Works, throughout the ages. The highest mountain believers will be asked to climb, in order that we might do the Works of God, is to set aside the traditions and teachings of man in favour of simply believing what the Scriptures say to us, through the interpretation of the Holy Spirit.

> *Jesus answered them and said, Verily, verily, I say unto you, Ye seek me, not because ye saw the miracles, but because ye did eat of the loaves, and were filled.*
>
> *Labour not for the meat which perisheth, but for*

> *that meat which endureth unto everlasting life,*
> *which the Son of man shall give unto you: for*
> *him hath God the Father sealed.*
> *Then said they unto him, What shall we do, that*
> *we might work the works of God?*
> *Jesus answered and said unto them, <u>This is the</u>*
> <u>*work of God, that ye believe on him whom he*</u>
> <u>*hath sent.*</u> (John 6:26-29)

God has declared all believers to be <u>positionally</u> of His perfect righteous nature, through faith in the perfect blood sacrifice of Jesus Christ, who paid so dearly for our perfection in Him. If the perfect sprinkled sacrifice of the blood of Jesus Christ on the Mercy Seat did not afford believers His perfection in God, then Christ's blood was of no effect, there was no redemption, and the Word of God would be null and void. Believers cannot <u>experience</u> in the flesh the perfection of Christ's nature within, because the Spirit and the flesh are two separate entities.

> *But this man, after he had offered one sacrifice*
> *for sins for ever, sat down on the right hand of*
> *God;*
> *From henceforth expecting till his enemies be*
> *made his footstool.*
> <u>*For by one offering he hath perfected for ever*</u>
> <u>*them that are sanctified.*</u> (Hebrews 10:12-14)

The core message of both the mystical body of Christ and the virtual denominational church is that men, need initially to repent at the foot of the cross. There is no salvation afforded unregenerated man except through faith in what Jesus Christ has accomplished, on the behalf of sinners, on the cross.

> *Or despisest thou the riches of his goodness and*
> *forbearance and longsuffering; not knowing that*
> *the goodness of God leadeth thee to repentance?*
> (Romans 2:4)

This message of the necessity of initial salvation is very true, but until both the mystical body of Christ and the denominational church are made aware of the many stages of further ongoing salvation afforded them, through the Covenants and the High Priestly ministry of Christ, at the right hand of the Father, they will never know of the gift of righteousness and perfection, which is their inheritance as the seed of Abraham. It is through faith in the shed blood and death of Jesus Christ on the cross, and belief in God's power to raise Him from the dead, where the unredeemed first find eternal life giving salvation, through repentance. However, until the redeemed, the born again believers, through the word of God, are awakened to the positional righteousness of God, which He has bestowed upon them, they cannot experience the rewards of further salvation and growing in His righteousness.

> *Awake to righteousness, and sin not; for some*
> *have not the knowledge of God: I speak this to*
> *your shame.* (1 Corinthians 15:34)

Only the Spirit revealed Gospel of Grace, can afford men the knowledge of God's plan of salvation to accomplish this further ongoing circumcision of the flesh. In order to awake to this further perfect righteousness it requires that believers follow the trail of Christ's blood, the crimson cord of the Gospel, from the cross to the Mercy Seat, within the Heavenly Throne Room of Grace. It is a glorious enlightenment when believers come to realize that it is through the present High Priestly ministry of Christ, within the Holy of Holies, that the sprinkling of His redeeming blood on the Heavenly Mercy Seat continually presents us in His righteousness to the Father. This was typified in the Old Testament on the day of Atonement.

> *For the law having a shadow of good things to*
> *come, and not the very image of the things, can*
> *never with those sacrifices which they offered*
> *year by year* <u>*continually make the comers*</u>
> <u>*thereunto perfect.*</u>
> *For then would they not have ceased to be*

offered? because that the worshippers once purged should have had no more conscience of sins. (Hebrews 10:1,2)

But NOW, in New Testament times, we see that it is through faith in the propitiation and redeeming blood of Christ that God's wrath toward fallen mankind has been mercifully expiated. And NOW, this same propitiation through God's Grace, imputes to believers God's very own righteousness and complete redemption from the guilt of our sin nature, past, present and future.

> <u>Now</u> we know that what things soever the law saith, it saith to them who are under the law: that every mouth may be stopped, and all the world may become guilty before God.
>
> Therefore by the deeds of the law there shall no flesh be justified in his sight: for by the law is the knowledge of sin.
>
> <u>But now the righteousness of God without the law is manifested,</u> being witnessed by the law and the prophets;
>
> Even the righteousness of God which is by faith of Jesus Christ unto all and upon all them that believe: for there is no difference:
>
> For all have sinned, and come short of the glory of God;
>
> Being justified freely by his grace through the redemption that is in Christ Jesus:
>
> Whom God hath set forth to be a propitiation through faith in his blood, to declare his righteousness for the remission of sins that are past, through the forbearance of God;
>
> To declare, I say, at this time his righteousness: that he might be just, and the justifier of him which believeth in Jesus. (Romans 3:19-26)

Until believers come to understand that it is God who supplies all our needs pertaining to life and Godliness, and it is He who sustains all life within us pertaining to physical well-being, we have no Holy reference with which to see the insignificance of our own finite power. Until we, through His Word, realize the gift of His righteousness given us through grace, we by default must remain dependent upon our own existentialism.

> *And he humbled thee, and suffered thee to hunger, and fed thee with manna, which thou knewest not, neither did thy fathers know; that he might make thee know that man doth not live by bread only, but by every [word] that proceedeth out of the mouth of the LORD doth man live.*
> (Deuteronomy 8:3)

The children of Israel were warned not to forget God's goodness, lest the Covenant of Abraham be taken from them, which unfortunately, is exactly what happened.

> *Who fed thee in the wilderness with manna, which thy fathers knew not, that he might humble thee, and that he might prove thee, to do thee good at thy latter end;*
> *And thou say in thine heart, My power and the might of [mine] hand hath gotten me this wealth.*
> *But thou shalt remember the LORD thy God: for [it is] he that giveth thee power to get wealth, that he may establish his Covenant which he sware unto thy fathers, as [it is] this day.*
> *And it shall be, if thou do at all forget the Lord thy God, and walk with other gods, and serve them, and worship them, I testify against you this day that ye shall surely perish.*
> (Deuteronomy 8:16-19)

For the believer, not to acknowledge the perfection of the righteousness of God within, is to disbelieve the Word of God and ignore the power of the blood of Christ, as well as to do despite to the Spirit of Grace. This doctrine of God's indwelling righteousness and perfection through faith in the blood of Christ, is the strength of the New Covenant, given to us at the expense of Christ's suffering on the cross. As Jesus prayed for us as our High Priest in the garden prior to His crucifixion.

> *Neither pray I for these alone, but for them also*
> *which shall believe on me through their word;*
> *That they all may be one; as thou, Father, art in*
> *me, and I in thee, that they also may be one in us:*
> *that the world may believe that thou hast sent me.*
> *And the glory which thou gavest me I have given*
> *them; that they may be one, even as we are one:*
> *I in them, and thou in me, that they may be made*
> *perfect in one; and that the world may know that*
> *thou hast sent me, and hast loved them, as thou*
> *hast loved me.* (John 17:20-23)

The knowledge of resurrection power only becomes a revelation to the believer through faith in the shed blood of the New Covenant.

> *That I may know him, and the power of his*
> *resurrection, and the fellowship of his sufferings,*
> *being made conformable unto his death;*
> (Philippians 3:10)

It was and is the blood of Christ alone which upholds the unconditional Covenants which God made to man. All the blood Covenants God made with man from Adam, through Noah and Abraham including the present New Covenant, were ratified through faith in the shed blood of the cross, after it had been sprinkled on the Mercy Seat in Heaven. It is here, at the blood sprinkled Throne of Grace where the believer receives grace and mercy. Not to understand or to lose sight of this central theme of the Word of God is to confuse the message which God would have us receive, that of the message of the scarlet thread of the blood of the Lamb who was slain from the foundation of the world.

> *Him, being delivered by the determinate counsel and foreknowledge of God, ye have taken, and by wicked hands have crucified and slain:*
> (Acts 2:23)

Until the Lamb returns with a vesture dipped in blood, this message, which is the central theme of the Bible, is the unshakeable witness of the perfect redemption given to all believers through faith in the blood of Christ. All unconditional Covenants were ratified by His blood.

> *And he [was] clothed with a vesture dipped in blood: and his name is called The Word of God.*
> (Revelation 19:13)

Wherefore we see, that unless we come to the knowledge of God's goodness, we have no appreciation of His power and love which produces humility within, and causes man to further awaken to His gift of righteousness. Until we see of His power we are not aware of our own insignificance.

Christ, after His crucifixion and resurrection, sprinkled His blood on the Mercy Seat in Heaven and so fulfilled the office of the promised perfect High Priest. Believers cannot receive the full benefits of the New Covenant, until we appreciate the power of His sprinkled blood on the Mercy Seat, within the veil, which speaks better things than that of Able. Likewise Abraham and all Old Testament believers waited in Abraham's bosom, and did not fully receive God's promise of perfection and righteousness, until the second veil of the Heavenly Tabernacle was rent from top to bottom.

> *And these all, having obtained a good report through faith, received not the promise:*
> *God having provided some better thing for us,*
> <u>*that they without us should not be made perfect.*</u>
> (Hebrews 11:39,40)

If we are not aware of the above facts, then we ignore our High Priest, and consequently have not accepted the benefits of continuing salvation. It is only through faith in the sprinkling of Christ's blood on the Mercy Seat, on our behalf, that guilt is purged, and believers are continually judged innocent and free from guilt, in the ever present NOW, by a merciful God.

It is for the unsaved to flee to the cross for justification, for we were brought there through the condemnation of the law. Now being declared righteous by God, (which is the meaning of justification), we are now free from the condemnation of the law of sin and death, the believer need not ever again look back to the cross for the declaration of his righteousness, for Jesus was crucified only once.

> *Who shall lay any thing to the charge of God's elect? [It is] God that justifieth.* (Romans 8:33)

Having been justified, or declared righteous by God, the redeemed are now eligible for further salvation, even unto the uttermost perfection, through faith in the mediating blood of Christ's perfect sacrifice, sprinkled upon the Mercy Seat. If then God has declared believers to be righteousness before Him, then I would ask... How righteous has He declared us to be?

> *Who [is] he that condemneth? [It is] Christ that died, yea rather, that is risen again, who is even at the right hand of God, who also maketh intercession for us.* (Romans 8:34)

And:

> *[There is] therefore now no condemnation to them which are in Christ Jesus, who walk not after the flesh, but after the Spirit.*
> *For the law of the Spirit of life in Christ Jesus hath made me free from the law of sin and death.*
> (Romans 8:1,2)

So there are two stages in the perfecting process. First, is justification by the blood of the cross at Calvary, second, is continual salvation to the uttermost through faith in the sprinkling of the blood of the cross within the Holy place.

> Much more then, being now justified by his blood, we shall be saved from wrath through him.
>
> For if, when we were enemies, we were reconciled to God by the death of his Son, much more, being reconciled, we shall be saved by his life. (Romans 5:9,10)

Complete salvation without sin, will be granted to the redeemed, when we are brought into the presence of our Lord, at the time He returns for His bride, the spotless church. However we are eligible to mature in His perfection (Teleioo), and receive further salvation, righteous judgement and sanctification NOW, and know further of the power of His resurrection, NOW, at the Throne of Grace, prior to His Second Coming.

If perfection of flesh or righteousness through the law were a criteria to enter into the presence of God, then no man would have needed justification through the cross and sanctification through the resurrection of Christ.

> I am crucified with Christ: nevertheless I live; yet not I, but Christ liveth in me: and the life which I now live in the flesh I live by the faith of the Son of God, who loved me, and gave himself for me.
>
> I do not frustrate the grace of God: for if righteousness [come] by the law, then Christ is dead in vain. (Galatians 2:20,21)

It is by grace, and grace alone, through which believers have been completely separated from their old sinful nature. God having mercifully set aside this old nature, we are encouraged to come boldly into His presence. We who were born with a sinful nature, and must needs continue to live this life in this body of flesh, through rebirth, have been given a new Devine nature within, which is the very nature of Christ, divided asunder and separated from our original sin nature. Here, within the secret place of the Most High, believers are given this, <u>the new perspective</u> at the Mercy Seat, the new and living way, which He has consecrated for us, through the veil. It is here, secure within the veil, in the presence of His Glory, that believers have no need to look back to the cross, to be once again reminded of their old dead sin nature. For he that is dead is free from sin.

For He has said in the New Covenant:

> *[Whereof] the Holy Ghost also is a witness to us: for after that he had said before,*
> *This [is] the Covenant that I will make with them after those days, saith the Lord, I will put my laws into their hearts, and in their minds will I write them;*
> <u>*And their sins and iniquities will I remember no more.*</u>
> <u>*Now where remission of these [is, there is] no more offering for sin.*</u>
> <u>*Having therefore, brethren, boldness to enter into the holiest by the blood of Jesus,*</u>
> <u>*By a new and living way,*</u> *which he hath consecrated for us, through the veil,*
> *that is to say, his flesh;*
> *And [having] an high priest over the house of God;*
> *Let us draw near with a true heart in full assurance of faith,*
> *having our hearts sprinkled from an evil conscience, and our bodies*
> *washed with pure water.* (Hebrews 10:15-22)

And again:

> *What shall we say then? Shall we continue in sin, that grace may abound?*
> *God forbid. How shall we, that are dead to sin, live any longer therein?* (Romans 6:1,2)

We would not be invited to come boldly before the Throne Room of Grace if God saw any sin or iniquity within us. It is humbling to know that, through the faithfulness of the blood of Christ, believers are presented in His perfection to the Father. Christ, the believers mediator, presents only our Divine nature to the Father, our <u>sin nature</u> having been removed as far as the east is from the west, to be remembered no more. Only faith in His blood cleanses believers conscience from the guilt of sin and all unrighteousness.

> *Behold, what manner of love the Father hath bestowed upon us, that we should be called the sons of God: therefore the world knoweth us not, because it knew him not.*
>
> *Beloved, now are we the sons of God, and it doth not yet appear what we shall be: but we know that, when he shall appear, we shall be like him; for we shall see him as he is.*
>
> <u>*And every man that hath this hope in him purifieth himself, even as he is pure.*</u>
>
> *Whosoever committeth sin transgresseth also the law: for sin is the transgression of the law.*
>
> *And ye know that he was manifested to take away our sins; and in him is no sin.*
>
> <u>*Whosoever abideth in him sinneth not: whosoever sinneth hath not seen him, neither known him.*</u>
>
> <u>*Little children, let no man deceive you: he that doeth righteousness is righteous, even as he is righteous.*</u>
>
> *He that committeth sin is of the devil; for the devil sinneth from the beginning. For this purpose the Son of God was manifested, that he might destroy the works of the devil.*
>
> <u>*Whosoever is born of God doth not commit sin;*</u>

for his seed remaineth in him: and he cannot sin,
because he is born of God.
In this the children of God are manifest, and the
children of the devil: whosoever doeth not
righteousness is not of God, neither he that
loveth not his brother. (1 John 3:1-10)

Above, we see once again, that the believers blood bought righteousness allows us to come boldly into the Holiest, we need not have a heart of a guilty conscience that regards the flesh as being of any eternal consequence. If the blood washed had not been given the required perfection to enter into the Holy place then the Lord would not have commanded us:

Be ye therefore perfect, even as your Father
which is in heaven is perfect. (Matthew 5:48)

Also:

For I [am] the LORD your God: ye shall
therefore sanctify yourselves, and ye shall be
holy; for I [am] holy: neither shall ye defile
yourselves with any manner of creeping thing
that creepeth upon the earth.
For I [am] the LORD that bringeth you up out of
the land of Egypt, to be your God: ye shall
therefore be holy, for I [am] holy.
(Leviticus 11:44,45)

God's Kingdom dwelling within believers is not something which is achieved by willful effort, but righteous perfection and Holiness have become all believers Divine sanctified nature, by a declaration of God, through His Sovereign Grace, by our acknowledgment of who He Is. He is the God who brings believers into His Kingdom, He is The Great I AM. It is The Great I AM who Covenanted the justified to be of His righteousness and perfection, as beneficiaries of the seed of Abraham, our father.

And when Abram was ninety years old and nine,
the LORD appeared to Abram, and said unto

him, I [am] the Almighty God; <u>walk before me,</u>
<u>and be thou perfect.</u>
And I will make my Covenant between me and
thee, and will multiply thee exceedingly.
And Abram fell on his face: and God talked with
him, saying, As for me, behold, my Covenant [is]
with thee, and thou shalt be a father of many
nations. (Genesis 17:1-4)

Also:

And he received the sign of circumcision, a seal
of the righteousness of the faith which he had yet
being uncircumcised: that he might be the father
of all them that believe, though they be not
circumcised; that righteousness might be
imputed unto them also:
And the father of circumcision to them who are
not of the circumcision only, but who also walk
in the steps of that faith of our father Abraham,
which he had being yet uncircumcised.
For the promise, that he should be the heir of the
world, was not to Abraham, or to his seed,
through the law, but through the righteousness of
faith.
<u>For if they which are of the law be heirs, faith is</u>
<u>made void, and the promise made of none effect:</u>
Because the law worketh wrath: for where no
law is, there is no transgression.
Therefore it is of faith, that it might be by grace;
to the end the promise might be sure to all the
seed; not to that only which is of the law, but to
that also which is of the faith of Abraham; who
is the father of us all, (Romans 4:11-16)

And again:

And when he was demanded of the Pharisees,

when the kingdom of God should come, he
answered them and said, The kingdom of God
cometh not with observation:
Neither shall they say, Lo here! or, lo there! for,
behold, the kingdom of God is within you.
(Luke 17:20,21)

Again we see, that God intervenes and declares those perfect whom he has chosen and declared righteous. It is obvious from the study of Scripture that Abraham was far from perfect in the flesh, but this observation only serves to further confirm and verify God's Sovereign Grace. This further awakens the believer to accept the fact that God does not judge those guilty for temporary lapses of faith, those whom He has declared righteous and perfect before Him. It is confirmation that believers, who receive the blessing of the Promise God made to us through Abraham, are separated from the spirit of sin and iniquity, for all believers are of the Spiritual seed of Abraham. It is the inheritance of the justified to receive this perfection through the Promise God made to Abraham, through the cross of Christ, who is NOW our High Priest in the order of Melchisedec.

Now to Abraham and his seed were the promises
made. He saith not, And to seeds, as of many; but
as of one, And to thy seed, which is Christ.
And this I say, that the Covenant, that was
confirmed before of God in Christ, the law,
which was four hundred and thirty years after,
cannot disannul, that it should make the promise
of none effect.
For if the inheritance be of the law, it is no more
of promise: but God gave it to Abraham by
promise. (Galatians 3:16-18)

It is not of the ten commandments, imposed upon the children of Israel through Moses, which works perfection, for God had not yet given the ten commandments when He made His everlasting Covenant to all believers through Abraham. It is the Sovereign Grace of God that would have us receive this Promise and so walk before Him in the perfection of this everlasting Covenant.

> *Even as Abraham believed God, and it was*
> *accounted to him for righteousness.*
> *Know ye therefore that they which are of faith,*
> *the same are the children of Abraham.*
> *And the scripture, foreseeing that God would*
> *justify the heathen through faith, <u>preached</u>*
> *<u>before the gospel unto Abraham, saying, In thee</u>*
> *<u>shall all nations be blessed.</u>*
> *So then they which be of faith are blessed with*
> *faithful Abraham.*
> (Galatians 3:6-9)

This everlasting Covenant, this Gospel of Grace through faith in Christ, was preached to our father Abraham four hundred and thirty years before the law was given to the unbelieving children of Israel, through Moses. This Covenant of Promise given to Old Testament believers through Abraham, was a figure or shadow of the New Covenant or Testament spoken of in Hebrews 8:8, which Christ ratified with His blood upon the cross at Calvary. For He said before His death:

> *And he took the cup, and gave thanks, and gave*
> *it to them, saying, Drink ye all of it;*
> *<u>For this is my blood of the new testament, which</u>*
> *<u>is shed for many for the remission of sins.</u>*
> (Matthew 26:27,28)

Jesus encouraged the born again to drink of the blood of the New Covenant, it is ours by inheritance, it is ours unto the perfection and Holiness which is of God through faith. If we do not receive this Promise of perfection through Grace, then we by default remain under the guilt of the law of the commandments of the flesh.

If we who are born again deny our perfection in Christ, then we deny the blood of Christ! If believers do not accept that our sin nature has been put into remission through faith in His blood, then we are asking Jesus to be crucified again. As pointed out in the Scriptures several times previously.

> *But this man, after he had offered one sacrifice for sins for ever, sat down on the right hand of God;*
> *From henceforth expecting till his enemies be made his footstool.*
> *For by one offering he hath perfected for ever them that are sanctified.*
> *Whereof the Holy Ghost also is a witness to us: for after that he had said before,*
> *This is the Covenant that I will make with them after those days, saith the Lord, I will put my laws into their hearts, and in their minds will I write them;*
> *And their sins and iniquities will I remember no more.*
> *Now where remission of these is, there is no more offering for sin.* (Hebrews 10:12-18)

If believers do not accept this truth of His indwelling perfection, and remission of sins through faith in His blood, then we do despite to the Spirit of Grace. The word here states very clearly that, we the sanctified through faith in the blood of Christ, have been given a perfected status forever. However, this does not mean that believers are totally mature in Christ, but we are graciously given the position and opportunity to be saved to the uttermost. We have been separated from our sin and iniquitous nature, under the New Covenant, as stated in Hebrews 10:17 above.

> *Wherefore he is able also to save them to the uttermost that come unto God by him, seeing he ever liveth to make intercession for them.*

> *For such an high priest became us, who is holy,*
> *harmless, undefiled, separate from sinners, and*
> *made higher than the heavens;*
> *Who needeth not daily, as those high priests, to*
> *offer up sacrifice, first for his own sins, and then*
> *for the people's: for this he did once, when he*
> *offered up himself.* (Hebrews 7:25-27)

The New Covenant is the Spirit of Grace, the Good News of the Gospel, it is the only true Gospel. Without the confessing of the Good News of God's Sovereign Grace, through the New Covenant, the true Gospel is not being declared.

The consequences of ignoring the provisions of our perfection through the New Covenant of Grace, are much more to be feared than unintentionally breaking one of the ten commandments. If we, of our own effort, try to accomplish righteousness, then we do despite to the Spirit of Grace.

> *He that despised Moses' law died without mercy*
> *under two or three witnesses:*
> *Of how much sorer punishment, suppose ye,*
> *shall he be thought worthy, who hath trodden*
> *under foot the Son of God, and hath counted the*
> *blood of the Covenant, wherewith he was*
> *sanctified, an unholy thing, and hath done*
> *despite unto the Spirit of grace?*
> (Hebrews 10:28,29)

We see from the above Scriptures, that it would be wise if believers were to give serious consideration to the provisions of the New Covenant. Without giving due consideration to the perfecting power of the blood, we ignore the goodness of God, and we would vainly attempt perfection of the flesh, either under the law of the ten commandments given through Moses, or some other self imposed law of our own self will.

Some of the methods of predetermination are: trying to keep the law of the ten commandments given to the unbelieving children of Israel through Moses; attempting to live by the Sermon on the Mount; using the golden rule as a principle or standard of conduct; adhering to a social Gospel that would attempt to convict us that we need to be "good people", or try to live up to some statement of faith. These are all desirable attributes but unless they are of the Divine motivation of the heart and are of the leading of the Spirit, they must be upheld by our own self will, and as such become mere man-made dogmas. All Scripture is doctrine and is upheld by the Word of His power, so to attempt to uphold any doctrine through any self determination or will of our own reduces these doctrines to human man-made dogmas, and ignores the provisions of Christ's High Priestly ministry at the Throne of Grace. Sacraments and ordinances only serve the law of the carnal flesh unless their prime motivation is generated through the moving of the Holy Spirit.

In the Old Testament, prior to Jesus Christ's manifestation and perfect sacrifice on the cross of reconciliation, the Mercy Seat was the focal point of the tabernacles made with hands, which were representative figures for the time then present.

> *And over it the cherubims of glory shadowing the mercyseat; of which we cannot now speak particularly...*
> *The Holy Ghost this signifying, that the way into the holiest of all was not yet made manifest, while as the first tabernacle was yet standing:*
> *Which [was] a figure for the time then present, in which were offered both gifts and sacrifices, that could not make him that did the service perfect, as pertaining to the conscience;*
> (Hebrews 9:5;8,9)

If the Mercy Seat in the tabernacles made with hands in the Old Testament spoke of redemption through faith in the sprinkling of the blood of Christ, and the perfect removal of a guilty conscience, then surely the same is also true today in New Testament times.

*Jesus Christ the same yesterday, and to day, and
for ever.* (Hebrews 13:8)

It is also God's intent that the Mercy Seat in the Heavenly
Tabernacle be the focal point of present day Christianity, the only
place where the believer may continually, in the ever present
NOW, receive mercy and grace in exchange for a guilty
conscience.

*Let us therefore come boldly unto the throne of
grace, that we may obtain mercy, and find grace
to help in time of need.*

(Hebrews 4:16)

And also as quoted several times previously:

*Having therefore, brethren, boldness to enter
into the holiest by the blood of Jesus,*

*By a new and living way, which he hath
consecrated for us, through the veil, that is to
say, his flesh;*

*And having an high priest over the house of
God;*

*Let us draw near with a true heart in full
assurance of faith, <u>having our hearts sprinkled
from an evil conscience,</u> and our bodies washed
with pure water.* (Hebrews 10:19-22)

Christ's intercession at the right hand of the Father is only
available to believers to the degree we know and accept the
Scriptures proclaiming His High Priestly ministry, and judge Him
faithful to intercede according to those Scriptures. We can only
know God according to the Scriptures the Holy Spirit writes in
our hearts. We might from week to week hear excellent sermons
delivered by the most informed and ordained of ministers of the
Gospel, but unless we take these Scriptures into our heart and
then allow the Holy Spirit to apply them to our lives, we do not
experience the knowledge of the truth. Neither can we hide and
treasure in our heart any Scripture or doctrine of which we are

unaware. It is incumbent upon every believer as well, to make sure any teaching that he might receive is consistent and in context with other Scripture. Much of present day topical preaching, although taken from Scripture, is not taught in context, and so can be very misleading.

This present intercessory High Priestly Ministry of Christ is probably best described in the Book of Hebrews. The Book of Hebrews seems to be little discussed in its entirety, and without a general overall view of this important Book, it is not readily understood, and consequently easily taken out of context.

As somewhat of an overview let it be said that this book speaks generally of the <u>better provisions</u> which are available to all believers who accept that their blessing comes to them as being the seed of Abraham and Jesus Christ. Also this inspired Book speaks of a <u>better</u> High Priestly Ministry at the right hand of the Father, where Christ is NOW continually making intercession for believers according to the will of God.

> *For the priesthood being changed, there is made*
> *of necessity a change also of the law.*
> (Hebrews 7:12)

A better priesthood, a better revealing of the law of love.

> *For the law made nothing perfect, but the*
> *bringing in of a better hope [did]; by the which*
> *we draw nigh unto God.* (Hebrews 7:19)

A better hope, affording believers perfection in Christ.

> *(For those priests were made without an oath;*
> *but this with an oath by him that said unto him,*
> *The Lord sware and will not repent, Thou [art] a*
> *priest for ever after the order of Melchisedec:)*
> (Hebrews 7:21)

A better eternal High Priest.

Wherefore he is able also to save them to the uttermost that come unto God by him, seeing he ever liveth to make intercession for them. (Hebrews 7:25)

A better mediation and ongoing salvation to the uttermost.

But now hath he obtained a more excellent ministry, by how much also he is the mediator of a better Covenant, which was established upon better promises. (Hebrews 8:6)

A better ministry, a better Covenant, better promises.

But Christ being come an high priest of good things to come, by a greater and more perfect tabernacle, not made with hands, that is to say, not of this building; (Hebrews 9:11)

A better Tabernacle, perfect and eternal, the mystical body of Christ.

Neither by the blood of goats and calves, but by his own blood he entered in once into the holy place, having obtained eternal redemption [for us]. (Hebrews 9:12)

A better blood sacrifice.

[It was] therefore necessary that the patterns of things in the heavens should be purified with these; but the heavenly things themselves with better sacrifices than these. (Hebrews 9:23)

A better cleansing and purification.

For the law having a shadow of good things to come, [and] not the very image of the things, can never with those sacrifices which they offered year by year continually make the comers thereunto perfect. (Hebrews 10:1)

A better sacrifice, perfect and eternal.

But this man, after he had offered one sacrifice for sins for ever, sat down on the right hand of God; (Hebrews 10:12)

A better propitiation, perfect and eternal.

For by one offering he hath perfected for ever them that are sanctified.(Hebrews 10:14)

A better, even a perfect representation before God.

Let us therefore come boldly unto the throne of grace, that we may obtain mercy, and find grace to help in time of need. (Hebrews 4:16)

And

Having therefore, brethren, boldness to enter into the holiest by the blood of Jesus, (Hebrews 10:19)

A better continual access, even boldness to enter into the Holy place.

We have an altar, whereof they have no right to eat which serve the tabernacle. (Hebrews 13:10)

A better Altar.

There are probably some "better" things not mentioned above. All these "better" things are a result of the provision of Christ's blood, and believers are the beneficiaries of these Gifts of Grace, through belief in the New Covenant in His blood.

Through continual study of His Word, we will discover, that it is only through His mediating ministry at the Mercy Seat, where growth and knowledge of the truth lead to continual ongoing salvation, affording believers freedom from sin and guilt. This blessing, the blessing of Abraham, is available NOW! SIMPLY BELIEVE AND RECEIVE.

You are most welcome to submit any and all questions and comments to the author at: www.aviewfromthemercyseat.com.